F

Recess is my *Best* Subject

Recess is my ~~Best~~ Subject

a memoir

by Peggy Mastel

FERGUS PUBLISHING
Sioux Falls, South Dakota

RECESS IS MY BEST SUBJECT
Copyright © 2013 by Peggy Mastel
www.peggymastel.com

Cover and interior design by Matthew J. Beier
Cover photo by fotogaby / iStockphoto.com
Author photo by Matthew J. Beier

Cover type set in Le Cochin BQ and Homemade Apple
Interior set in Adobe Caslon Pro and Homemade Apple

All rights reserved. No part of this publication may be reproduced or transmitted in any form or by any means, electronic or mechanical, including photocopy, recording, or any information storage and retrieval system, without permission in writing from the publisher.

Requests for permission to make copies of any part of the work should be submitted by e-mail to peggy@peggymastel.com.

Library of Congress Control Number: 2013951973

ISBN: 978-0-9897701-0-1

FIRST TRADE PAPERBACK EDITION
Also available in e-book format
Fergus Publishing, 2013
www.ferguspublishing.com

To Shannon and Ian

Author's Note

I TRIED TO BE AS HONEST and thorough as I could while writing this book. I disguised the children by giving them different names and by using as few descriptive phrases as I could. I could have painted a complete picture of each child in order to make the narrative more interesting, but I didn't want any of them to be identifiable. The teachers' names are also aliases. I used names I haven't heard since my childhood eons ago, so I hope few (if any) people will make the connections.

I hope you laugh, and I hope your heart is touched by some of the stories. I hope you're moved to make life easier for children in need. I don't think I made a lasting impression on anyone when I worked as a sub. But what I saw certainly changed me.

Chapter 1

I'M NERVOUS. I SHOULDN'T BE. Very little is expected of substitute teachers. I'm a fifty-six-year-old college graduate with years of experience pacing and talking in front of adults, teaching them how to get along in the workplace. I've faced hostile turkey-processing-plant employees who were forced to attend training after working ten-hour night shifts. I've trained white, male, middle-aged government employees on the benefits of working with women, people of color, and people who are gay, lesbian, bisexual, and transgendered, all while they sat with their arms crossed, never touching the handout material. I've risked the wrath of casino employees because I would not allow them to smoke during customer service training. Today, it's just a bunch of third graders in Sioux Falls, South Dakota—the heartland of America. They'll be the Opie Taylor types, from extended families with old-fashioned values, morals, and church affiliations. I can handle it.

Plus I truly enjoy spending time with kids. I come from a large family with ten children. My first paying job was when I was just eleven years old, babysitting for three little girls—Candy, Tammy, and Sherry Nelson, all under the age of five. From that summer until I turned sixteen, I built a career out of babysitting, working hundreds of twenty-five-cent hours. By the end of my run, I knew more about teething, potty training, temper tantrums, and double-diapering at bedtime than most first-time mothers. Now, I've raised two children of my own. Substitute teaching should be a breeze.

It's a glorious day in early September, with a light breeze and bright sunshine. We haven't yet had our first frost, so the trees are green, and faded potted flowers dot the yards. Crayons are sharp; shoe laces are intact. Hope for a good year flutters in the hearts of students and teachers.

I find my assigned elementary school, one I didn't know existed, in an established neighborhood that consists of large, old trees and single-family homes. I walk around its perimeter fence until I find the main door. All other doors are locked and require an access badge for entry—something I don't possess. When the administrator took the photo for my substitute ID, the staff told me sub IDs can't be used to open any school doors.

Most of the schools in our area were built years ago, when no one worried about armed intruders or bomb threats. The architects didn't have to spend a great deal of time determining the clearest tactical routes for SWAT teams, should the need arise. So, even though there are many doors, all of them are locked, except for the door closest to the administration office. I follow the instructions posted for all visitors and register in the office, hoping I don't look too nervous.

It's 7:20 a.m. I expect to be greeted with a welcoming smile and handshake from the principal, then walked to my assigned classroom, given time to ask pertinent questions, and left with assurances of help should I need any. Nah-uh. It seems passing the background check (with the ten-dollar fee coming from my own pocket) and dredging up my ancient college transcripts to prove I graduated were the only two requirements for becoming a substitute teacher. No matter that I haven't a clue how an elementary-school day should proceed.

Subs don't have to check in before 7:30 a.m., but I'm pretty sure I'll need extra time, because it's my first day. I want to do well. I *have* to do well. I have no other job options right now.

By the time I arrive in the school's office, the day's routine is in full swing. Women—presumably school employees—are answering phones and directing incoming students and parents to their appropriate destinations, such as the counselor's and principal's offices. Teachers are picking up mail and supplies while greeting each other, visiting with students, and reminding the women on the phones about who is leaving when, ending their brief exchanges with "remember to call me if . . ." It feels like the trading floor of the New York Stock Exchange without the bells or the guys in blue jackets.

I stand alone, waiting for a break in the movement or a flicker of eye contact from someone. I know there is paperwork to fill out and that I'm not supposed to leave the office area until I have permission. Traffic swirls around me, increasing as the clock moves closer to 7:30. I hear a woman say, "His stepdad will pick him up today, but I'll do pickup tomorrow and Friday," and then I watch as she hands over a small child, whom the women greet by name and send to the proper classroom. Some children are directed outside to join their classes. I'm sure there is a system being used for this inside-outside sorting, but it's too busy right now for me to crack the code.

Finally, out of pity I'm sure, one of the multitasking women gives me a form to fill out, a set of keys on a lanyard, and a clipboard with sheets of information and construction paper. She says, "You have Mrs. Bowersox's room, 302, down the hall and to the left. Take the first turn after the double doors, and don't leave the key in the door. If it doesn't work, come find me. Sorry I can't walk you there, but it's too busy for me to leave the office. Call me if you have questions. Bring the paperwork back at the end of the day—wait until 3:15 or so—and I'll give you your copy."

I realize I'm staring at her as though she is speaking another language, so I fake a smile and start walking. I have a lousy sense of direction, so I try to remember her instructions and follow them carefully. The noise level in the building creeps up as I get closer to a cafeteria-like space. There are about thirty children eating breakfast with adult supervision. I think of remarks I've heard from some parents who complain about spending tax dollars to feed breakfast to kids from low-income families. I'm glad someone braved criticism and developed a program to feed the hungry, because these kids look tired (and sort of dreamy) as they munch away.

I find 302, unlock the door, turn on the lights, and take

a deep breath. How bad can it be? I can do this. It takes me a couple of minutes to scan the chock-full bulletin boards and determine that this is a third-grade classroom. And then I make the connection: the room starts with the number three, so of course this is third grade. I roll my eyes at my own ineptitude.

The clipboard in my hand contains all the information I'll need if administrators order a lockdown. I glance through it. "Turn off the lights and lock the door, take the children to a corner of the room where they would not be seen from the door, and keep them quiet. Put a green card in the window of the door if none of the children are in need of medical attention. Put a red card in the window if you or someone in the room is in need of medical attention. The police will respond to the rooms with red cards first as they conduct their room-to-room search. Be prepared to spend several hours in the classroom with the children." I find I'm taking quick, shallow breaths, hoping God will not allow a lockdown today. He or She knows I couldn't handle it.

It's now 7:45, and school starts at 7:55. I head for the teacher's desk and hope her absence was planned and that she had time to put together whatever it is that will get me through this day. I am lucky. She has meticulously written instructions for each subject and time period of the day. She has highlighted the lessons' main themes and secondary messages. She has copies of the assignments to hand out during class, sticky notes in the teachers' manuals for each subject, and books to read aloud should the work be finished early. Six full typewritten sheets of instruction.

An electronic bell sounds through the PA system, not

a clanging schoolyard bell but a gentle ding like a computer announcing, "You have mail." I'm frantically skimming through the instructions when one of the other third-grade teachers pops her head into the room and invites me to walk with her to pick up the students. She says the day will go well, because "it's a good group of kids—a little chatty, but good." Because I try to listen to her as she tells me her name and her phone extension in case I have questions, I forget to mark the way to the outside door with bread crumbs.

We step outside to find each class lined up in a tidy row, awaiting the signal to come inside. My students are in the third line, their twenty-two little faces staring at me, the stranger in the teacher group. They look worried, so I smile and tell them I'm the substitute teacher for Mrs. Bowersox today. I observe the other teachers say, "Give me five!" They put their hands in the air, fingers spread apart. It seems to quiet the kids, who then stand quietly until the teachers nod. The lines then move in an orderly fashion through the door. My class, however, is starting to wiggle, whisper, and get pushy, and they are ignoring me. I give the magical instruction, "Give me five!" They stop talking. I don't know what it means, but they do, so we head for our room.

As we walk, I mentally count, "First graders are six, and second graders are seven, so third graders are eight or nine years old." I remember they can follow instructions like "Open your book and turn to page thirty-four." They don't need help in the restroom, and they can read. I have yet to learn that they know how the day goes and don't expect everything in the schedule to happen before recess. Most can't lie without some telltale sign.

They like order, routine, and for things to be done the way their regular teacher does them. They have line leaders who get to be the first ones out the door for the whole day. They also rotate weekly the highly prized jobs of handing out papers, taking the lunch count to the office, and turning off the lights. This information will eventually seep into my brain, but on this first day, all I can do is punt.

The kids get noisier as we get closer to room 302, but I ignore it. Not a smart move. By the time we're all inside, two boys are in a shoving match, and one hits the floor. I don't want to be a crabby substitute and start the day off with a corrective lecture, so I firmly say, "Stop it, both of you, and sit down." They meet my attempt at leadership with a chorus of "We have to put away our backpacks and turn in notes to Mrs. Bowersox and read the morning message *before* we sit down!"

Later, when I finally have time to read further in the six-page Epistle to the Substitute, I find all of this noted. The teacher also included the names of the students who can be expected to help if I have any questions about the daily routine.

We take roll call. I can say most of the names without help, and the kids with unusual names don't have to repeat their names too often, because the helpful spokesperson students blare the names in my ear. Phonetically.

"ALL-vee-OH-LEEN!" "MAD-a-gas-GAR!"

When the phone rings, I know I'm taking too long. I try to follow the sound but look harried, so my little helpers point toward the phone and shout, "Over THERE!" The secretary politely asks for the attendance list and lunch count. Lunch count is not just the number of children who will eat hot lunch that day; it also comprises the number of those who will take milk with their cold lunch and the number of those who think they will eat hot lunch *tomorrow*. That entails another scramble on my part to locate a menu, because the kids want to know what their options are. In the process, I learn that the lunch menu isn't to be confused with tomorrow's breakfast menu. That one is color-coded.

I triumphantly send my numbers to the office with a reliable child and scan the Epistle to see what is next. We're ten minutes behind schedule. I introduce myself and ask them to be patient with me, because I have never been in their school before. I tell them to call me "Mrs. M." Knowing how important it is to make connections with people before asking them to work with you, I inquire if anyone has any questions about me or substitute teaching.

One little girl raises her hand so urgently that she is nearly on her feet, waving at me. When I nod at her, she says, "How come all the substitute teachers are so old?"

I say, "Because they are," and reach for the Epistle.

I call for Morning Meeting, a gathering of students with teacher used to reinforce days of the week, months of the year, seasons, holidays, the number of days left in school, and types of weather and weather patterns. It's a grounding exercise to start the day. Songs and clapping exercises accompany each part. Students also practice introducing themselves to each other so they can become comfortable with that particular social skill. Monday adds an extra opportunity to socialize in an adult-supervised setting, because each child gets to share something interesting about his or her weekend.

The kids sit in a circle at my feet, and we size each other up. My smile must look forced, because their faces are serious, their eyes wary. If they were meerkats, they'd be standing on their hind legs, watching for cues whether to dive back into the burrow or go play.

I follow the Morning Meeting notes. Like an annual meeting of corporate shareholders, it drags on forever, and I feel my jaw muscles lock. No wonder this ritual is phased out by fourth grade. The kids with shorter attention spans are wiggling out of their assigned spots on the floor. Some are talking loudly while the meeting leader is counting out the number of straws to match the number of days spent in school. The "Can I go to the bathroom?" and "Can I get a drink?" parades have started. I let the children leave one at a time until a sweet-faced girl with green glasses tells me, "Mrs. Bowersox doesn't let us go during Morning Meeting unless it's an emergency." For a couple of minutes, they stop asking, but the floodgates open again when one kid realizes that saying "It's an emergency!" gets approval.

How can I determine whether a kid really has to go or just wants a change of scenery? I don't have time to come up with a solution, so I just follow the lesson plan.

It's time for the first subject of the day, but we're half an hour behind schedule. The "students who can be counted on," the spokespeople, inform me that they have "specials" today. I remember my own children using that term for Music, Computer, Art, and PE, so I check my instructions and blissfully find we are only thirty minutes away from Music. They go to another room for Music. I can hang in there. Math first.

Math is my least-favorite subject, but I can handle third-grade math. Besides, I have the teacher's manual with all the answers. The spokespeople have hands in the air, so I select one of them to do a few problems on the whiteboard. But first I have to explain why we can't use the SMART Board, which is a computer system that projects the lesson on a large, interactive screen. (The screen can be written on with special markers so the whole room can see the work.) The children don't accept my reasoning when I say, "Substitute teachers don't have the passwords and can't open the file." Some shout out passwords and numbers they have used when in the computer lab. I remind myself to smile and plow ahead. Three boys distract me with their antics as I attempt to maintain control of the classroom.

"Bradford, stop singing and please sit down."

"Please keep your hands off of your neighbor's desk, Lawrence."

"Evanston, where are you going? Please do not touch things on the teacher's desk."

"Bradford, feet on the floor please."

"Lawrence, please stop talking and listen to instructions."

"No, Evanston, it is not recess time. We just started the day. No, you may not take a nap. Please listen."

"Bradford, please take your head out of your desk."

"Lawrence, take your feet off Michael's desk, and pay attention."

"Evanston, give the pencil back to Bradford and sit down."

We are about halfway into the assignment when the music instructor comes to the classroom to collect my students, because, yes, we're running behind schedule. She doesn't look too upset, though it's clear no regular teacher would commit such a heinous crime. It's obvious the room is in the hands of a sub. "No problem," she says after I apologize, and she neatly lines the kids up.

"We always get a bathroom break before music!" they wail as they march out, bladders bursting, to the music room. I promise them they will get to go when music is done. Half of them have already been to the bathroom at least twice since they got to school. What are they having for breakfast? Triple mocha lattes with a Big Gulp to go?

I get thirty minutes to regroup and gain control. I study the lesson plans. Recess is right after Music. Sing hallelujah! More time to study the notes. I'll also use the time to walk around the room and read the names taped on the desks, so I can say each child's name, not just those of the three who needed constant correction and redirection.

While the kids are gone, I decide I'd better locate a teacher's restroom. As tempting as it is to use the students' restroom just down the hall, I figure that is verboten. Kids peek at each other in the toilet area. I do not need the image of me using a toilet to be burned in a child's memory for life, so I begin the search. I walk purposefully and see kids sitting in the halls outside their classrooms. I smile. They look upset, angry, guilty. It takes me awhile to figure out that they are in the hall as punishment for not completing assignments or behaving in unacceptable ways.

"Music is a fun special," my kids tell me when I collect them outside that classroom a few minutes later. I can feel their energy level rising at the mere thought of recess. I stop by the bathrooms, and only two have to go. I walk them to the outside door, and they explode onto the playground. I feel refreshed until another teacher tells me apologetically that I have recess duty. I hide my disappointment, because I don't want anyone to think I'm lazy cow or that I feel anything other than pure joy for being a substitute teacher. Oh hell. The weather is wonderful, and who doesn't need a midmorning walk?

The playground is so busy that it's tough to focus on any one child, but I keep moving. I don't know the rules about acceptable behavior on the playground structures, but I figure it out quickly. If they're doing something that is not allowed, they stop doing it as soon as the teacher gets near. And they tattle on one another shamelessly. It's like having paid informants all over the playground. The major complaint from the girls is, "She says I can't be her friend!" I vividly remember my daughter and her friends using this phrase to torture each other, and I now realize it may take genetic engineering to eradicate. I say to the perpetrator, "You can't say that, understand?" and take the hand of the sniffling child and tell her to walk with me, and we'll find more friends. It surprises everyone involved when it actually works.

With my new little friend in hand, I check out a group of third- and fourth-grade boys who have worked their way into a shady corner of the fenced playground, their backs forming a tight shield. Someone is on the ground. As I approach, they start to move away from a crying kid lying in the leaves and sand. He is dirty, his hair looks as though someone has cut out chunks, and his clothing is too small and has holes that clearly didn't happen in this skirmish. He is the poster child for Victims-of-Bullying. I round up the larger, older boys and ask them to tell me what happened. One boy is wearing a wife-beater and has a mohawk haircut with both sides of his head shaved to the skin. He has pen ink on his arms. Another boy is clothed all in black and also has a shaved head. They seem to be the leaders, and they tell me the boy on the ground started it. I help the boy up and tell him to stay with me. I tell the bigger boys that I don't believe the victim asked to be pushed or hit. They scatter. I ask the victim why he hangs out with the bullies. He tells me no one else will let him play with them. When the bell rings, he disappears into the hundreds of children hurrying to line up. I know I should find a regular teacher and report what happened, but it suddenly seems too overwhelming—it's already all I can do to keep it together and finish the day. I collect my sweaty little kids, and we head back to the classroom.

The remaining time before lunch is supposed to be spent studying spelling words with partners, followed by a pretest so they can work on words that give them trouble. Most students buckle down right away, but Bradford, Lawrence, and Evanston spend the time avoiding both me and the assignment. They ask to sharpen pencils, and when I allow it over the spokespeople's warnings that "Mrs. Bowersox doesn't let us sharpen pencils until after lunch," they noisily grind theirs down to two-inch nubs and have to start over on a new pencil. They wander from desk to desk, distracting others. Two girls almost succumb to the lure of these Three Unwise Men, but I stand over their desks and hold them in place with a fierce look. I'm so distracted that I miss Bradford and Evanston digging in their desks, pulling out toys and trinkets they aren't allowed to have at school at all. When I finally do notice, I confiscate them, saying, "They're mine until the end of the day." The boys are furious. They punish me by claiming not only that they can't find their spelling word lists but also that they *never heard* of a list for that week. Feeling manipulated, I end up putting all three in Time Away chairs in separate corners of the room. I then get the feeling this is what they wanted in the first place.

Finally, lunchtime arrives. With the day half-done, I get a second wind. Some conversation in the staff workroom (formerly known as the teachers' lounge) should give me a boost. By the time I actually find it, I have only twenty minutes to eat. Even so, I have just an apple and a granola bar, and I'm looking forward to some adult conversation.

At any given time, there are nearly two hundred substitute teachers working in the Sioux Falls school system, so I'm not an oddity. Still, I feel invisible today. Most of the teachers in the staff workroom are deep in their own discussions or working over their lunch breaks. I notice no one is eating what is being served in the cafeteria. I tell myself their behavior is understandable, because lunchtime is so short, and why would they get to know me when I'll be in another school tomorrow? Maybe I'm actually relieved. If I were to talk with them, I'd probably reveal how little I know about teaching.

After lunch, I make only one wrong turn on my way to the door where my students stand waiting after lunch recess. I'm not the last teacher to arrive, which means I'm making progress! I lead the children back to the classroom. With a mere two hours and fifteen minutes before dismissal, I'm all smiles as I remind the students it's now time for quiet reading.

They have books or magazines from the library, approved by Mrs. Bowersox, and they know what to do. That's what page three, paragraph four of the Epistle says. I love to read, and for some reason I'm certain they do, too.

I expect them to sit at their desks absorbed in their books, but no. The children burst into a loud discussion about who gets to use the futon and the beanbag in the corner. But I'm lucky—the matter settles quickly when I check my instructions and locate the names of those who have earned the coveted places for that day. Others stake out places on the carpet near their friends. One quiet girl squats under her desk, reading a book that is typically middle-school fare.

My three repeat offenders are on the move. I catch myself getting irritated with them and remind myself how little I know about these three boys. Can they read at a third-grade level? Are they on medication for ADHD? Why are they so immune to correction? I put each boy in a separate corner with his reading material. By the end of the allotted time, two are reading (or at least pretending to), and one is back in a Time Away chair. I grind my teeth. A more experienced teacher would know how to reach not just the good students but also the troublemakers.

The social studies lesson is all about the early settlers in America. The afternoon begins to drag, and I feel compelled to raise the energy level in the room. I ask them some of the questions listed in the book. The good students politely answer, the dreamers have disconnected, and the repeat offenders are sizing up opportunities for fun.

I scan the room, remembering how my own kids always

complained about how "boring" pioneer history was. *What the heck*, I think. *I won't be back here tomorrow. This may get noisy, but I gotta try it.*

I start describing the life of an imaginary child in one of the colonies. Carrying water, chopping wood, watching for animals coming out of the woods. What did he eat? What did he do to play? No school? Why? Who needed to read?

I walk around the room, peering at names taped on desks so I can call out the dreamers, the doodlers, and the good students with their waving hands. I even aim to engage BradfordEvanstonLawrence. To my surprise, the kids pick up their energy. I make jokes. I answer the inevitable "What did they do when they had to go to the bathroom?" without mincing words. The children are shocked and giggle guiltily, as though someone has said a bad word. For a few seconds, I envision their garbled version of my answer relayed to the teacher tomorrow. I almost lose my nerve and go back to the book's suggested discussion topics.

I ask who likes to hunt. It's South Dakota, so a lot of hands shoot into the air. I describe the old muzzle-loaders used by the settlers, how hungry people had to make each shot count. The girls all curl their lips and noses when talk turns to skinning and tanning hides. We define "hardships"—taking care of siblings, maybe a sick parent, no bathtubs, cold, dark houses, bugs, snakes, loneliness—because they don't know the meaning of the word when I ask.

The noise level is so high that I don't hear the first bell for dismissal. Bradford does, and he sounds the alarm. The students slam their books shut and grab their corrected papers from mail slots. Bus riders climb over slow-moving kids to snatch backpacks from the closet.

"Hurry up! We're supposed to leave first, because we ride the bus!" come shouts from several sources. They're aimed at me.

A boy stands inches from my shoulder and bellows three times, "Kids Inc. leaves now, too!" Evidently, the people who run this after-school program in the multipurpose room/gym are very strict about students arriving within minutes of dismissal. I feel a little dizzy from the decibel level of the boy's voice, so I merely nod and tell the children to line up. Even the spokespeople look at me as if I'm demented.

Next, I dismiss the bus riders and the after-school-care students. They all try to get out the door at once and end up wedged together like the Three Stooges. I try to help unclog the pipeline, but they squirm free without any assistance and frantically run-walk down the hall.

I look at the remaining students and tell them to line up as the second bell chimes. The leader strides out the door, and I fall in at the end of the line. The hall is full of children leaving in weaving lines with fatigued faces. Many have open backpacks, completely empty. I get to say good-bye to only one of my students, the last out the main double doors. I stand for a second to take a breath and am bumped by a second wave of big kids, maybe fifth graders, who are half-running by the time they touch the double doors. The school grounds are swarming with parents, childcare providers, teachers on outside duty, aides for students in wheelchairs, and hundreds of kids. I'm too tired to watch.

I walk slowly back to room 302. My shoulders droop when I see what messes were abandoned in the scramble to get off the Titanic. A few chairs have been placed on desktops; the good students know what to do even if the substitute is derelict in her duties. Other chairs are tipped over. Paper scraps, pencils, and pieces of crayons litter the room. Closet doors stand open, even though at least a dozen students slammed them shut before they left. The doors' deep bass banging echoes in my ears.

I spend about forty-five minutes cleaning up and writing a note to the teacher. She will no doubt deduce how clueless I am from the reports of her students tomorrow morning, so it's useless to embellish the list of assignments we actually worked on today. We finished about half of her list. I apologize and try to acknowledge positive student behaviors as well as the behaviors that got in the way of learning. Though it's early in the year, she knows her class, and nothing I write will surprise her. I try not to dwell on how many times I found BradfordEvanstonLawrence acting up and wasting everyone's time.

My lower back and left leg are reminding me that standing for hours comes at a cost. I limp to the office to pick up my paperwork and am thanked several times by the administrative women. When they ask whether I would consider subbing at this school again, I automatically say yes. The job market won't change before 6:00 a.m. tomorrow, when the automated system will start calling for substitutes again.

I sit in my car for what seems like hours, running through scenes from the day in my head. I shake my head and sigh over my own shortcomings. Why did I get annoyed so quickly? What should I have done differently? Why didn't the kids listen to me? Did even one child learn anything at all from me? Half an hour later, I have no answers and feel too tired to drive home. But I'm parked across the street from the school, and people from the neighborhood are watching me from their front lawns. I mentally dare someone to approach my car and ask me what I'm doing here. If they do, I'll tell them what level of hell I've just lived through and lay rubber as I leave. Instead, I drive slowly through the school zone and head home to wallow in self-pity.

I made ninety dollars today, and I won't see the money until the end of *next* month. I used to make more than that in one hour as a corporate trainer. I realize now that I've never worked so hard for so little.

Chapter 2

A SUBSTITUTE TEACHER relives the first day of a new job over and over and over. The adrenaline pumps as you locate the school, find a place to park, hike to the front door, and check in, hoping to make a good impression.

You spend the day working with children you don't know, doing tasks that the other teachers assume you're familiar with, and you are evaluated for proficiency and potential by unknown administrators who may or may not catch a glimpse of you in action. If the teacher you replace for the day finds the room in decent order, some of the lesson plan properly executed, and students who seem to have liked you, you may be asked to sub at that school again. The only contact with other adults you'll have during the day will most likely be cursory greetings in the halls. You might improve if you keep showing up.

Days pass. When I tell people what I'm doing, the response is unsettling.

"My cousin subbed for a year in Minneapolis and said it was the worst time of her life!"

"How do you dare do that? I could never face a different room of kids every day! You are so brave."

"I tried that and I will *never, ever* do it again! It was horrible!"

Those words of support and comfort roll through my head as I step out of my car, into the crisp fall air. It's my ninth day as a sub. The sky holds traces of sunrise, and frost sparkles on the grass. It's still mid-September, so the day will warm nicely, and everyone will shed jackets by lunchtime.

The early-arrival students shuffle into the building with me. This school has many children from low-income households who need subsidized meals and before-school care. I wonder how these people from Africa, the Middle East, Bosnia, Central America, and Ukraine chose our conservative, white-bread community. Did they throw a dart at a map? Are they happy to be here?

I'm feeling a little better about subbing. I've learned some survival skills and am less vulnerable. As the school day starts, I take attendance and lunch count with the help of a dependable student. My helper scans the room, tells me who is absent, and asks, "Who is having hot lunch today?" I now send a student to the Time Away chair after two warnings. The pack will sense uncertainty if you show weakness, and then the rest of the day will be chaos. I look for any reason to give positive feedback. "Thanks for standing quietly in line." "You wrote your name so clearly!" "Thank you for finishing the assignment. I appreciate your hard work!"

I've had to purge from my mind the belief that I shouldn't have to praise kids for doing what they're told to do. My mother, who raised ten children with the biblical belief that God gave rods to parents for the specific purpose of spanking, would have choked on thanking a child for following an order. I remember my many corporate training employers smiling and saying, "Positive feedback is what they get when I pay them to do what they're told to do."

By now I've also had some nice, warm-the-cockles-of-your-heart experiences. A little second-grade girl gave me a note with a drawing that said she "liked me a lot, almost as much as her real teacher." I happily remember the faces of some little boys as I held a coat tree over my head to show them how tall the T-Rex stood compared to the Triceratops. A few times, I received high fives when the kids left at the end of the day. A few kindergartners have given me hugs.

I have fifth grade on my next assignment. Fifth graders are a curious mixture of kids and adolescents. There are more boys than girls in this group, and they don't look too threatening as they line up outside the building. Some of the boys are talking, pushing each other into the chain-link fence. The girls are chatting but keeping it hushed, so the boys get the first correction of the day.

"501 boys, get away from the fence!" shouts the teacher standing next to me. "You have been told that over and over."

I look more surprised than the students, who take their time getting back in line.

"Give me five, 501!" Same teacher, this time with more of an irritated edge to her voice. "You guys had trouble listening yesterday when you had a sub. Want to lose a recess?" She stares at my students with a fierceness that should set off diving submarine warning whoops in my head. The students look away as though embarrassed, but they quiet down. Classes have to stay in line until all kids are quiet. Mine is the last to move through the doors.

By the time all twenty-three students are inside room 501, it is bedlam. I cannot shout loud enough to get anyone's attention, so I clap my hands together, making three sharp cracks. They look my way but continue yelling across the room, throwing whatever they can find—erasers, shoes, pencils, and notebooks. A wrestling match is underway inside the closet. Even the normally well-behaved spokespeople have joined in the riot. I'm afraid the noise will attract the principal, and I will get sent home, humiliated. The two diet colas I downed before 7:30 jolt me into action.

I head for the wrestlers in the closet first. Giggling girls have surrounded them—two tall boys who are competing for an audience. I get in the face of the tallest one, who is my height, and say, "Get. In. Your. Seat." I stare until he slouches and heads for his desk, then I do the same for his opponent. The girls saunter to their seats.

I find a short, slender boy tucked in the back of the coat closet under some sweaters, sucking on the sleeve of his shirt. It's wet halfway up to his elbow and around his neck. I don't know if this is his usual behavior or if something traumatized him and he needs immediate attention. When I ask him if he is all right, he nods and wanders to his desk, still sucking on his sleeve.

I try to get the morning checklist done, and the students sit down. Well, most of them. Several wanderers travel from the pencil sharpener to paper trays to books on shelves to their backpacks in an endless quest for proper supplies and someone to play with. A boy who answers to "Edward, are you having hot lunch today?" is cutting paper into confetti squares, which, he says, are for his art project. Most of it ends up on the floor around his desk. Another boy, much smaller than everyone else, keeps following me with questions.

"Where is Mrs. Hager? Is she coming to school today? Do you know when I go to the resource room? Can I go now?"

He tells me his name is Randall and that he doesn't have to do the same work as the rest of the kids in 501. His desk is nose-to-nose with the teacher's desk so that when he is seated, he faces her.

Randall begins his round of questions whenever I try to quiet the rest of the class. We are on the fourth round of "Where is Mrs. Hager? Is she coming to school today?" when I figure out he is not intentionally being a royal pain; he is developmentally challenged. I ask him if he has some work to do. He nods and starts rummaging though his desk, which is overflowing with scraps of paper cut into ruler-sized pieces. He starts gluing the paper strips together and sits quietly.

During the two or three minutes it takes me to focus on Randall, the rest of the class ratchets up the noise level. They are not fighting or arguing, just talking loudly. I glance up at them, hoping I look fierce, even frightening.

"Take out your math books, please, and turn to page forty-one."

The silly conversations swirling around the room stop abruptly. As if a switch has been thrown, they start to protest.

"I don't want to do math!"

"I hate math. It's so stupid!"

"Why do we have to do math now? Can't we just read?"

Even the students who find their math textbooks and slam them open join in the whining. Randall rummages in his desk, grabs a notebook with paper scraps trailing from it, and heads for the door.

"I go to the resource room now, and I won't be back until lunchtime," he says.

The carpet around Edward's desk is covered with litter. I get all the other students to follow the math lesson, but Edward ignores my polite, firm directives to join the class. He isn't belligerent or angry. He simply continues cutting, coloring, and drawing. The two wrestlers from the closet banter with each other and try to make everyone laugh, especially the girls who flip long forelocks of hair over their shoulders and lean over desk tops so the boys will take notice. The parade to the bathroom has started. I tell the students they may be excused one boy and one girl at a time and must use the bathroom passes hanging by the door.

Dread washes over me. If this is how the entire day is going to go, I don't know how I'll last until dismissal.

I'm attempting to lead the class into another subject when

a tall, imposing man appears inside the door to the classroom. He looks like an ex-football player/drill sergeant in sweats. He's carrying a clipboard, and two boys are with him, looking subdued and guilty. The first boy belongs in my classroom; the second is from another. All the kids fall silent. I prattle my cheeriest greeting as though I'm a happy hostess at a home-decorating party.

"Hi, welcome! How can I help you?" Even from the back of the room, I'm certain he can see the sweat dripping down the sides of my face. I'm also sure he heard the noise from my classroom all the way down the hall.

He tells me he is Mr. Landau from "the office" and that he found the two boys throwing water and paper towels around the restroom. He says they will spend their recesses and lunchtime with him so they can learn to make better choices.

I notice all the students are perfectly silent as he speaks. The wanderers are seated. The shirt-sucker has his hands in his lap. Feet are miraculously on the floor.

"I'll be back in a few minutes, and I'm going to sit in for awhile, if that's all right with you," he casually mentions. "These kids know the rules, and they know they're supposed to listen to the teacher." I want to turn my head toward the window and see if a ray of golden light from heaven is shining on me. I listen for violins and an angelic choir.

I say, "You're welcome any time!"

"I will be right back," he says as he gives the whole class an eye-squinting, chin-lowering warning frown. I sense a fantastic opportunity to learn how to maintain order with fifth graders. I can't wait until he returns.

The boy from my class who is facing the no-recess sentence shuffles back to his desk. Another boy whispers, "Aww, man, now you're really screwed!" I glare at him. He quickly slumps over his textbook while I give the rest of the room the stink-eye. The students look at their books, their feet, anywhere but at me.

Mr. Landau spends almost an hour sitting at a table in room 501. The students follow the lesson. They answer questions without making bathroom jokes or teasing whichever kid is politely talking. Mr. Landau makes eye contact with Edward-the-artist, tells him to put away his artwork, and gets him to open the same book as the rest of the class. No one argues with him. He never raises his voice. He respectfully reminds them of the consequences of not following directions. I feel calm. Lunchtime is near.

When Mr. Landau leaves, he reminds the students of their responsibility to follow instructions and act respectfully. Two more boys have earned the honor of spending lunch with him, because they ignored orders to work without talking. He tells me to send any other troublemakers to his office. I know I have a big grin on my face as he leaves. The kids look as though I've cancelled all birthdays for the next five years.

When Randall returns from the resource room, I walk them all to the lunchroom. When I get back to the classroom, I turn off the lights and eat my sandwich in cloistered silence. I don't have to put up with bad behavior, I tell myself. If I can separate the troublemakers from the rest, I can actually teach. They will like me, and I will like them.

They are sullen and sweaty when I collect them from the

line outside after lunch recess. The day has turned warm, and the temperature in the building has climbed to the high seventies. The lesson plan says "independent reading" for thirty minutes. Some roll their eyes and mutter, but everyone finds a book or magazine. I closely monitor the bathroom passes so that only one boy and one girl are out of the room at a time. When several girls complain about waiting times, I race-walk to the girls' restroom and find one of my fifth graders singing and dancing in front of the mirror. Not a bit surprised or embarrassed, she smiles at me as though I'm an adoring fan. I tell her she just used up her warning and will get sent to the office after the next infraction. She strolls dreamily back to her desk.

The boys seem to be more than sweaty. Water is dripping onto their shoulders. Some T-shirts are wet all down their backs. When I see a boy playing with the puddles of water on his desk top, I ask him for the source of the water. He mumbles something I can't understand, and when I ask him to repeat it, the room gets very quiet.

Mr. Landau is again in the doorway, this time with his hand on the shoulder of Charles, once again a boy from my classroom. Charles's entire upper body is soaked, his hair is sticking to his head, and he looks so busted. Mr. Landau explains that Charles contributed to a second watery mess in the boys' restroom and will be in detention for the rest of the day. The other wet-heads in the room try to disappear by sitting very, very still. Mr. Landau beckons to two more boys, who leave the room without uttering one sound of protest. Charles and his posse have been disruptive all day, so with a sense of relief, I lead the fifth graders through their history lesson.

When I announce that it's time for afternoon recess, Randall is working on another paper-and-glue project and doesn't want to put it away. The rest of the kids line up, but Randall, with pieces of paper sticking to his wrists and fingers, can't be hurried. He shouts "NOOOO!" and arches his back when I try to help him clear the mess. I can see he will need more time to disengage, so I tell the kids standing in line, "You are fifth graders, the role models for all the kids in school. You know the rules. Can I trust you to walk quietly to the outside door while I help Randall?" They assure me they are worthy of my trust. I nod to the line leader to proceed.

I've taken about half a dozen steps toward Randall's desk when I hear shrieks, shouts, and the thunder of fifteen pairs of pre-adolescent feet in full gallop down the hall. They run past four classrooms in session, trumpeting like a herd of rogue elephants.

I forget Randall and sprint after them, wondering what the hell am I going to do. I see another teacher fly out of her classroom so fast she has to grab the door frame to keep from spinning into the lockers across the hall.

She shouts, "501, stop right now!" as she races for the doors to the playground. She is a long-legged woman on a mission, and I don't catch up with her until she is standing outside, hands on hips, glaring and shouting at about half of my students. She has made them line up against a brick wall and is definitely *not* reading them their rights. She uses their names as she describes the disobedient, unacceptable behavior she has witnessed in the last couple of days. I stand like a mute dolt. She tells me to go round up the rest of them, and I hurry to comply. The kids act stunned to be included with any group of students who would break school rules by running in the hall. They protest all the way to the brick wall.

"It wasn't me! Belinda and them others ran first."

"I didn't do anything! The girls started it!"

"I didn't run! I walked all the way to the doors!"

They act so unjustly accused that I waver for a moment before I realize they would not have been on the other side of the playground without a running start.

As I bring the rest of the runaways to the wall, the still-very-angry teacher is in full rant. She tells me the principal is on his way, that he will deal with all them, and that I should go back to the classroom. I obediently walk back to 501.

Randall passes me in the hall, telling me, "I had to wash the glue off a my hands, so now I will go to recess." I try to tidy up the teacher's desk, just because I don't know what else to do. Will I get sent home? Today, that may not be such a bad thing.

The principal, who is young enough to be my child, smiles as he comes into the room. I shake my head and apologize for losing control. He is very kind and won't let me take responsibility for what happened. He says this class tends to push limits, and this is not the first time they have taken advantage of a substitute. I feel stupid but relieved. He tells me that not only will they all lose several recesses, but they'll also have to spend time discussing their behavior with Mr. Landau and the teacher when she returns. He instructs me to send any students who don't listen or follow instructions directly to his office.

He says something I store in my memory. "You are here

to teach, and they are here to learn. Don't put up with any behavior that gets in the way of that."

The bell rings to signal the end of recess. I am not prepared for their outrage over the punishment, because every single one of them, with the exception of Randall, claims to be innocent of raising a voice above a whisper or running in the hall. They loudly accuse classmates, then argue when someone rats them out.

I clap to get their attention. I tell them they have a choice. They can continue to argue and go to the principal's office, or speak only when I call on them and stay in the classroom. I relay the principal's message and tell them I intend to follow his instructions to the letter.

They spend the remainder of the day in an ugly, pouting, silence. I don't try to jolly them out of it or give a lecture on what they should have done differently. I talk through the rest of the language arts lesson and give them a worksheet.

Dismissal mercifully ends a thoroughly unsettling day. The students stomp out without making eye contact with me, and I don't call anyone back to put their chairs on their desks so that the custodian can vacuum more easily. By scoping out other classrooms at the end of the day, I learned that if the kids don't do it, I have to hoist the chairs myself.

"Not coming back here!" I mutter to myself as I make neat piles of assignments for the teacher. "What was I thinking? I can't do this!"

I write my notes for the teacher and try to include details. I try to avoid whimpering that it was not my fault, but I don't want to make the kids sound like evil, hard-hearted hellions.

They are fifth graders. This was their second day with a sub. I was a new sub who hadn't worked with kids their age. Together, we became perfect ingredients for the Recipe for Time Spent Up Against the Wall.

I slink past the principal's office when I collect my paperwork at the end of the day. I want to run as soon as I step through the outside doors, but I've seen that teacher with the long stride, and I worry she'll run me down before I reach my car.

I'm too tired to cry. I'm subbing because I spent hundreds and hundreds of hours in the last three years crying. My son died at noon on November 25, 2006, and I'm still here because his sister, my daughter, needs a mother, and I didn't want her to believe even for one second that she was not enough for me.

After my son's death, I got out of bed each morning to make sure my daughter got breakfast and went to school. My husband heroically went to work, and I went back to bed. I got up later and walked the dogs, made something for dinner, and never missed any school plays, conferences, concerts, or recitals.

I tried to work. I spoke to and trained groups of people who had been warned not to ask me about my family. They did anyway, and whenever they asked if I was doing better, I'd just start crying. I cried while driving, shopping, and cleaning. I spent hours at the cemetery, sobbing. The calls stopped coming.

Our family's budget relied on two incomes. When my husband asked if I had any potential work projects and I didn't answer, he used credit lines and credit cards to pay bills. We began to sink. The recession only made us sink faster.

So now I substitute teach—elementary schools only, because high-school kids scare me, and I can't look at middle-school or junior-high students without looking for a boy who looks like my son. He was thirteen years old, brilliant, handsome, and talented.

I see no light at the end of the tunnel. I am lost.

Chapter 3

I SHOULD HAVE LISTENED closely this summer when I attended the school system's mandatory "Soooooo, You Think You Want to Be a Substitute Teacher" all-day seminar. It was actually called the Student Support Staff Conference, and everyone who showed up and stayed for the day got paid fifty dollars.

There were hundreds of people in the auditorium, most of whom seemed . . . well . . . old. I bet the average age was about seventy, and I'm being generous. Some struggled with the stairs, gripping handrails while peering through trifocals and cautiously feeling for every step. I can't jump out of my chair these days without making a grunting noise, but I felt positively young compared to the rank and file.

I also noticed a few Generation Xers and Yers who texted and worked their BlackBerries. They smiled at their chatty elders but didn't leap at offers of conversation. They breezed through paperwork and quickly decided which small-group sessions they had to attend: "Why Do Adolescents Act the Way They Do?"; "Intruder/Bomb Threats in a School"; "The Impact of Poverty in Our Schools"; or "The Educator's Response to Child Abuse."

I was still in denial about being a substitute. I still believed at least one of the many regular-job interviews I had smiled through (while projecting competence, professionalism, and a positive attitude) would pan out before the first day of school. I pretended the recession hadn't tightened training budgets, and clients who hadn't heard a word from me in three years would magically reach for the phone and beg me to train all their employees for twice my former fee.

I should have keyed in on conversations at the lunch table as retired teachers described how they worked only with certain schools, certain teachers, and specific ages of children. I should have taken notes and underlined the phrases "Do not accept a substitute job unless you know the teacher and the school" and "The little kids are adorable, but they are so much work." It's possible one of the silver-haired elders said with conviction, "If an educational assistant position pays the same amount as a substitute teacher, there is a very good reason."

If I had taken advantage of the gathering to network and ask solid questions, I would have been prepared for a particular call that comes early one morning, during the first week of October. The system is automated, so a computer-generated voice asks for the substitute by name and doesn't make the job offer until he or she enters the proper number codes. All or parts of the job can be repeated while the sub scrambles for paper and pencil.

This morning, when I hear "EA position paying the same

as a substitute teacher," I accept the job. I figure it will be a great opportunity for me to watch another teacher and learn not only how to maintain discipline in the classroom, but also how to approach the core subjects of math and science—my weakest subjects.

I find the school without getting lost, park close to the front door, and spot a teachers' restroom on my way to the second-grade classroom. It's only 7:30 a.m. Bright sunshine fills the room, and all the posters, charts, and primary-colored teaching support material make me feel as if I've landed on the set of Sesame Street. The young teacher working at her desk welcomes me with a warm handshake and a nice smile. Her name is Ms. Campbell, and she has huge brown eyes that remind me of the Ewoks in *Star Wars*. I have learned that most people in the school system think I am a retired teacher because of my age, so I'm treated cautiously until they determine whether I am grandmotherly, a know-it-all, competent, or clueless.

I tell Ms. Campbell that today is the first time I'm working as an EA (we used to say "teacher's aide"), and she should feel free to give me any and all instructions that will help the day go smoothly. I envision myself seated at a little table with sweet, eager-to-learn second graders, helping them read *Clifford the Big Red Dog*. After reading, I imagine we'll make posters explaining how plants grow from seeds, then work on adding columns of two-digit numbers.

Ms. Campbell angles her head slightly to one side and says, "You will be working with Darrin exclusively today. He has autism but is higher-functioning. You sit with him while he is here in the classroom, accompany him to PE and lunch, which he attends with the rest of the class, and take him to the various resource rooms for help with reading, math, and speech therapy."

Her Ewok eyes seem to radiate empathy when she tells me she doesn't work with Darrin very much, because he is out of the classroom for over half the school day and isn't expected to participate in the same lessons as the rest of the class. His daily schedule is taped to his desk top, and a three-ring binder contains his lessons. His desk is located at the front of the room, at the end of the last desk row. A second-grade-sized chair sits next to it. After a few seconds, I realize it's for his EA—*me*.

Ms. Campbell apologizes for having to get back to her lesson preparation. This is perfectly understandable, as it's nearly time to start greeting her twenty-five students.

I sigh. It's louder than I intend, and it attracts her attention. She glances up and tells me I should go out to the playground and collect Darrin from his mother, and that I should take it slowly with him, because he doesn't like changes in routine. Ms. Campbell tells me Darrin has really bonded with his regular EA, so he may be resistant.

"Oh, and he's a runner," she says. "So stay close to him, and don't let him get away."

I'm staring at her.

"Where does he run to?" I ask with wide eyes.

"Well, the outside doors are all locked, but he tries to get out anyway. And he's pretty fast!" She emphasizes that last word. Maybe I don't resemble the superb athlete I was as a young person, but I can feel my ego stinging a bit.

"Thanks for the warning," I say, trying to smile. I head out the door.

The playground is swarming with kids and parents, many of them sleepy-eyed and rumpled. A few pajama-clad toddlers are in tow, toting juice cups. Other parents dressed for work, already in a rush, stride purposefully up the slight hill from the street, tugging at their children's hands.

"Hurry up, Mommy has to get to work. I'll see you later. Give Mommy a kiss. Have a good day!"

Some of the younger children wrap arms around a parental leg and make pitiful sounds. Little fingers have to be pried open for the separation to continue. Plenty of fathers have drop-off duty, and their good-byes are less wordy.

"See ya later, pal. Have a good day."

"Be good, have fun."

"Love you. It'll be okay."

I don't see anyone who seems to be looking for me, so I ask the teacher in the bright-orange and lime-green safety vest if she could point out Darrin and his mother. She walks me to a mom who has a small boy sitting on her feet, holding both her wrists in his, crooning something that sounds like a repetitious song. Darrin's mother is reminding him that Miss Leslie, his EA, is at a meeting today, but school will be fun anyway.

I introduce myself and stand by quietly. Darrin's tugs on his mother's arms increase in speed and strength as I get closer. He hasn't made eye contact with me, and he drags his mother's attention away by scooting behind her and twisting her arms across her chest. As she attempts to break his hold, I ask her how his morning is going.

"Oh, he's doing pretty good," she chokes out as she tries to break his hold. "He's just a little upset, because he doesn't know you, but he'll be fine. And he's going to eat hot lunch today, so that's a big step for him."

Darrin hasn't let go of her. She starts using a louder, stronger voice.

"Darrin, stop that! You are hurting Mommy! If you are not good today, you can't watch any Pokémon movies when I pick you up. Stop that!"

Darrin's sort-of-singing gets louder and louder until the whole playground can hear him chant, "The following attraction is coming to a theater near you!" I realize he is repeating a line from a movie trailer. He follows the chant with "Nooooo! Nooooo! Nooooo!" as his voice travels up and down the vocal scale. He takes a breath and continues his loop of chant and song.

The kids and parents watch the performance for a moment, then shrug and turn to their circles. Evidently this is nothing new, and they had hoped for a different tune.

Darrin's mother tells me she has to get going, because her toddler is in the car, and she has to get to work. Together, we gently detach Darrin's octopus hold on her, and she walks quickly toward the gate in the fence. I wonder if it's ever a relief to walk away from him for a few hours.

I try to speak calmly over Darrin's shouting while hanging on to his hand, which he shakes and pulls in a constant attempt to free himself. When he works one hand loose, I take hold of the other. For a skinny little seven-year-old, he's strong. The first bell, which signals the time to line up, has not yet rung. We are a long way from the second-grade line.

I decide he's too worked up to answer any questions, so I tell him we will read stories today, and he will get to choose the stories. I name some of my favorite stories and keep chatting as I try to make some forward progress. Seeming to run out of energy, Darrin stops fighting me and sits down on the pavement with his legs stretched out in front of his body.

I let go of his hand, and we both catch a breath. The first bell rings, and all the other children, as though drawn by a giant magnet, make their way to their assigned places in line.

"Darrin, let's go say good morning to Ms. Campbell, okay?" I lean over him with a smile. He swings his head side-to-side in large, slow arcs. I decide to wait for him to change his mind.

As lines of kindergartners begin moving through the school doors, I stand over Darrin, who is still seated on the pavement. He begins muttering something, and before I can lean over to decipher it, he springs up and starts to run.

As Darrin makes a beeline for the far edge of the school grounds, I distinctly hear him shout, "The following attraction is coming to a theater near you!" I head after him in my fastest walk, but I'm not terribly concerned—a sturdy five-foot-high chain-link fence encloses the playground, and I can certainly catch him before he gets near it. The fence is half a block away, I tell myself, and he would have to scale it.

As I warm up and begin to sweat, I pick up my pace until I'm jogging. Darrin is heading on a straight course for the corner of the fence that meets the building. I question his route for a second or two until I see a parent with two small kids open a gate in the corner, which, of course, I had not seen.

Stop, you little turkey! I want to shout, but I can only think it, because I have no breath left. I'm now running at the top speed my fifty-six-year-old body with fibromyalgia and fifty extra pounds can manage. I feel like a lumbering bear. My athletic shoes with extra arch support slap the blacktop, and my arms pump. The makeup I carefully applied at 6:30 this morning is running down my face. And Darrin has heard me coming. Sprinting on his toes for the gate, he reaches for the latch, jabbering on about coming attractions.

I grab his shirt collar with one hand and his waist with the other. I don't care who is watching or listening. I don't care if I'm using an inappropriate method of restraining a child. I slide down the fence with him straight-jacketed in my arms. His legs are free to kick my shins, but I'm concentrating on breathing and can't move away or correct him.

Sensing defeat, Darrin collapses as if I have poleaxed him. When I stop sounding like a winded buffalo and realize I'm going to live, I decide we should get into the building. Now I have to stagger to my feet *and* lift his body when all I want to do is lie down with multiple ice packs and feel sorry for myself.

"Darrin, we are going to go inside now. Come on," I grind out between gasps for air. He is fussing listlessly but will not stand up. I pick him up and plant his feet on the ground, keeping a vise grip on his arm. I try to walk him forward, as if I'm coaxing someone on stilts. He collapses. I pick him up and drag him a few steps. He collapses again. I put my hands under his arms and hoist him to his feet. He throws his arms over his shoulders and sinks all the way to the ground.

We are now the only people on the playground. The cavalry is not coming to help.

I tuck Darrin like a surfboard under my arm and start walking. He is wiggling and protesting, but I'm not listening.

He makes a few feeble kicks, which I ignore, because I'm on a mission. I will deliver him to the teacher and slip to the floor in a genteel faint so they will take pity on me, call an ambulance, and find another sub. The daydream comforts me as I make slow, steady progress.

As we approach the door, I almost surrender when I remember my ID is useless in the keycard system. But someone has seen me and my strange burden, and the door opens magically.

"Are you having a tough day, Darrin?" someone asks as I ease him to the floor, keeping his hand in mine. "Good catch!" the woman says to me and walks away.

My feet are numb, my back muscles are in total spasm, and we are not yet in the classroom. I take an extra twist of Darrin's shirt material in the back just for safety's sake, and we proceed to Ms. Campbell's room.

I may look as if I've taken an airboat ride through the Everglades, but Ms. Campbell just says, "Good morning, Darrin," and continues with Morning Meeting. Darrin does not join in. He goes to his desk and begins to rummage through its rat's nest of papers. He pulls out a fairy-tale picture book. I ask him if he wants me to read it to him, and I take the seat next to his desk.

Darrin isn't seated, but he is listening to me, so I begin reading.

"Once upon a time, a handsome king and a beautiful queen lived in a castle on an island full of magical trees." Darrin rocks restlessly on his heels, but he knows the story so well that he quickly turns the page as I read the sentence, "As long as the people on the island obeyed the Laws of the Trees, they were protected from invading dragons." When we get to the page with a drawing of the dragons, Darrin turns the page before I can finish. "Three dragons fly from their mountain caves, heading for the . . ."

I read faster. He turns pages faster.

"The king and his soldiers, wearing armor and carrying—"

"The dragons show no fear of the king's —" We are bouncing over entire paragraphs now, and I sound like a skipping CD.

"The magical trees dance around the castle—"

"'Stop!' cries Queen Margaret, sheltering—"

"The dragon's fiery breath melts—"

"'I promise you that we will find—'" I can barely glimpse a single phrase as the pages fly by.

"As the dragons descend—"

"The king remembers the promise—"

"The trees surround—"

". . . *happily ever after.*"

Darrin claps the book shut, tosses it into his desk, and strolls along the shelves on the side of the room, touching books in baskets and talking quietly. I check his schedule and notice we have only ten minutes before he has to report to the speech therapist.

Morning Meeting has concluded, and the children are going to their desks. I turn to Ms. Campbell to ask where the speech therapist's office is, and I see a blur in my peripheral vision headed for the door. I lurch out of the little chair and give chase as Darrin sprints for the double doors at the end of the hall.

Darrin is shaking the heavy metal doors, shouting, "No! No!" when I catch up. He seems so upset by having his escape foiled that I let him shake and shout for about a minute. I stand ready, poised to scoop him up if he tries another evasive maneuver. He suddenly crosses his arms, turns, and walks back to the classroom. I get directions from Ms. Campbell for the speech therapist's office and take Darrin's hand, and we make the trip without incident. I talk about going to PE later in the morning; he answers "yes" when I ask if he likes PE.

I go to the teacher's restroom and sit in the locked stall for ten minutes. I am alone. My pride is wounded, and I think my antiperspirant quit. I need to learn how to work with this child.

I go back to the speech therapist's office, stand outside the door, and listen. I hear repetition, refocusing, rewarding, constant requests for eye contact. Clear, brief instructions. Patience.

We have time for one more story before PE, and I ask Ms. Campbell if she knows anything about Darrin's fascination with movies. She says his mother uses movies to reward him and to keep him quiet in the evenings.

Darrin is less agitated with me now, and we speed-read *Cinderella* as the rest of the class completes a reading assignment. He stands up to wander along the book shelves again, and I race across the room, cutting him off at the door. He returns to his desk, swinging his arms and humming as though I misjudged his intentions. His classmates and Ms. Campbell hardly glance our way.

I keep Darrin's hand in mine as we walk single file to the gym. I assume I will hand Darrin over to the PE teacher and observe from the corner. The PE teacher reminds me what happens when we assume.

"You stay with him and keep him on task," she says, hands on her hips.

She sends Darrin and me to his assigned blue-tape spot on the floor. I'm told not only to do the exercises myself but to "help Darrin follow along." Darrin climbs into my lap as I attempt to sit cross-legged. It puts additional stress on my protesting joints, which barely want to hold my own weight, much less his. I don't make him sit on the floor, because I'm pleased that he sees me as a refuge from the PE teacher, who scares me as much as she seems to scare him.

We stretch and wave, stand and dance our way through the class. Darrin sticks close by my side and needs only a few reminders to follow along. He smiles at me during a silly song, and I clap my hands for him when he finishes.

I am by far the sweatiest person in the gym as we line up to leave. Darrin is no longer attempting to wriggle his hand away from mine, and his body is less rigid than before. We troop back to the classroom and, after a bathroom and hand-washing break, get lunch cards and head for the lunchroom. The kids don't understand "cafeteria." To them, it's the "lunchroom."

The food served to the approximately twenty-two thousand elementary-school children in Sioux Falls's twenty-four schools is prepared at a central location, trucked to the individual schools, and served in gymnasiums or large rooms equipped with picnic-style tables and bench seats. The tables fold up and are rolled away each day so the rooms can be used for assemblies, before- and after-school care, and conferences.

The teachers deliver their students to the lunchroom on a strict schedule, then leave for their own lunch period unless they have lunchroom duty. Each grade has assigned tables, and the kids are supposed to sit in line order so they can't exclude anyone or sit only with friends.

The women who serve the food from large trolley carts seem to know all the students. They wear hairnets and gloves, and some circulate among the tables, helping kids with condiment packets and milk cartons and generally keeping the peace. In some schools, the principal and counselor walk between the tables, chatting with the kids while monitoring noise levels.

The principal calls out, "Give me five!" every five to ten minutes. Everyone has to be perfectly quiet until told otherwise. The kids who shout, throw food, mess with someone else's food, compare the food to unflattering things, or ignore directions are sent to a separate table, where they will wait in silence until their class has left for recess and the principal or counselor has explained the consequences of bad choices. Some kids don't get any recess time because of exceedingly obnoxious or repetitive behavior. They get taken to the office.

I remember I'm supposed to stay with Darrin during lunchtime, so I walk the line with him, helping him balance his tray. He has always eaten a lunch prepared at home, so I tell him how good it is to try new things.

Today's lunch is cheese pizza, carrot sticks with ranch dressing, half an apple, and milk. The large, rectangular slab of pizza is more than enough for most of the kids, who take mouse-sized bites or pick at the cheese.

Darrin stares at his tray while I kneel next to him and coax him to take a bite. One of the lunch ladies clomps up to me and says, "You don't just sit there and help him! You get a hairnet and gloves and move around and help the others. And you get a bucket and rag and wash the tables between the classes."

I apologize and follow orders.

The hairnet makes my head even hotter, setting off another hot flash, and my lower back, which still hurts from my race with Darrin earlier in the day, screams for relief. I wander the room, opening dressing packets and milk cartons, mediating arguments, and telling kids to use indoor voices. I check on Darrin whenever I'm near his table, and he is not eating. He is staring at the pizza, which looks less appetizing each time I pass.

He finally pinches off a tiny piece of cheese and puts it in his mouth, then shakes his head and pushes the tray away.

When Darrin's class is excused for recess, I'm relieved, believing I've also been given a reprieve. As I reach up to remove my hairnet, another EA takes Darrin's hand and tells me that he goes for reading assistance now. She says I have to stay and help with the rest of the lunch shifts. I spend another half hour in Cafeteria Hell with a smile on my face, fingers puckered from bleach water, and a steadily-worsening attitude.

I swallow Extra Strength Tylenol with my sandwich as I slump in a corner of the staff workroom. I'm embarrassed, because I am doing such menial work. I'm also ashamed of feeling that way—as if I'm somehow better than all the other people who do this demanding job on a daily basis.

Darrin and I spend the afternoon comfortably in each other's company, sort of like an old married couple. He makes a move to run, and I anticipate his actions like a good cutting horse and block his escape. He finds a book, and I read bits and pieces at warp speed until he's satisfied. We walk hand-in-hand to his sessions with different specialists, admiring the artwork hanging in the halls while he quotes lines from his favorite movies.

The high point of the afternoon happens during the spelling lesson. Ms. Campbell gives her second graders their weekly spelling list and directs them to print the words in their notebooks. Darrin is not expected to do the work, but I have seen his printing and believe he could complete the list.

"Darrin, you're a good printer," I whisper to him. "You could print the spelling words, don't you think? You know those words. They're easy! You can do this!"

I have no idea why he decides to comply, but he whips out a piece of paper and starts printing. He leaves no spaces between the words, but he copies the list perfectly. When he shows his work to Ms. Campbell, she smiles and tells him what a good job he's done.

At the end of the school day, I limp with Darrin across the playground to deliver him to his mother. She is delighted that he tried the school lunch and that he printed the spelling list. I tell her Darrin is a great kid, and I had a good time helping him today. As they walk away, I listen to him tell her which movies he wants to watch when they get home.

Ms. Campbell tells me Darrin seemed to work well with me and that she thought he would be more resistant to a new EA. I'm hoping to sit down (in an adult chair) and talk with her about her class, what she hopes to accomplish with them by the end of their second-grade year, how Darrin fits into the picture, and why he is in this room but not this class. But she has a staff meeting to attend and piles of papers to correct. I simply thank her for her words of support and wish her well.

The walk to the car takes forever. I have to stop and lean against the fence to ease the muscle spasms in my back. I wonder if I would have been a good mother to a child with special needs. I'm completely used up after a single school day.

When I get home, I make an appointment to see a physician. My back hurts like hell.

Chapter 4

Late October in Sioux Falls is usually lovely—warm, sunny days and cool, star-speckled nights. Some years, an early frost bleaches the dazzling autumn leaves, but typically, the weather stays perfectly agreeable. The kids can be hyped about Halloween without having to worry about covering their costumes with snowsuits and boots.

Historians tell us that indigenous people gave time periods specific names to note the beauty of the seasons, the struggles they faced to stay alive, or great disasters that swept their corners of the world. "The Season of Falling Leaves." "The Time of the Great Flood." "The Year of Great Sickness."

October 2009 will live in teachers' memories as the beginning of the Long Winter of Indoor Recess. When the ambient temperature is below zero or the windchill pushes the temp below zero, elementary students stay inside for recess.

Rain and heavy, wet snow are also causes for indoor recess. Sioux Falls's weather may meet the indoor-recess criteria for a few days here and there during a normal year, but the winter of 2009 and 2010 starts out especially cruel.

Rain, wind, and colder-than-normal temperatures get October off to a rough start. Two snowfalls before the fifteenth of the month surprise everyone. Children and parents receive repeated written reminders that warm coats, boots, caps, gloves, or mittens must be worn; it's the rule. Snow pants are also required if the child wants to play, sit, or dig in the snow.

Organizations in Sioux Falls make constant pleas for donations of new or gently-used winter clothing for needy kids. Many teachers have stockpiles of extra caps, gloves, mittens, and even coats and snow pants in their classrooms. When that supply is tapped out, these kids are sent to the offices to dig through bins of donated clothing. It's not enough. Many immigrant and low-income parents are unable to provide enough warm clothing for their kids, or they have no idea how long and cold our winters can be. Some kids show up in flip-flops and T-shirts, shivering in the cold wind.

Students who are not properly dressed for the weather spend recesses indoors and must be supervised. Some kids are sent to the office, and some are sent to the counselor's room to read or draw. Neither the adults in charge of them nor the kids themselves like the arrangement. More notes are sent home encouraging parents to dress children appropriately for South Dakota winters.

Teachers build extra time into the daily schedules for kids to deal with all their winter gear—taking it off in the morning, putting it back on for recess (and then taking it off again), and finally putting it back on in the afternoon. Anyone working with small children can appreciate how long it takes for one or two kids to get bundled up. When it's twenty-five children under the age of six (and that's just in one room), any adult's sanity will be tested. Boots end up on the wrong feet, little fingers can't close zippers, and brains lose focus. Some kids wander around the room in a daze, and others forget their snow pants, so they have to take everything off and start again.

The sounds of clomping boots in the halls compete with sniffling, coughing, and sneezing. "It's too early," teachers and EAs mutter as they schlep their own boots, furry hats, triple-layered gloves, and long coats in case they're called for outside-recess duty.

The school classrooms are still too warm for me, but I now know to crack open a window when the kids aren't around. Hot flashes are my constant companion, but I'm a five-year breast cancer survivor, so I can't take advantage of soy supplements, natural estrogen, and progesterone creams. These treatments can reduce hot flashes, but they can also cause a recurrence of tumors. So, I sweat, hoping my classrooms will have industrial-sized fans like those used by firefighters to clear a room of smoke.

I've taken substitute jobs in thirteen schools since the beginning of the academic year, teaching all ages from preschool to fifth grade. I have a better idea of daily routines now, and I'm more comfortable with following lesson plans and dealing with negative behavior. I don't work every day. I can't. Physical therapy hasn't improved my back and leg pain, so I have to devote time every other day for recuperation.

I still get lost in the larger schools, wondering why each wing is not clearly marked. I spend far too much time trying to retrace my steps while collecting my students from the library, the music room, the gym, and the doors they file through for recess. I feel it must be my dirty little secret, this inability to find my way in the maze. I try to memorize the artwork on the walls, but lately, every school and every grade is doing pumpkins and hand-turkeys, so I plod on, peering around corners, sighing in frustration.

I SPEND A FEW DAYS teaching kindergarten classes and find the children adorable. They are as easily distracted as Doug the dog in the animated movie *Up*. Just like Doug and his knee-jerk "Squirrel!" attention shifts, one of my kindergarten classes' focus jumps with equal intensity from a classmate with a small paper cut to the book I'm reading out loud to the sugary cereal that passes for their midmorning snack.

Each child jockeys for my full attention when I walk by, reaching out to tap my arm or leg and saying, "Teacher, Teacher, Teacher!" I calmly ask them to take their seats as I proceed to do whatever their *real* teacher instructed me to do next. No matter how many times I slowly try to explain our strict agenda for the day, they leave their tables (no desks in kindergarten) to tell me what they think is very important.

"I have a new baby sister. I'm losing a tooth, see?"

"My grandma has shoes just like yours."

"Don't let Prescott sit with Lori, because they talk too much and don't listen."

"We have to sit criss-cross-applesauce with our hands in our laps, or you aren't allowed to read to us."

I discover my instructions are not as clear as they need to be for five-year-olds. I repeat, clarify, walk among the tables, and work with each child until I'm certain they know what to do. I try to encourage those who gave up before they started, refocus those who made a bit of an effort before deciding to play with a classmate, and give specific, positive feedback to the kids who are actually working.

Of course, that puts me far behind schedule, and no matter how I attempt to hurry these kindergarten children along, they move at their own pace. They cry, and I feel terribly guilty for potentially scarring their young psyches. I fear someday I will be strolling in a park with my dogs, and a child with his or her parent in tow will step in front of me and screech, "That's her! That's Mrs. M! She's the one who made us finish our rabbit pictures before we could go to PE, and that made us late!"

On one particular afternoon, my bachelor's degree in nursing actually serves me well. I arrive during lunch period, because the teacher needs to pick up her sick child and go home. She takes a few minutes to brief me. "Good class, easy afternoon, here is the lesson plan. No children with special needs, etcetera. Oh, and they're at K02 for indoor recess."

Some schools send all the children from one grade to the room of the teacher whose turn it is for recess duty. There, they watch movies or play quiet board games. Some schools send several grades to the gym with a few drawing and coloring supplies, and EAs are in charge.

In spite of the over-heated room, I feel relaxed. Two-and-a-half hours of teaching kindergarten kids is a pretty simple gig.

They stare at me when I pick them up from K02, then burst into chatter when we enter our room. I let them go for a few minutes before saying, "Please go to your resting places for quiet time." Each child finds a spot on the floor and lies down. I turn off the lights, play soft music, and tell them to close their eyes. For twenty minutes, their little bodies are (mostly) still and silent. When they start whispering or playing with some nearby classmate's shoes, I have only to look at them with raised eyebrows to make them squeeze their eyes shut and stop moving.

When rest time is over, I turn on the lights and tell them to join me in the circle for a story. The only student who doesn't comply is Raymond. His eyes are still closed, his body sprawled on the carpet by one of the tables. "Raymond, please come and sit on your mark in the circle so I can read a story," I firmly request. The rest of the class gapes at him, worried, silenced by his stillness.

I tell them to stay in their places while I go to Raymond. I check his pulse, listen to his breathing, hold his hand, and tell him to squeeze my hand. No change. I roll one closed eyelid open and see a blue-gray iris with a normal-sized pupil staring back at me. When I let go of the lid, it snaps shut. I watch his eyeballs roll around under his tightly-closed lids and note his normal heart rate, good color, and breathing. The teacher hasn't left any of the usual, required paperwork for a child with a chronic or life-threatening condition, so I figure he's playing possum.

While I complete my assessment, all of his classmates

have quietly crept up, forming a ring around Raymond and me. I bump into three little heads as I raise mine and tell them, "Raymond has decided he doesn't want to listen to the teacher today, so if he doesn't get up now, he won't be able to play in Centers when it's time."

There is a collective intake of breath. Centers is the best part of the day for most kindergartners. They love the thirty minutes at the end of the afternoon spent playing with Legos, wooden blocks, art supplies, little cars and trucks, dress-up clothes, individual whiteboards, and (most popular of all) the kitchen set with dolls, cribs, strollers, dishes, a table, and chairs. Each play area is first-come, first-served unless the teacher specifies otherwise. She carefully watches the clock and tells them to switch Centers every ten minutes. By October, they are well trained in the daily routine, but fights can break out if someone ignores protocol and stays in a Center too long.

Raymond's eyelids continue to move, and his breathing stays normal. I lift his arms and try to stand him on his feet. His limbs are limp, and his head rolls back. I'm not sure what to do. Can kindergarten kids be sent to the office? Is a substitute a complete failure if she can't deal with a five-year-old pretending to be narcoleptic?

I tell the class that we are going to ignore Raymond, and he will miss afternoon recess unless he joins us in the circle. Raymond must feel committed to his cause, because he remains on the floor.

I read the book with appropriate emphasis and insert questions to make them think. They respond well. We move on to a cut-and-glue math assignment that makes a huge mess of sticky blobs on the tables, floor, and one boy's lap. I tell him to go to the sink and clean up with paper towels. The other kids watch, hopefully learning that taking the lid off the glue has consequences.

"See all that glue on Graydon's pants?" I say for good measure. "You don't want that to happen to you!" But I'm glancing at Raymond's inert form still lying in the room's main traffic area. I gently pull him aside and check his eyes. They remain closed.

When I turn back around, I immediately have to confiscate all glue bottles, because many of the children have decided to avoid Graydon's fate by pouring glue directly onto the table tops. We leave early for bathroom break and a much-needed washing up, and then it's recess time. I deliver them to another kindergarten room so they can watch a movie.

I cannot ignore Raymond any longer. I find another teacher in my wing and ask her what should be done if a child refuses to get up after rest period. She throws me a shocked look before dashing to Raymond's side, asking, "How long has he been like this?"

I describe his behavior while she shakes him, calling his name.

"His heart rate, breathing, and eye reflexes are all normal," I tell her. "He just doesn't want to get up."

The teacher goes from scared-that-a-child-may-be-in-a-medical-crisis to annoyed-with-said-child in a nanosecond.

"This is ridiculous! Raymond, we are going to the principal's office!" She lifts him to his feet and, with her hands under his arms to propel him, walks him to the door and down the hall.

His eyes are still tightly closed.

I don't know if her familiar voice was enough of a catalyst, if he's simply tired of lying on the floor, or if he thinks we haven't figured out his game. His odd behavior will be analyzed and addressed by educators far higher in the pecking order than a substitute teacher. I let out a big, nostril-stretching sigh before I collect the rest of the class from the other kindergarten classroom.

The kids are happily involved in the play areas when Raymond returns with the principal, who assures me he is ready to come back to work. Raymond apologizes for being disrespectful and sits alone at his table, watching his classmates build, draw, play make-believe, and read.

I let him stew for ten minutes before I revoke his sentence and let him join the fun. The group playing house welcomes him and gives him the coveted role of Daddy. Raymond hardly has time to sit and enjoy his pretend dinner before it's time to get ready for dismissal.

With a pleasant smile, I start helping all the students with their darling little snow pants, boots, coats, caps, gloves or mittens, and backpacks. While I help one, others wander off into corners to play. Someone starts a game of throwing mittens and caps in the air, and by the time I get it under control, three kids are crying because they "didn't want to play" and can't find their things. The first child I helped dress tells me she "is too hot" and removes her coat, cap, and mittens. My smile disappears when two more follow her lead.

Someone, another teacher maybe, pops her head into the room and says, "There are a lot of impatient K03 mothers outside, wondering where their kids are." I resist the urge to snarl a vulgar comeback and keep stuffing feet into boots, hands into mittens, arms into sleeves. She takes the four kids who are ready and delivers them to their mothers. I keep corralling a few at a time near the door so I can finish the dressing process and nudge them into the hall.

The last children left in the room are two boys I have ignored, because they are just too hard to catch. They have been playing Tag since we started the get-ready-to-go-home process. "You must want to stay in school and help me clean up," I say, because they aren't listening to instructions. It's lucky I'm still using my Nice Teacher voice, because their mothers appear in the doorway a second later, looking peeved at having had to park and come all the way into the building to collect their sons. I help gather the boys' clothing, which is scattered all over the place, and hand it to the mothers. They wrestle the boys into coats as they leave the room.

The H1N1 flu arrives before the official start of winter. It apparently thrives in the petri-dish environment of warm school buildings crammed with many bodies for hours and hours each day. Gallon jugs of hand sanitizer show up in the classrooms. Some teachers enlist students to help clean desks before dismissal. Proper hygiene posters are hung everywhere, and kids learn to cover coughs and sneezes. Some even wash their hands.

There are so many sick teachers that phone calls for substitutes now start coming shortly after 5:00 p.m. the evening before. If I don't accept an assignment, I have no reason to fret; more calls will flood in at 5:45 a.m. I can sub every day if I am so inclined. Miraculously, I don't catch the flu, even though I'm exposed to sick kids every time I go to work. I carry sanitizing wipes and clean every surface possible before school starts, before I eat, and before I leave for the day. I wash my hands constantly, singing a nasty version of "Happy Birthday" that would get me sacked if I turned up the volume. If I could figure out a way to bathe in anti-germ liquid without burning my skin, I would. I suffer through endless cold symptoms and spend evenings slumped on the sofa, channel-surfing and blowing my nose. But it's better than the flu!

Hidden in the pile of doo-doo that is subbing in the winter, I find the pony. I don't have to get up early each day. Teachers are going home sick (or going home to care for sick children) at midday, so I can accept jobs for the afternoon only! I realize my standards are sinking pretty low, but I have always wanted a pony.

I accept an afternoon job at one of the first schools I worked at this school year. I'm certain I remember the route to get there, and I leave with plenty of time. Plenty of time, at least, for someone who has a clear sense of direction and the presence of mind to check the address on a map before departing.

I drive to another school across town and don't catch my mistake until I see the wrong school's name printed on the sign. I panic. As I flip a U-turn in the school parking lot, I call the substitute program administrator, who has already rescued me too many times this year. She calmly talks me through the correct route without a hint of "You are too stupid to live" in her voice.

I squeal up to the school at 11:30 a.m., arriving at the time I'm supposed to be stepping into the classroom. The playground is empty. Another indoor recess day—I'm now experienced enough to deduce that by looking at the clock. I jog into the building, snow blowing into my open coat. The office is locked, but I can see a woman working at one of the desks. She looks startled but opens the door for me. I tell her that I'm subbing but have forgotten the name of the teacher I'm replacing. This is a serious faux pas, and with a confused look, she says she has no idea which teacher is leaving for the day.

Murphy's Law has me in its grip, so the woman sends me to the staff workroom to ask the secretary, who is on her lunch break. Whether it's because she's trying to enjoy her half hour of solitude or because I am inept enough to arrive late without knowing which classroom I belong in, she instantly turns up her nose at me, even though she's sitting down. She tells me to call the sub administrator and that I'm supposed to know where I'm going before I show up to work. If I had taken a moment to think, I would have come up with that same solution. I leave the staff workroom feeling about two inches tall.

I cannot apologize enough to the kindergarten teacher when I finally find her classroom. She hurriedly shares the afternoon schedule with me before trotting out the door. Her twenty-eight students, along with two other classrooms' worth of indoor-recess kids, are a wriggling mass on the floor. They're no longer giving a whiff of attention to their PBS movie; they seem far more interested in the babbling mess that has just walked in. Some stare with open mouths, others with fingers in their noses.

Two other kindergarten teachers arrive at the end of recess to take their charges, leaving me with my large, loud group. They begin to form the customary kindergarten mob, all talking at once, beginning with, "Teacher, Teacher, Teacher!"

I check the schedule and am surprised to see that it calls for quiet rest time.

I have my doubts about making them rest. They have not had outdoor recess for three days. The cold, snowy weather has certainly kept them indoors at home, too. I turn off the lights and turn on classical music. No one rests, so I issue stern reminders while separating piles of kids who are wrestling like puppies.

Math is next, and we cover how many pennies equal one nickel, one dime, one quarter. A few kids protest loudly that they already know this, but I plow ahead anyway, since the rest of them are looking at me with wide-eyed wonder.

They are seated on the carpet in a circle near the SMART Board, talking continuously with classmates despite my attempts to get them to focus. I'm seated on a low office chair with swivel wheels. I direct the four chattiest kids to sit near my feet, about a foot away from the others, so that they won't have a chance to be distracting with their silly noises, head-butting, hugging, and touching. I reach out to separate offenders, get their attention, or move them back to their assigned spots when they try to creep closer to their pals.

I'm wrapping up Math when the two loudest talkers initiate a shoving match. Still seated, I make a quick forward motion to intervene, but the chair rollers catch on a wad of bunched-up carpet. My body continues forward without the chair, making a squatting, arm-stretching lurch at the boys. I don't want to crush them like bugs, so I try to abort the launch and fling myself sideways. The chair bounces to safety, and I fall in a heap on the floor.

There is a half second of stunned silence, then a roar of kindergarten laughter. I have to laugh along as I sit up, legs splayed in front of me, my ID lanyard wrapped around my forehead. A couple of little girls ask me if I'm okay before they join in the laughter.

For the rest of the afternoon, I'm unable to recover from my complete loss of dignity and control. They sense defeat and remind me how funny I looked when I fell off the chair. I know the story will be told and retold, getting a laugh each time.

I allow half an hour for wrapping up the day. Before they can put on coats, they say, they have to help clean. They crawl on the floor to pick up paper scraps, wash desks with antibacterial wipes, and put away books and markers. They love the activity, and even the drifty kids lend their hands.

The classroom is next to an outside door, so it's an easy task to release two or three children at a time to their afternoon caregivers. It takes the pressure off those who want to sit in the coat room and talk about superheroes and pets. A few older siblings appear in the doorway, fully dressed for the weather, backpacks strapped on, ready to provide a proper escort home. That hurries the kindergartners more than anything I say or do.

The absence of noise and motion is startling when the room finally empties out. The floor is clear of debris, ready for the custodian's vacuum cleaner. I write a short note to the teacher, including another apology and a description of my catapulting off the chair, so that she won't think the kids are hallucinating tomorrow when they tell her what happened.

It's 3:10, and I'm done! I meander toward the office to sign out and collect my copy of the paperwork. The secretary whose lunch I interrupted with my stupid question is staffing the desk alone, and with a scowl. A young man standing nearby in a tie (a student teacher, or another substitute?) hangs up the office phone, saying, "I'm not getting an answer. What should I do?"

He motions toward two boys, who are playing catch with a wad of crumpled paper, throwing it up so it bounces off the ceiling, laughing in their outdoor voices. They are fully swaddled in winter gear from head to toe. I take a wild guess and decide their ride is late, has forgotten them, or has packed up and raced for the border, purposefully leaving them behind forever.

The secretary tells the young man he can leave, that she "will handle it." She makes several calls before connecting with a parental unit.

"No, you need to come now. This behavior is unacceptable!" she barks. I can't tell whether the parent is being snotty, or the kids are getting on her last nerve. She has a tight grip on the phone, and I think I hear her molars grinding. She tells the boys, "Sit!" and they comply. She goes back to work, mumbling something with a lot of hissing sounds.

I see an announcement on the wall warning substitute teachers that they're expected to stay until 3:30 p.m., and if they do not, they may not get paid the full day's wages. I could return to my classroom for ten minutes and practice my chair-somersaults, but I decide to put my head in the lion's mouth.

"Excuse me, how strictly is this enforced?" I ask, pointing at the notice. "I was wondering if it's okay if I leave now?" I am using my nice-person, conciliatory, "I'm-on-your-side" tone.

The secretary's eyes flare red.

"You came in late today, you didn't know which teacher you were subbing for, and now you want to leave early? I can't believe this!" Her lower jaw juts at me, and I wonder if her teeth know how to sharpen on their own.

I start backing away from her desk, saying, "No, no, I was just asking; I will stay."

"Did you leave the classroom in decent order? Did you clean up?" she snaps. "That rule was made because people weren't cleaning up the classroom at the end of the day."

I'm nodding and babbling about cleaning and probably look as embarrassed as I feel, so she rolls those blazing eyes and says, "Fine, you can go then!" She hands me my copy of the job assignment. The boys have started to act up again, so I trot out the door without putting on my coat, relieved to have escaped further scolding but so upset that I can hardly breathe.

The secretary's words bother me for the rest of the day. She was correct about my character flaws, but I decide I can't go back to that school. I can feel inept and helpless in twenty-three other schools, thank you very much. I have my standards.

Chapter 5

Some people take comfort in knowing what each workday will bring. Not me. I find daily, repetitive routine suffocating. Maybe the pioneers were similar, pushing ever-westward in search of adventure, figuring that crossing prairies, mountains, and deserts couldn't be any worse than showing up for some monotonous day's work. It's also possible they hitched up the wagons before they knew what to expect.

I accept an assignment for subbing in a Cluster Classroom in early November. I haven't received an automated call by 6:00 a.m., so I punch in the number of the program administrator and ask if she has any jobs in the elementary schools. I hear nothing suspicious in her voice when she tells me there's an EA-paying-the-same-as-a-teacher job in a Cluster Classroom, so I naively answer, "Yes." I have no idea what it entails, but I thank her and pack supplies for the day: lunch and snacks, books in case my students leave the classroom for specials, Band-Aids, tissues, hand sanitizer, and warm clothes. I bring boots, earmuffs, and warm gloves in case the snow stops falling and we can all go out to play.

The assignment is at a school just minutes from my house, so I won't get lost this time. The secretaries in the office are multitasking, smiling at everyone, as I get pushed through the door by a gust of wind.

"Have you worked in a Cluster Classroom before?" asks one of the friendly secretaries as I fill out the paperwork. I notice a glint of concern in her eyes.

When I tell her I don't even know what a Cluster Classroom is, she tilts her head to one side and pauses, looking as though she's deciding how much information I can handle. But suddenly (and with obvious relief), she points to another middle-aged woman who has just shuffled in, shaking snow from her head. "Oh, there's Deb," the secretary says. "She'll be working with you today. You can walk with her."

I fall in step with Deb, who walks with the speed and confidence of a woman with experience.

"Ever worked in a Cluster Classroom before?" Deb asks, using just enough words to convey her suspicion that she's been saddled with a rookie.

I shake my head and ask, "What *is* a Cluster Classroom, anyway?"

"We used to call it Special Ed," she answers, glancing at my face for a response. I shrug, picturing the children I've watched leave classrooms for extended periods of time, many with severe learning disabilities. "Just tell me what to do," I say.

She relaxes just a bit, and we chat on our long trip down the maze of halls, to a far corner of the building.

We pick up another woman, Lynn, who is evidently heading to the same classroom. My attention wanders as they chat about the cold weather, but soon, the straps of my canvas supply bag start cutting into my fingers. As I shift the load, a snippet of their conversation reins me back in.

"When he gets like that, we should take off his shoes."

"I don't know if one person can do that alone."

I feel my brow wrinkle and my lips squeeze into a straight line, but before I can ask for clarification, we arrive at our classroom. It has some of the usual pieces of elementary-school furniture, such as semicircular tables with chairs, lockers, shelves with books, and toys. But there are other things, including metal bars on rollers with canvas swings, that I cannot identify.

When we all introduce ourselves, the teacher, Marcia, asks whether I've worked in a Cluster Classroom. She seems distracted or preoccupied or medicated, talking to me in a kindergarten-teacher voice that is slow and calm, ending each sentence with "okay?"

"Our students have multiple challenges, and some are not able to verbalize, okay? Just help Deb and Lynn, because they know the students quite well. And you should take your ten-minute break at 9:30, okay?"

I am about to tell her the concept of taking a break is new for me when Deb and Lynn tell me it's time to meet the buses and get our kids. As adults travel to the rear of the school to claim their charges for another day, the halls grow noisy with stomping boots and the swishing of outdoor coats.

The wind has blown most of the snow off the parking lot and away from the doors, and it's wicked cold. Three short buses with wheelchair lifts are unloading, and as I watch the drivers and attendants secure the children in the chairs, I almost bolt. I've always thrived in new situations. I've learned how to put together local news stories by watching and listening to reporters. I've learned how to write advertising copy by working in a bullpen with writers much more experienced than I. I've learned how to swim in the corporate training pool by being thrown into the deep end without having any formal instruction. But I don't know if I can handle this. The kids are so needy, so impaired. They will know I'm squeamish about changing their diapers or feeding them. I don't want to hurt their feelings, and I am afraid.

Some of the children sit motionless in their wheelchairs, making no response to the adults who rode on the bus with them or the EAs who greet them loudly, lowering their heads so they are face-to-face. Some children make spastic, jerky movements and give noisy answers with wide-open mouths. A few are physically handed over to the EAs, who grip their young hands as tight as handcuffs. The buses keep coming.

Swirling ice crystals and brilliant sunshine make my eyes water. I duck my head and notice how the kids in wheelchairs can't move a muscle to protect themselves. I am the only adult who is not helping a child. Deb is gripping one well-swaddled child in her left hand and pushing another wheelchair-bound one with her right. She points her chin toward two more wheelchairs, each with a small boy strapped in, and says, "You take those two and follow me. That's Xavier and Collier."

A lifetime of doing what I have to do kicks in, and I hustle to unlock the wheelchairs' brakes and start moving them to the doors. I realize I have not introduced myself, so I get the boys out of the wind and lean over so they can see my face. Their huge brown eyes roll in my direction as I tell them my name, that I'll be helping take care of them today.

When I say, "If I make a mistake and do something wrong, will you tell me?"

Xavier laughs out loud, snapping his head to one side. His feet stick straight out from his body, and his tiny hands lift off the chair arms.

"Yes!" he shouts, so happy to be asked. The added emotion starts his head swinging faster from side to side, and I'm not sure whether I should do something. Collier doesn't say anything, but his extra movements cause him to slide to the left until his head is hanging over the side of his chair.

As I attempt to prop Collier back up, I hear the sound of countless little boots shuffling down the hall. I move the boys in wheelchairs to one side, because the kindergarten and first-grade students are heading for their classrooms. I envision Xavier, Collier, their wheelchairs, and myself buried under five- and six-year-olds who keep coming like bundled-up, red-cheeked miniature soldiers on a parade march.

We make slow progress in the crowded hall. Some of the children say hello to Collier and Xavier; others stare at them. I see Deb and Lynn round a far-off corner with three wheelchairs, followed by a couple more kids who are able to proceed without wheels. One child holds a looped end of a thick rope, jumping with both feet in a sort of bunny-hop movement. Lynn grips the other end of the rope, her shoulders lurching with each hop.

The usual buzz of children's voices is missing when we enter the classroom. Lynn and Deb make small talk with each child as they unload backpacks from the wheelchair handles and remove coats, hoods, and caps.

The hopping child is crawling on the floor by the lockers. Deb patiently helps him to his feet so she can remove his coat, reminding him that he is supposed to go to his chair. His name is Ross. He appears to be about seven or eight years old, and his buzz-cut hair reveals a network of scars on his head. He resists Deb's efforts by locking his arms to his sides and pulling away, drooling saliva and making birdlike screeches and caws. His eyes circle constantly, never connecting or making contact. Deb tries to dodge Ross's hands as she works his arm out of a jacket sleeve, but he clamps onto her wrist and yanks her to the floor with him, starting the hopping movement from his knees up. She rolls her eyes, peels his fingers away, gets off the floor, and stays with the task.

I'm still standing near the door with Xavier and Collier, hesitant to take the next step, because it appears there is some type of system to this getting-settled process. Marcia, Deb, and Lynn help the children who are somewhat mobile first, keeping them away from the now-closed door. One child, the only girl, is seated as soon as her coat is removed in what looks like an adult-sized high chair with a locking tray. Her face is animated and smiling, and she responds with a happy noise when Lynn asks if she had a nice ride on the bus.

Deb finishes with Ross and hops him to a chair, then looks my way with impatience.

"Go ahead and get their coats off!" she says with an edge to her voice. She reaches for Collier's wheelchair, and we all roll to the lockers. It's a tight fit with two large women crouching back-to-back, helping the little boys. Xavier is in constant motion as I squat next to him and gently attempt to ease him out of his coat. It should be simple. Unzip it, slide his arms out. But his muscle spasms get stronger as he tries to help, and it seems to take forever. His head rolls from side to side, and I feel like a clumsy oaf.

Xavier's little shoes almost make me cry. He is wearing black athletic shoes, neatly tied. The soles are clean and unmarked; the suede uppers unsoiled, unscuffed. He will outgrow those shoes without ever taking a step.

The teacher, Marcia, is talking with a tall boy who doesn't seem to belong in this classroom. He has removed his coat and is standing casually with his hands in his cargo-pants pockets. I'm surprised when Marcia calls him Derek and tells him to take a seat.

We pull the wheelchairs into a ragged semicircle, and Morning Meeting begins. Derek looks bored but joins in the songs with the adults. A couple of the kids croon along and clap hands energetically. I scan faces, wondering how much the silent children hear or understand. I see more shoes that haven't touched the floor.

But Ross sure has. He's back on his hands and knees,

corralled inside the circle, rocking back and forth. The teacher winds her way through the days of the week, the month and the season, how many days we've been in school, and the schedule for the day. Derek's responses are clear and correct. He moves restlessly in his chair, but I can tell he's engaged with the lesson.

Deb and Lynn take turns returning Blake, an ambulatory boy who is about ten years old, to the circle. He chirps and chatters away, but most of his words are unintelligible to me, often followed by a high, shrieking laugh. The school's clock says 8:35, and I wonder if it's broken. I check my watch and exhale loudly, because it's not.

Without warning, we seem to be done with the circle. The teacher and Derek go to a corner table and begin what sounds like a fifth-grade math lesson. Ross hops out of the room with an occupational therapist. We move the children in wheelchairs to separate work stations as Blake takes a seat at a miniature cubicle. For the next hour, I work with two children at a time, helping them with their individual lessons. Blake and I review colors and shapes, and he makes me smile when he calls me "Mama." I've forgotten about his tendency to shriek laughter, and while I'm arranging his next exercise, he catches me off guard with a high-decibel hoot. His face is two inches from my ear, and I stumble backward in shock, bouncing off the lockers.

Xavier spends his time finding matching words on laminated cards, much like the card game Concentration. It is a lesson in patience for me as I sit quietly beside him, hands in my lap, as he struggles to turn a card. His fine-motor skills are those of an infant, but his focus is fierce, and he doesn't quit. His head and shoulders rock with the extra effort it takes to move hands that aren't getting the message. When he finds a matching pair, Xavier raises his little arms over his head and says, "I did it!" I want to hug him, but I settle for cheering him on.

When it's time for my break, I find the staff restroom, guzzle some water, and head back to the classroom. Deb and Lynn have told me I'll be spared from diaper-changing duty today, because it's too hard to train someone just for one day. I figure I'll be able to handle the rest of this one easily enough, but I suspect I won't be calling the sub administrator to ask for another Cluster Classroom assignment anytime soon.

I work with Christopher and Jacob when I return. Both boys are in wheelchairs, and neither has made a sound all morning. Jacob's lesson is listening to a tape-recorded story with headphones. I ask him if he's comfortable, but I get no answer, no flicker of movement. Deb tells me his medication was changed yesterday, and it may have been increased too much.

Christopher is a well-fed fifth grader with severe cerebral palsy. He and his clothes are meticulously clean, and he smells of soap and fabric softener. A bungee cord is wrapped around his wheelchair near his chest, above his chair tray. On the cord is a rubber teething toy in the shape of a *C*. He spends his time maneuvering the toy to his mouth with his hands. I'm told to park Christopher's chair in front of a computer that has colored shapes moving in a constant pattern. After twenty minutes, I ask if I should move him to another lesson. The teacher is working on her computer, and Ross is back in the room, so the EAs have their hands full. They tell me to leave

Christopher where he is. Bathroom breaks and diaper changes are consuming their time and attention, so I decide to keep a low profile. After another twenty minutes have passed, I see that Christopher has worked the teething toy off the cord and is holding it in his mouth. As I reposition the toy on the cord, I take a long look at Christopher's face. He studies me for a few seconds with his large, dark eyes, then tilts his head away. It feels wrong to leave him without trying to reach him. I kneel down beside his chair.

"Christopher, are you tired of watching the shapes?" I ask quietly, because I don't want to irritate the others and risk losing my exemption from diaper duty. He keeps gnawing on the toy.

"Should I read a story?" No change.

"Should we pretend to play the drums?" I ask him, running out of options. I haven't told many people that I'm taking drum lessons, because most people think it's more than a little strange that, at my advanced age, I'm interested in an instrument that's usually played by young boys and old Dead Heads. I've found, however, that drumsticks are a favorite toy for most kids.

I take Christopher's hand and tap his fingers on the palm of my own, counting out a simple rhythm. I repeat it several times, then switch hands. He shifts his attention from the slobbery toy, and I hold both his wrists, tapping the fingers of his right hand into the palm of his left. We switch and repeat. It doesn't feel as if he is making any effort, but I keep going, trying a new rhythm. His gaze is fixed on some point on the ceiling, so I don't know if I'm anything more than a diversion from his toy. When Deb says it's time for his diaper check, I tell him he's a good drummer, and I will see him later. As I stiffly get up from my knees, Christopher hooks his wrist around my arm, pulls me close so I can watch, and begins to tap one hand into the palm of the other, mimicking our drum lesson. I look at his face, and he seems to be smiling. His head remains still for just a couple of seconds, and I focus on his eyes. His irises are so dark that I can hardly see any pupil. I get a sense that he understands what I was trying to do, that some kind of connection was made. I feel honored and humbled. And I hope he didn't sense how afraid and uncomfortable I was this morning when the buses rolled up.

Deb commandeers Christopher and whisks him out the door. It's my lunch break, and I don't have to be told twice. I munch my sandwich in a corner of the staff workroom, lost in a book for a full twenty-five minutes. I don't want to think about my morning's work or talk it through. I have to put the images and sounds in storage for later. If I process it now, I will invariably think about my own son and be consumed by grief. The doctors told us that, even if they had been able to restart Ian's heart when it failed, there could have been serious complications. He could have suffered paralysis or other permanent neurological deficits. He could have been like the children in the Cluster Classroom. I was ready to make that deal with God, but it wasn't offered.

I think I know what to expect for the afternoon. We will be inside, because the windchill is well below zero. Today's special is music, and I'm looking forward to watching the kids respond to a lesson that will probably be presented at the preschool level. I feel confident that I'll be able to help each child with the parts that are customized for them.

There is a definite difference in the classroom energy from the morning. The kids seem restless, shifting in their chairs as though physically uncomfortable. I ask Deb if something happened, and she tells me that most of the kids get meds in the morning, so they feel and act differently by early to mid-afternoon.

Marcia, the teacher, leaves the room for her lunch break. Blake is playing in a corner of the room that has shelves of toys and beanbag chairs for quiet time. I join him for a few minutes and wonder about the location of the play area, which includes a window about a foot off the floor and some computer cables trailing along the wall. Blake hands me toys from the shelves as I sit on a beanbag, asking him for the names of each piece. Lynn and Deb are working with a few of the other children, and Derek is pacing at the front of the classroom. I get the impression that this is what happens every day after lunch.

Derek joins us in the corner, even though the space is just big enough for the two beanbags, but I figure he's in need of company, and I'm not doing much more than holding a football and a truck full of blocks. He sprawls on a beanbag, bumping some of Blake's carefully piled toys, which topple to the floor. Blake doesn't make a sound as we replace the piles. Deb told me earlier that Derek is a recent addition to the classroom because of disruptive behavior. She said he has autism and, while very high-functioning, "has a lot of angry outbursts." She was telling me something about his interesting choice of words when the call of duty interrupted us.

"I'm too hot. I'm gonna open a window," Derek says as he twists his upper body around and unlocks the crank-type window. I give Blake the football and quickly reach for the crank, almost touching Derek's hand in the process.

"We can't open a window, Derek," I tell him. "It's too cold outside. Some of the kids' hands are ice-cold already, and we don't want to make it worse." The window takes only a few cranks to close. I make sure it's locked. Derek looks upset and frustrated, and his eyes are moving in a rapid side-to-side manner.

He then rolls on his side and begins to play with the computer cables. Blake is standing near Derek's knees, watching him. I tell Derek to leave the cables alone, please, that they are not to be messed with. He ignores me. I repeat the order, and again he acts as though he hasn't heard it. I'm on shaky ground here, and both of us know it. He is almost as tall as I am. I'm heavier, but it's obvious he's quicker. Do I tell him he'll be sent to the principal's office if he refuses to comply? I ask Deb for advice. She comes to the corner and sternly tells him to let go of the cables and get out of play area.

Derek launches into a full-blown angry outburst before I have an inkling of what is happening. He kicks, slaps, shouts, starts to sob. Deb drags Blake to safety, but I am pinned between Derek and the side of metal filing cabinets. His open hands slap my forearms, startling me more than hurting me, so I grab both his arms and hold them tightly to his chest. He tries to bite my arms, and my surprise instantly turns into anger. I use my sternest parent voice and tell him to stop what he is doing. I might as well be reciting the daily special. His well-aimed kicks are connecting with the shelves, and toys are flying. He's showing no signs of weakening, and I wonder how long I'll be able to dodge his teeth and feet if reinforcements do not arrive.

Deb reappears with another woman, who fearlessly steps into the corner between kicks and captures his legs.

"When he gets like that, we should take off his shoes" suddenly makes sense as Deb reaches for Derek's sturdy, leather shoes and begins to pull. The indignity of shoe removal adds to his frustration, and he intensifies his efforts—twisting, snapping his teeth, shouting, trying to wrench free of us. I know I can't let go, and I get a fleeting mental image of a clown in a barrel at a rodeo.

The frantic activity stops suddenly when he runs out of breath. The three of us are panting, and Derek is yelling, "Fricking, fricking, fricking!" through clenched teeth. He starts bucking and fighting once more, continuing for a few minutes until he has to rest again.

"Derek, it's Dawn. We want to help you," the newest arrival says. Her voice remains calm even as he throws a few more kicks her way. "I want you to take some deep breaths, and I will help you calm yourself," she continues.

"I want my shoes! Where are my shoes?" Derek says through tears.

Dawn tells him he will get his shoes when he is calm, but not until then. She tells him that we all want to let go, but not until we're certain he won't hurt himself or anyone else. I'm still holding his arms, staying out of range of his teeth, when I feel his body start to relax. For the next half hour, Dawn carefully, quietly talks him out of his anger and fear.

My arm and back muscles are in full spasm when we release Derek. He coolly stands up and asks for his shoes, but I'm still a heap on one of the beanbags in the corner. Deb tells me I will have to go to the office and write up an incident report.

Dawn says, "It's just so hard to know what triggers these outbursts. I don't know him that well, so I don't know if I really was able to help."

I assure her that she made all the difference and thank her for what she did. Dawn heads back to her classroom, and I pull myself to my feet. The rest of the afternoon slips by without another upsetting incident. While the kids go to music, I go to the office, write an incident report, and speak to the principal. This is not new behavior for Derek, so there will be follow-up with parents, his counselor, and possibly his physician. I stop feeling sorry for myself when I think about the problems he will face next year in middle school, then in high school, and how limited his life will be.

I limp back to the classroom in time to help students get ready to board their buses. We stuff notes into their backpacks and wrestle their coats back on. As I fit hoods over heads with hair flattened by headrests, I wonder why these very special, needy kids do not wear gloves or mittens. Their hands look frozen a few minutes later as they wait for the bus, get loaded on the lift, and wait for the rest of the riders to get loaded. I'm so distracted getting everyone aboard that I forget to look them all in the faces and tell them how much they taught me today. But they can't even turn their heads to say good-bye. The bus doors close, and they are gone.

We trudge back to the classroom, remove our coats, and

get the room ready for tomorrow. Fatigue shuts down conversation as we put away toys, clean desks, and customize each child's schedule, attaching pictures of activities to Velcro strips on the lockers. The camaraderie I felt earlier melts away as we hurry to get out the door. Deb and Lynn leave ahead of me. I turn to say something to the teacher, but her eyes are reflecting the computer's glowing screen, and end-of-the-day chatter seems intrusive.

The principal is in the office area as I pass. She asks how I'm doing after my incident with Derek. She tells me it has happened before, and that the professionals involved are trying to pinpoint his triggers. She says he seems to lose control when he is told he cannot do something, especially when multiple corrections are given in a short time.

I leave shaking my head, thinking about Derek and his problems from a parent's viewpoint. What would I do if I were alone and had to tell him "No"? Would I be afraid of him? Can you stop loving a child?

I am exhausted and stunned. The bruises won't show until tomorrow, but I'll remember those children's faces for a very long time.

Chapter 6

November brings the anniversary date of Ian's passing. I am haunted by the image of my son lying in his casket, wearing the suit jacket he so proudly picked out in the men's department, the white shirt I ironed for the last time, the tie he wore with his kilt when he played with the bagpipers. Tears pool in my eyes almost constantly, and I swallow compulsively. When people ask about my red eyes and nasal, muffled voice, I say I have a bad cold.

The official cause of Ian's death was eosinophilic myocarditis, heart failure brought on by a rare allergic-type reaction to an antibiotic prescribed thousands of times each day. I have taken the medication. My husband and daughter have taken it. Ian took it and died. Grief makes me brittle and antisocial.

The forces of weather play a joke on us and turn the month into the fourth warmest November on record in Sioux

Falls. We need sunglasses to protect our eyes from snow glare as temperatures shimmy up into the forties and fifties. The playgrounds once again teem with bundled bodies running, throwing balls, screeching, and burning up energy generated from hours of sitting and eating. As the snow melts, we dole out high numbers of Band-Aids to cover bloody knees, hands, and elbows. The kids are still required to wear boots, which turns running into a contact sport with the now-bare pavement. Snow pants, especially the boys', look bedraggled and torn.

I read "What I Am Thankful For" essays hanging in the halls as I wait for my kids to finish Music or Art or Gym. Moms and dads, dogs, computers, and video games lead the usual lists. I carry tissues as runny nose protection, as there are children who are thankful "because Mom doesn't have cancer anymore" or "for my baby sister and her medicine that will make her better." The kids who have a family member in the military add "for our country's freedom" to their drawings of Mommy or Daddy in uniform.

I spend a few days a week covering classrooms for teachers who have collaboration/planning meetings. Some schools allow half a day per teacher; others give them two hours to meet with peers and administration and make sure they are on track to meet their goals as measured by standardized tests. Kindergarten and first-grade teachers meet together to ensure a smooth transition when the students move up next fall. Second- and third-grade teachers spend time together, and those teaching fourth and fifth are linked.

The teachers' absences are planned and short-lived, so collaboration subbing sounds like a relatively easy assignment. I bring an extra book in case I need a change of pace from the "woman-faces-a-midlife-crisis-and-has-to-build-a-new-life" fiction books my daughter has so aptly, sarcastically named. Nonfiction should provide a nice change of pace. I include a new notebook so I can jot down interesting ideas about how to discover my strengths and live a balanced, fulfilling life.

My first assignment of the week is at one of the oldest schools in Sioux Falls. Wooden floors and narrow halls give away its age. The number of kids having breakfast in the ancient gym is large, and most are children of color. Our local multicultural center keeps track of numbers of immigrants and reports that about 4,500 people from Sudan, Ethiopia, and Somalia live in Sioux Falls. Their first winter here must be frightening.

I join the line of substitute teachers in front of the secretary's desk. We all look tired and unenthusiastic, knowing we will bounce from classroom to classroom before we return to this line and sign out at the end of the day.

The secretary reminds me of the plate spinners who used to appear on *The Ed Sullivan Show* when I was a kid. The phone system has at least four incoming lines that never stop ringing. She is taking "My kid is sick today" and "My child will be late today" calls, juggling paperwork for half a dozen substitutes, acting as school nurse for kids who feel feverish or nauseated, and taking messages for the principal. She doesn't seem the least bit frazzled. I want to stay and watch her, but she gives me my classroom list for the day and turns her multitasking attention to five other people.

The winter sun is warming the windows as I begin the school day in a third-grade classroom. The teacher has everything organized and spends about ten minutes with me before she leaves for her meeting. She advises me to be firm with her class, because they can be noisy. A third of her students will leave after Morning Meeting to get extra help with English and other subjects, because they are recent immigrants. Two kids have learning disabilities, so I shouldn't expect them to complete the lessons.

I ask her to help me pronounce the names taped to desktops. I stumble over two of them even with her help. She points me in the direction of the outer doors and whisks herself off to her meeting.

My line of children seems too short, but the noise in the hall makes asking for help impossible. Metal lockers slam with such force that I'm afraid I'll find severed fingers on the floor. Some kids have hat hair, and others are victims of static electricity that lifts their hair off their heads. Fresh choruses of laughter accompany each hat removal, despite the large signs on each wall proclaiming, "This is a Quiet Zone." Kids argue, chat, empty backpacks on the floor, and take their sweet time getting ready for the march to their classroom. The lockers are too small for heavy coats and all the winter gear, so boots must be placed on the floor in front of the lockers. I learn this by watching older, bigger kids further down the hall.

I don't know which kids are mine except for the girl who led the line. I realize I can't rely on the other adults in the hall to help me identify my students, because we're all substitutes, conspicuously clueless. I find my one recognizable student and tell her to point out the kids in her class. She points to two boys who are stuffing themselves into a locker, plus ten other children. I ask her why there are so few students. She looks at me with disdain and tells me, "The other kids are at breakfast! They come when they're done."

We straggle back to our classroom, and I notice some of the little girls in the hall are wearing Muslim head scarves and long skirts. They shyly look away when I smile to show I'm friendly.

I have learned to let the line leader take us to the correct classroom. Even the youngest children lose faith in substitutes who don't know the way, so I walk with the kids but shorten my steps so I can round up stragglers and keep from tipping my hand.

As the kids get settled, I try to take attendance. My attempts to pronounce unfamiliar names embarrasses both me and the kids whose names I mangle. A few of the students react predictably and shout the correct version, but the kids who are new to this country don't laugh. They look away or down, and I apologize. A couple of little girls with empty-looking eyes sit very still.

The intercom startles me with announcements, which the children ignore. A few more kids wander in from breakfast. We stand to recite the Pledge of Allegiance. Some of the recent immigrant children steal glances at me as I say the words, but they don't join in. Their faces hold more than curiosity. I think they are afraid of having yet another stranger in their lives.

I cut the Morning Meeting short, because it seems pointless. The mouthy, smart-aleck kids won't stop talking, and the immigrant children huddle together in clumps, silent and staring. When asked for their favorite flavor of ice cream (the teacher-recommended question intended to get a response from each child), several of them hide behind others in an attempt to avoid answering.

We play a math game of addition and subtraction that rewards fast answers. The same kids win over and over, cheering for each other. One little girl bursts into tears when some boys cheer for their buddy, who beats her on the answer. I stop for a minute and ask everyone to remember what it feels like to come in second. I ask them to turn down the volume of the cheers.

When it's time to end the game, I wade through a chorus of "Ahhhh, no! One more round, please?" The adrenaline rush from the competition makes it nearly impossible for some kids to sit. I'm feebly pointing to chairs and calling names when the principal pops his head into the room. He calls the name of each child who is not in a chair. When all are seated, he calmly reminds them what proper behavior looks like.

"What should we do when our visiting teacher is talking?" he asks. "And what should we do when we want to say something in class?"

The kids raise their hands and give the correct answers. I like being called a "visiting teacher." It sounds more as if I donned my gloves and hat and came for tea and less as if I ran through a dark maze and found myself on a dead end.

I read to them after the principal leaves. I wander up and down the aisles using different voices for the characters as I read, trying to draw their attention to the story. But some kids cannot be distracted from whispering with their neighbors or digging through their desks. Do they really think I can't see both hands rummaging under the lid? Still reading aloud, I hover next to the rule-breakers and touch them on the shoulder to get their attention. The boy who has not been able to stop talking since he entered the room gets my final warning. I tell him he will have to go to the office if he can't be quiet, and his teacher will be so disappointed. He is able to control himself for the remaining reading time and nearly explodes from his chair when I tell the children to line up for Music.

When the class is safely delivered to the music teacher, I return to my assigned room to tidy up and write my note to the classroom teacher. Having finished her meeting, she will pick them up from the music room, and everything will return to normal.

I cannot shake the frightened looks on the faces of the immigrant children—dark eyes holding images and memories of refugee camps, deaths of loved ones, other things I can scarcely imagine.

I take my lunch break in a cramped, windowless staff workroom and then head toward my afternoon assignment, a Combination Classroom. After wandering through the school, I get confused, because two doors have the same number. The teacher sees my frown and waves me in while filling out a form for one student and attempting to refocus a trio of boys who are obviously not listening.

Any self-confidence I have earned as a teacher evaporates as I glance around the room. There are about thirty kids in this double classroom, talking, laughing, hanging across desks, arguing. The only child seated is in a wheelchair. They're roughly an even mix of Caucasian, Native American, Hispanic, and African American.

My face reveals my feelings as the teacher quietly explains, "These are fourth and fifth graders who have been sent here from their regular classrooms for various reasons. Most have some sort of developmental challenge or have exhibited behavior that can't be allowed."

"Don't you have any help?" I blurt. "An EA or another teacher for a few hours during the day?" My eyes widen and my jaw drops when she says, "No, it's just me."

"You must be joking!"

"No, sorry," she answers apologetically. Then, in a worried voice: "Do you think you can do this?" She seems genuinely concerned, and I don't want to disappoint her. The woman is either the most dedicated teacher in the northern hemisphere or has a totally consuming, expensive addiction like scrapbooking and needs the money worse than I do. I nod and hide my coat, purse, and bag of supplies under her desk.

The kids have taken full advantage of our momentary distraction and increased their activity level. As the teacher raises her voice to get their attention, I stand beside her and try to take it all in. The six girls, exhibiting true herd instinct, have staked out one clump of desks and appear to be engrossed in conversation. The bigger boys, who look far older than fifth graders, are camped about a foot away, elbows on knees, barking witticisms understood only by other prepubescent males. The smaller boys slink around desks on the perimeter like jackals, yipping to draw attention from their leaders.

There is a five-foot-high cage in the corner of the room, the kind used for birds, with ladders between levels and barred floors for easy cleanup. I dismiss it as empty, figuring some poor creature spent every evening and weekend chewing through the bars to escape, because that's what I would do.

The teacher gets most of the kids to sit or perch on their desks, then turns to me and says words that raise my core temperature to the uncomfortable range.

"You can cover Math Lesson 14 while I'm gone. It's fractions and figuring common denominators."

She smiles and hands me the teacher's manual, open to Lesson 14.

"Just do your best, and I will try to hurry back. Good luck!"

She is gone.

"Everyone, please take out your math books," I bellow. Their reaction is instantaneous. Shouting over each other, they laughingly explain fourth grade has one book and fifth grade has another, and I have to pick one. For a couple of minutes, I try to sort it out while the noise level rises.

"Who in here is good at math?" I ask, book in hand, herding some of the smaller boys back to their desks. A tall boy in the center of the room gets most of the votes, so I ask him if he would be interested in working a problem on the whiteboard. He gets a few catcalls as he saunters to the board, but it's obvious he is the male leader of the pack. I read the problem and ask him to write so we can all see his work. The girls watch him through forelocks of swinging hair, then hunch down over their own calculations. Many of the boys shout insults, then instructions, jumping to their feet as if we're watching a soccer match.

I challenge everyone to check the pack leader's work and raise hands if they get an answer that differs from his. Several hands shoot into the air, and I ask for another volunteer to explain what could have been done differently. The pack leader slumps against a desk, arms crossed, eyebrows arched, curious. From their table, the girls send a thin, scared-looking cohort with fingernails chewed to nubs to correct a multiplication mistake. That stumps the pack leader for a second as he peers at the board, then graciously accepts her correction. She tosses her hair and dashes back to the safety of her peeps. I compliment our brave volunteers and lead some applause.

The class seems engaged, so I ask for another volunteer, whom the others cheer every step of the way to the whiteboard. I ask whether the last problem was too easy, if I should find a more difficult equation. They loudly vote for the "same kind," so I oblige. They are giddy with success, and I want to keep them in good moods.

As I circle the room rounding up strays, I realize there are about half a dozen kids who cannot or are not following the lesson. It's painful to watch them act out, but I'm stuck, because I need to keep the rest of the students involved.

Suddenly, a tall, thin young man appears in the doorway. He is wearing the male teacher's uniform of a shirt and tie with khaki pants. A lost look brands him as a substitute even before I notice he has his ID badge on a lanyard, not a clip. The "regulars" never wear lanyards.

"Are you looking for someone?" I ask as the kids shout corrections and answers to the students at the board.

"I'm not sure," he says, checking his list. He reads off the names of five boys who are supposed to join him for help with reading. The list includes the smaller boys who have been unable to understand the math lesson. They cluster around the substitute as he tries to figure out what to do and where to go. The whole group leaves the classroom, then surges back in a moment later to settle in a circle on the floor near the back. The boys argue with each other about which book they are supposed to read.

The math lesson continues on my end of the room, noise levels rising as the boys cheer for their comrades and the girls challenge their work. I sense their interest waning after about thirty minutes and wonder how best to transition to another subject. It will require me to step away from the action, get to the teacher's desk, and find her lesson plan.

Suddenly, the cage in the corner rattles, thumps, and shakes. It takes me a couple of seconds to locate the source of the sound. A very large gray-and-white rabbit is flinging itself against the bars of the cage, then climbing up a ladder to repeat the behavior on a higher level. The poor thing is a blur, and I'm afraid it will end up a bloody mess. The kids notice me staring at the cage. One of the girls strides up to it and begins to open the door.

"He does this all the time," she says as she reaches for the rabbit.

"No! Please leave him in there!" I shout, visualizing the uproar if the rabbit gets loose.

I have to repeat my directive sternly several times and am tempted to get in her face and screech, "This behavior is exactly why you're in this class! Listen when the teacher gives you an order!" But the girl finally closes the door and stomps back to her desk. I check to make sure the cage door is latched. The rabbit is breathing heavily, and I want to whisper to the poor, demented thing that I will be back to rescue it later. I can see how PETA gets new members.

The reading circle in the back of the room has settled down nicely, but the rabbit's antics have signaled the end of the math lesson. I shuffle through the teacher's plan, praying for Art, Music, recess, or an all-school assembly.

"God always answers your prayers," the nuns told us many years ago when I was a student. "Sometimes the answer is 'No.'" Yep, they were right. I have another forty-five minutes to fill before marching them off to PE.

"Take out your writing journals, please," I announce.

Their moans and groans are well practiced but not convincing. I give them their assignment for the day and get creative with the incentive. If they finish the assigned writing before going to PE, they may read quietly or draw until it's time to leave. I raise my voice to tell them I must check their work before they put away their journals.

The assignment from the teacher is: "Write about someone special in your life. Use descriptive words and phrases. Tell me why the person is special to you."

I make the rounds of the desks, making suggestions, breaking up conversations. The students who can't find their journals are given sheets of paper. The parade to the pencil sharpener begins.

"How many lines do we have to write?" asks a boy who has not written one word.

"Half a page," I answer, and sounds of suffering roll out of their mouths. They hold their heads in agony, faces contorted.

"No way! I can't write that much!"

"Start writing, and if I see you're making an effort, I may let you write a little less," I stupidly say. "But you have to try! If you don't write anything, you won't get to draw."

I spend the rest of the allotted time reading sentences that would make a third-grade teacher weep.

"My sepchal persin is my broteher."

"My dadd is special person for me."

"I dont have no specal person can I draw no."

One of the girls writes three sentences that make sense and are somewhat legible. I compliment her writing, and she blushes. The boy pack leader shows me his half page and grins. He has left huge spaces between words and repeated one sentence four times. I stand next to his desk and ask him questions about sports. He tells me about a coach who told him he could be a quarterback if he works on his passing. I try to get him to write about it, but he looks away and puts down his pencil.

I look for students who are actually writing and give them loud, positive feedback. I help them finish sentences and spell any difficult words. I praise the smallest effort and tell them what great writers they are. I ignore the kids who give up and occupy themselves with markers, crayons, colored pencils. If they are quiet, we can all pretend writing time has been a total success.

By the time they march off to PE, I've detached myself from the class. It's the only way to survive the day. Each child needs so much more help, attention, structure, guidance, reassurance, and encouragement than I can give with my limited time and skills.

I conclude that if we treated each child as though he or she was gifted or had other extremely special needs, we would have no child left behind. We would not have rooms full of children who have failed so many times that they believe they cannot change. I shake my head over and over as I clean up messes around the room. What would I do if my child was part of this group and I could not afford anything else?

I stand in front of the rabbit cage for a long time, my tired brain tossing out more questions than answers. Could I find another home for him? How would I approach the teacher and tell her I think the noise in this classroom has driven Mr. Bunny to madness? Is he in danger? But he looks well fed, his cage is clean, and his water bottle is full.

"I'm so sorry you're stuck here," I tell him, avoiding eye contact, before I walk away. I think I hear him whisper, "But you're supposed to help me!" as I leave.

Chapter 7

I DON'T REMEMBER ever having a substitute teacher when I was in elementary school way back in the day. Saint Therese of the Little Flower Catholic Elementary School in Rugby, North Dakota, was run by Franciscan nuns from far, far away.

Their motherhouse/ship/convent was in Hankinson, North Dakota, 280 miles southeast of our little farming community, but my family didn't travel much beyond the fifty miles to Grandma and Grandpa's house. The world outside was exotic, dangerous, mysterious.

I thought our school was a mission outpost for the nuns. I knew about missions, because one of my uncles served as a missionary priest in Papua, New Guinea, for all of his adult life. Father John got to come home every five to seven years and would mesmerize us with his stories of trekking through the jungles to reach "the natives," who didn't wear shirts and ate only sweet potatoes.

As a student, I didn't question whether non-nun substitutes were allowed. If a nun was sick, another one appeared and filled in for the day. One nun left in the middle of my eighth-grade year because she got a promotion to teach in a Catholic high school. Her replacement was a young, newly-minted nun, Sister DeLourdes, who laughed when a strong wind blew off her veil at recess one day. She had short, dark hair that was the topic of conversation for the rest of the year.

The nuns who operated Mount Saint Benedict Academy in Crookston, Minnesota, where I attended high school, must have been paragons of health as well. If one teacher was "indisposed," a retired nun was propped in front of the classroom for that day. No student was foolhardy enough to act up or smart off to an elderly nun, because retribution would be swift and painful from the younger nuns the next day. The Benedictine sisterhood protected its own.

Teachers and their substitutes are far more approachable now. Many are parents themselves who know only too well that their students need every boost they can get.

I would rather stay in bed for the rest of 2009, but I accept an EA job in an Early Childhood classroom shortly before the Thanksgiving break. Early Childhood programs are preschool concepts presented to children who need extra time in the classroom environment before kindergarten. Some of the kids have special needs, and some are from families with limited resources. "It's Head Start with expanded responsibilities," says the secretary as I check in at the recently remodeled elementary school, which lies at the center of Sioux Falls.

The Early Childhood classroom is a small, windowless, and stuffy space, packed with toys and books on low shelves. It has its own bathroom next door and is fairly close to the outside doors. Introductions are brief, because the morning class of thirteen children will be arriving very soon, and their snack needs to be quickly gathered from various coolers and carts. Mindy, another EA, shows me the ropes while the teacher, Bonnie, busies herself at her desk. Three adults for thirteen kids. *Good odds, zone defense, easy gig*, I muse.

"Do they actually eat this?" I ask as I count out thirteen slices of white bread and thirteen individually wrapped pieces of processed cheese. Mindy shrugs and reminds me to get the milk cartons from the hall cooler. The menu includes orange wedges as well, which we peel and tear before the bell sounds.

Mindy is out the door before I can even wash my hands and find my coat, which is hanging in a cabinet with childproof locks. The teacher agrees that the locks are a hassle, but they're a necessary precaution "for the kids' safety and our own protection." I want to ask for clarification, but she says, "Mindy will need help with the children," and I hurry outside.

Bus drivers are helping small children maneuver down the steps and into the wind as I search for Mindy.

"Zander, Ahmed, Jade, come with me!" Mindy calls as she pulls little bundles with boots and backpacks to my side.

"Stay here with them while I get the others," she shouts over the rumble of diesel buses and the voices of kids and aides. "There are more on the next bus."

I grip mittens from two children and corral a third child between my body and a line of frozen shrubbery. Mindy reappears with a gaggle of five more and tells them all to stay with me. I have to adjust caps and hoods that have slipped down over their eyes, but I manage to say hello to each child. They all stare at me and watch as the lanyard with my name badge blows around my head in the strong wind. My coat is open, and I know it's the last time I'll feel the right temperature until I leave the overheated building this afternoon.

"Got 'em all!" Mindy yells as she leads the way back to the classroom. We stop at a long, low row of coat hooks outside the room and begin the disrobing process.

"I can do it myself," is the mantra I hear as I offer help to each child. I have to fold my hands as if I'm praying so I don't jump in and do the untying, unzipping, and debooting myself. When they step in puddles of melting snow with stocking feet or jam their coat zippers and cry, we intervene. I break up a pillow-fight-with-backpacks and herd the children toward the teacher in the doorway.

The teacher welcomes each child and begins Morning Meeting in the circle. The kids who aren't staring at me are wandering, talking, or taking toys off the shelves to play. Bonnie reminds them to come and join her. Mindy and I help with the redirecting, which is a misleading, far more Zen-like way to describe the herding we're actually doing. The kids try to avoid what's coming, slipping from our hands as soon as we place them in the carpet circle. For a few seconds, I wonder if many might be hearing-impaired, because they appear oblivious to our repeated directions.

I suddenly have a flashback of a Bill Cosby routine from years ago in which he mimicked a mother trying to control her hyperactive child during a long flight. The mother shouted, "Jeffrey, Jeffrey, Jeffrey! Stop that! Jeffrey, come here! Jeffrey, don't do that! Jeffrey, no! I said, 'No!' Jeffrey, listen to me!" as the child climbed around the cabin as if it were a jungle gym. Jeffrey could have learned his first lessons in an Early Childhood classroom.

The children range in age from four to six. For some, this is their second year in the Early Childhood program. About half of the class is able to sit for Morning Meeting and sing, chant, and clap along with the teacher through the days of the week, the months of the year, and weather for the day. The others stroll around until we gently return them to the circle and tell them to sit on their bottoms, criss-cross-applesauce, hands in their laps, eyes on the teacher, mouths closed. Two boys are so hyper that we settle for keeping them in the circle, allowing them to hop in place and shout their answers. I worry that the only way they'll be ready for kindergarten next year is if the teacher is a kangaroo and the classroom is outside with high fences.

One little boy, Joachim, sits quietly with vacant eyes and motionless hands in his lap. He is wearing three long-sleeved, wool sweaters. His family recently immigrated from one of the African countries that has been at war for too long. He is in the room physically, but that is all.

When we complete Morning Meeting, the teacher reads from a huge picture book. It's an old favorite, *The Little Red Hen*. The children who can follow the story listen with open mouths and big eyes. The concepts of cutting wheat grown from seeds and grinding flour to make bread are so alien to them that they listen as if hearing a story about magic. The teacher shows remarkable patience when one little girl gets stuck in a question loop.

"What is a hen?"

"That's a good question, Maya. A hen is a chicken."

"But what is a hen?"

"Maya, a girl chicken is called a hen. Can you say the word 'hen'?"

"What is that hen called then?"

"This chicken is called the Little Red Hen, because she is a girl chicken. She lays eggs."

"Where are her eggs?"

"Her eggs aren't in the picture."

"Why is she a hen?"

We are saved from more chicken questions by Zander, one of the extremely hyperactive boys, who throws his arms around Alex in an arm-pinning hug that causes both of them to topple over. Alex kicks wildly in an attempt to break free of the python hold, screaming, "Dop! Dop it, Dander!" I'm able to interpret the scream, because Alex told me a long, involved story about "Dorm Doopers" and "Daath Dader" and the "Demperor" this morning as I helped him get out of his coat and boots. We were nearly finished before I figured out he was talking about *Star Wars*.

The melee takes three adults to sort out, because some of the kicks land on Shane, who jumps into the fight like a sailor on shore leave. Two little girls see their chance for unstructured play and start dumping bins of wooden blocks and miniature cars on the floor. I step on Brittany's fingers while trying to avoid turning an ankle on the toys, then maneuver around Parker and Davinia, who calmly watch the struggling adults drag the wrestlers to their corners.

Brittany takes several minutes to calm down while the boys glare at us from their Time Away corners. Bonnie tells the girls to put away all the toys so we can have our snack. The girls ignore her and move on to the treasured kitchen set, where they start playing house. Mindy has Zander blocked in a corner, tranquilly ignoring his shrieks of rage at being contained. I crawl on the floor, scooping up toys as the teacher places the children in a line for the bathroom in preparation for snack time. Hand-washing takes forever, so I have time to don a hairnet and pass out the unappetizing snack.

"Are you a boy or a girl?" A little girl asks me while she smears bits of cheese and bread around her space at the table. The sweat is collecting under my hairnet, and my lower back is radiating pain down my left leg.

"What do you think?" I reply in as neutral a tone as I can manage.

"She's a girl!" answers a girl who looks older than the others. She easily led the Morning Meeting songs and gave correct answers to the questions about *The Little Red Hen*. She must be a veteran of the Early Childhood curriculum.

"She has girl earrings, see?"

The questioner stares at me, hoping for a more obvious clue to my gender. My short hair has confused her, and I don't feel up to explaining how to tell girls from boys.

Snack time is over in about fifteen minutes, and the children rejoin the teacher on the carpet for another lesson. Accompanied by music from a CD, the kids sing "Right Hand, Left Hand" while I clean up the tables and the floor. The familiar smell of bleach fills my nose as I wipe up and sweep. Mindy keeps a hand on Zander's shoulder while encouraging the kids on the fringe to sing along. About half of the class is engaged in the lesson. Whining, wriggling away, or wandering to the play areas, others make it clear they have reached the end of their attention spans.

"You have GOT to be kidding!" nearly pops out of my mouth when I hear what activity is next. With help from adults, the children are supposed to cut pictures of Thanksgiving foods from grocery ads and glue the pictures to paper plates. Using scissors is a stretch for most kindergartners and even many first graders, and to combine this with identifying grainy food photos just seems ridiculous. Not to mention that glue sticks, always easier than glue bottles for small children to work with, are nowhere to be seen. Glue bottles it is.

I'm assigned to four children seated at a round table. I pull up a very small chair, thinking I can sit. I glance at the four little faces and count myself lucky, because they are sitting and might actually be listening. I ask them to help me find Thanksgiving food pictures, and not one makes a move.

"Here's a turkey!" I exclaim as though I have found gold in them thar hills. "Who wants to cut the turkey out and glue it to their plate?"

One child carefully picks up a pair of scissors and owlishly examines them as if they were a lab specimen.

I try to drum up interest by cutting out the orange-colored turkey and applying glue to Anastasia's plate. She has had her fingers in her mouth since the teacher plunked her in the chair and has uttered not a sound. Maybe she's had enough of cheerful adults telling her where to sit and what to do. Her big blue eyes fill with tears, and she wails, "Nooooo!" flicking the turkey off her plate onto the floor.

The teacher comes by to comfort Anastasia and drop off another little girl who "needs to work in different group." I give up my chair and squat or walk around the low table on my knees, attempting to involve each child. Whenever I can get away with it, I hurriedly cut out pictures of anything a kid points to and let them squeeze the glue bottle. I can hear the teacher telling her students at least to try using the scissors, but I make an executive decision to do whatever it takes to get through the assignment without looking irritated or in pain.

The plates at my table are full of food pictures by the time the teacher calls for cleanup time. I don't care that two of the plates have only ketchup and bread, one has a photo of oranges, and Anastasia's plate has peanut butter and jelly. If the parents complain tomorrow, I will be in another school.

We release the children to Centers for free play until lunch is ready. Lunch is served family-style in the classroom so that the children can learn to sit quietly until the food arrives, serve themselves food (some of it new) from a bowl, and use manners.

"So they don't go to the lunchroom to eat?" I ask Mindy, puzzled.

"No, it's better for them to stay," she tells me. "It's not as distracting for them as it would be in the big lunchroom with so many other kids, and we can take better care of them here."

Hairnetted and gloved, I join a shuffling chain gang of EAs who must have drawn the short straw this morning. We collect lunch from carts full of food prepared at the central kitchen: chicken fingers, green beans, rolls with butter, milk, and cake. The women are helpful but hurried with explanations of where to pick up and return dishes. The schedule to feed, clean up, and send the morning class on its way must be followed carefully in order to have time to set up for the afternoon class, which eats lunch shortly after arrival.

The hairnet will stay on my head for another hour.

I must be dawdling, because Mindy has taken charge and is waiting for me at the classroom. The chicken goes directly onto each child's tray, but the bowls of gray-colored beans are placed on each of the three tables with measuring cups in place of serving spoons. Milk, a roll and butter, and a dessert also go on each tray, accompanied by one packet of ranch dressing. Each place has plastic silverware and a napkin.

We call the children to take their seats and begin the meal. The adults circulate through the room, opening milk cartons, silverware bundles, and condiment packets. I'm surprised at how well the kids are able to scoop some of the beans from the bowl and put them on their trays. The measuring cup is a great idea. Soon, some are begging for more dressing or ketchup, because they have stashed multiple packets and eaten only that.

"No, you are allowed only two dressings," Mindy reminds them. "Try a bite of something, please."

Half the kids are licking butter out of their miniature tubs.

True to form with preschool kids, some eat a decent meal (and even try the beans), some eat only the cake from its plastic wrap, and others eat nothing. The mess is mounting, and it has my name on it. Pieces of cake, cellophane wrappers, chicken chunks, and squashed green beans are everywhere.

I remember swooping the food away from my children when they were toddlers if they did nothing but play with it. As four- and five-year-olds, they certainly knew making a mess wasn't going to fly.

"You'll have to do a better job of keeping your food on the tray next year in kindergarten!" I want to scold with a wagging finger. "What you're doing is not acceptable!" I allow my inner judge to rant in my head for a minute or two before I rein her in and remind myself that these kids are in the Early Childhood program because basic life lessons are not being taught and reinforced elsewhere, or because they have some sort of barrier to learning.

The process of getting children ready to leave begins while I wipe, scrub, sweep, and throw away all the remaining food, including any unopened milk cartons. Bowls of beans join piles of chicken parts drenched in leftover milk in a huge trash can on casters. I trade the gag-inducing mixture for a can with a clean liner from the custodian, gallop to a sink to wash the serving dishes, toss my hairnet, and grab my coat.

It is time to send the morning students to their afternoon caregivers or programs and welcome the afternoon Early Childhood class. The cold wind feels refreshing as we clomp to the bus-loading area and make sure each child gets on the correct vehicle. Some of the other women huddle near the building to wait for the afternoon kids' buses to roll up to the door. I stand away from the others with my coat open, fantasizing about saying I'm sick and going home for the day. I'm being paid nine dollars per hour for babysitting and cleaning. The work is backbreaking and monotonous.

But a new batch of bright snowsuits kicks me back into gear. The kids totter off the bus into Mindy's and my care. We tramp back into the building for another round of winter-cocoon removal. The afternoon group is no less rambunctious than the morning children, but I am too tired to care about sticking to the schedule.

My attitude takes a nosedive when the hairnet goes back on my head.

Mindy tells me I can take my twenty-minute break as soon as the children are seated and served. She will leave for her break when I return. I'm hungry but can't imagine being hungry enough to eat what I'm serving, so I leave the room with half an appetite. By the time I take a quick bathroom break, find the staff workroom and wolf down half a sandwich, my break is over.

I return after cleanup chores are finished to hear the teacher covering the same material as earlier. The afternoon children's reactions mirror those of the morning: fights, fidgeting, and teeny, tiny attention spans.

The Little Red Hen begins to irk me. Why does she keep asking the other animals if they will help? How many times does she need to be rejected before she figures it out? And aren't we teaching a lovely lesson in revenge by emphasizing how Red will flaunt it and eat the bread all by herself because the others refused to help? Stupid chicken.

During free play in Centers, I listen as three little girls play house. Luckily, there are extra toy telephones, because all three girls talk with the phone tucked between their shoulders and chins while cooking and caring for their dolls. One orders pizza "with extra pefferoni," one wants to know "when you're coming home, 'cause I gotta go shopping," but the third wipes the smile from my face. With her hand on her hip, she shouts, "Don't you call the police on me! I'll call the police on you and get a 'straining order!" She slams the phone back into its cradle and turns to the stove to stir her soup.

Shrieks of protest suddenly distract me, and I turn around to catch Kobe playing Giant, stomping on carefully-placed blocks, miniature cars, and the hands of the builders. Enraged and injured, Aaron beans Kobe with a toy truck before the adults can get close enough to stop it. No blood, no foul. The teacher sends Kobe to a Time Away chair in a quiet corner, and everyone returns to their toys.

EARLY CHILDHOOD WORK is not the same in each school. I discover that later in the week, when I beep my acceptance to the computerized caller looking for a half-day EA in an Early Childhood classroom across town, which will pay the same rate a substitute teacher would make. I arrive on time with a bit of cockiness, because I know what to expect.

"Have you worked with autistic children before?" Mariel, the young, pregnant teacher asks me.

"A few," I answer. "But not as a teacher. Tell me what you want me to do."

I nod as she describes how children with autism need structure and routine, how I need to go slowly with them, because they will not be happy to see a new face in the classroom.

"We will have only two boys today, so as I work with one child, you must stay very close to the other. And keep them safe," she stresses. "Until they get used to you, try to avoid touching them unless they are going to hurt themselves."

Mariel explains how a touch from a stranger can be extremely upsetting for a child with autism and could spark some explosive behavior. I think back to how often I've put my hand on children's shoulders to calm them down or get their attention, how I've taken their hands to bring them back to their seats, how I've given them high fives when they make efforts to try something new.

This restriction will take concentration on my part.

"And they are both named Robert," she adds. "I call one 'Robby' so it's not so confusing for them. Robert is higher-functioning and can say some words and phrases. Robby doesn't verbalize at all yet."

Robert arrives just then, hand-in-hand with his father but tucked behind the man's right leg like a shadow. A cute little guy with sandy blond hair, he seems simply to be shy. As his father helps him out of his coat and cap, he leans back into him, saying, "Don't wanna go to school. Wanna go home!"

Mariel approaches his father for the handoff, reminding him to close the door as he leaves. Then, she gives Robert her full attention. He's on the move, having clearly stated his opinion of school, and Mariel has to be quick. Instead of taking her seat in the circle and telling Robert to come to her, she spends about ten minutes corralling him, calmly explaining how he needs to listen, follow instructions, and use words to describe what he is feeling.

Robert flies around the room, throwing toys on the floor, hollering, "No! No! Don't wanna!" at the top of his lungs. He dodges the teacher like an agile receiver headed for the end zone. I try to block him, but Mariel warns me to stay motionless until he is caught. Never losing her composure, she pins his flailing arms to his sides and, facing him away from her body, holds him closely to her chest until he calms down.

The classroom door opens again, and another father dressed for work tenderly walks a slight, dark-eyed boy with curly hair into the room. Robby has the disconnected look so common in children with autism. He processes all the things in the room but doesn't yet seem to notice the people in it. His father bends over to say good-bye and give him a kiss, but Robby shows no response. I step forward to introduce myself and tell them I'm helping Mariel today. The grief and sadness on the father's face stuns me. When he leaves, Robby stands in the same spot, quiet and alone.

I take small steps toward this adorable little boy, who takes no notice of me until I am about a foot away from him. Robby then turns his face in the direction of familiar Mariel and, walking on his toes and dribbling saliva, begins to meander toward her.

I follow at a discreet distance, like a bodyguard. When he strolls too close to Mariel and Robert, I ask Robby to come with me and find a toy. Mariel is ducking Robert's flying feet and hands, saying, "Use your words! Tell Mariel what you want!"

She shows no irritation or impatience, which amazes me. I hear her repeat and correct him while she watches for any sign that her message is getting through. When he stops attacking her and moves one Velcro square on the felt board, she cheers and rewards him with about thirty seconds of jumping on a small exercise trampoline.

By trial and error, I find that Robby will approach me if I avoid eye contact and simply play with toys, making noises that mimic buzzing airplanes, beeping car horns, and howling fire-truck sirens. If I try to interact with him, he skitters away, fingering his saliva bubbles, making little humming sounds. He climbs on the trampoline as soon as Robert is finished but cannot manage more than one hop by himself. I figure Mariel will let me know when Robby is ready for contact with me.

Robert's lesson proceeds, and I move around the room with Robby. I don't know if his inability to focus on one toy for more than a few seconds is due to his discomfort with me or if that's just how his day goes. I sit down, get up, kneel down, stand up, and follow Robby for what seems like hours, keeping him out of the bathroom, away from the teacher's desk and papers, off the work and lunch tables, and in the room until I am dizzy. The clock says the boys arrived twenty-five minutes ago.

I get too close to Robby at times, and he responds by breaking into a run or growling, bubbling out more saliva, and baring his tiny teeth at me. How do his parents cope and not lose heart?

When Robert's time with Mariel comes to a close, a speech therapist escorts him to her office for another lesson. He isn't exactly doing cartwheels at the prospect of yielding to more adult direction, but he isn't fighting either. Routine whining and foot-dragging seem so tame after his earlier behavior.

Our attention turns to Robby. Mariel carefully brings him to the front of the room, where she has arranged her teaching materials. She directs me to sit on the floor next to him and introduces me as "Ms. Peggy, the helper." She shows me how to fold his hands into mine so we can clap as we count. Now that he is engaged, Robby surprisingly seems less hostile about physical contact. He settles into my lap.

As the minutes pass, I forget Robby has special needs. He's a little kid propped against me, and we're singing silly songs. Soon the synapses in his brain misfire, and he struggles to get up and away. I hold him with very little effort, but it's enough to make him angry. He faces me, forms his hands into claws on my face, and growls. Mariel quickly corrects him, telling him, "Only nice touches, Robby," and the lesson proceeds. I hold Robby's hand for balance as he triumphantly bounces on the trampoline.

When bathroom break time rolls around, Robby does his business and waits for me to clean him up. He lets me wash his hands without resisting. Robert returns from speech therapy, and we serve him a bland snack of white bread, cheese sticks, and sour, unripe oranges. He refuses to eat, so we throw it away.

Every surface and toy touched in the room has to be thoroughly cleaned with bleach water after the boys are swaddled in winter clothing and delivered to their after-school caregivers. I ask Mariel what happens to children like Robert and Robby when they get to age eighteen.

"Oh, you would be surprised," she answers as she sets up her lessons for the next day. "Many of the children, with a lot of help, will be able to live in supervised settings, maybe hold a job. They aren't lost causes, and we don't give up on them."

I have the uncomfortable feeling that I learned much more today than the children did, and my education is far from complete.

Chapter 8

NOVEMBER 25 PASSES. I feel less anxious and guarded. I can suppress the memories of that day for another year. I have something to be thankful for—none of the boys in my many, many substitute teacher classrooms share my son's name. I doubt I could call a child "Ian" and keep from crying.

Flu season is on us with a vengeance. Phone calls with the computer-generated voice offering substitute teacher jobs keep coming until I crack and push the #1 key to accept. The schools are full of subs, and the kids are full of pre-holiday exuberance.

The month of December starts with a fifty-one-degree day, and dirty puddles of slush make us forget that snow shovels are usually well worn by this time. The very thought of spending another day standing patiently while the kids get rid of their winter gear, taking attendance and lunch count, and sitting through a mind-numbing Morning Meeting makes me throw caution to the wind and accept an assignment of the unknown. I think the recorded voice says something about "Suspension." I envision a quiet day of reading while occasionally glaring at offenders hunched over their schoolwork.

The school secretary sizes me up when I tell her I am subbing in the Suspension Room. Without blinking, she asks me if I have ever worked this particular assignment before. I say, "No!" and give her my "Don't know nothin' about nothin'" smile. She leans toward me, widens her eyes to show her misgivings, and says with strong emphasis, "Make sure you read all the instructions before you come back here to pick up the students." She hands me a key and points me in the direction of the stairway.

A little click of concern registers in my brain, but I'm not a quitter, so I find my way to the Suspension Room at the top of the stairs. I unlock the door, flip on the lights, and stare. This room must be the only space in the twenty-four elementary schools in Sioux Falls that is completely devoid of colorful posters, dancing mobiles with uplifting words, children's artwork, and baskets of books. There are five cubicles, one in each corner and another in the center of the room. The teacher's desk near the door has nothing on it except a laminated sheet of instructions, which I grab, hoping for a full description of how I am to get through the day.

> THE STUDENTS ARE NOT TO SPEAK UNLESS GIVEN PERMISSION BY THE TEACHER, AND THEN THEY MAY SPEAK ONLY TO THE TEACHER.

The students are to be delivered to the school by a parent and picked up at the end of the day by a parent.

The students must have a completed Behavior Contract signed by a parent and by the student before being admitted to the Suspension Room.

If the student does not follow the agreed-upon Behavior Contract and complete all work assignments, the student will spend another day in the Suspension Room.

The students will get their lunch trays and bring them back to the Suspension Room. They will eat in their cubicles without speaking to anyone.

The students must be accompanied to the restroom by the teacher.

The students are never to be left alone in the room or the restroom.

The students are to complete the work assignments sent by their teacher from their respective schools. The students must work alone.

RECESS IS MY BEST SUBJECT

READ THESE RULES TO THE STUDENTS.

AFTER THREE DAYS IN THE SUSPENSION ROOM, THE STUDENTS WILL BE HARVESTED FOR ORGAN DONATIONS.

Okay, the last part is mine, but the seriousness of the situation registers in my brain, and I feel scared, which in turn makes me feel silly.

I remind myself to think this through. The students who will arrive in a few minutes have pushed the envelope of the discipline policy at their schools. They have been given many chances by their teachers, counselors, and principals to shape up. Notes have gone home to their parents. They have spent time in the hall, in the office, and in detention. They are frequent flyers and potential future delinquents. This full day of sort-of-boot-camp is intended to scare them straight and make them see the harsh consequences of their behavior choices.

The last line of the laminated instruction sheet tells me to call the principal immediately if the students do not follow all the rules. I notice neat, orderly piles of textbooks and worksheets on the desks in three cubicles. Is it possible that I will be responsible for only three children today?

The clock tells me it's time to pick up my miscreants, so I report to the office. The secretary hands me a packet of papers and points me to two pairs of mothers and sons. None of them look happy to see me. I forget to be serious and smile, then realize my mistake and put on a serious, sober face.

One mother, dressed for professional success, is on her phone while her son slumps in a chair. The information packet states his name is Boyd, and he is in fourth grade.

As I wait, she cuts off the call with a snap of her phone, then tells her son to "Do your work today, and pay attention to the teacher, okay?" She turns to me and adds, "He is getting tested for ADHD this week." I nod, showing polite, blind support for the idea. A second later, she is gone.

The second mother and son are standing very closely together, taking up as little space as possible. The boy, Michael, is a slender third grader with a fresh haircut and big eyes full of apprehension. His mother must have already said her good-bye, because she disappears when I ask, "Are you ready, Michael?"

"Follow me, please, and no talking," I order before leading the way. There must be a cloud of shame surrounding us, because the well-behaved children pause to gawk as we parade through the hall and up the stairs to our classroom. The boys are silent. Someone has told them the "Don't talk unless the teacher asks you something" rule, and I don't know whether to be glad for a respite from reminding kids that the halls are Quiet Zones or to feel sorry that they're being treated like little prisoners.

We meet the third perp, Gavin, at the door. He tells me some convoluted story about his mother not coming today, because she has to work and can't be late again, the way she was yesterday after dropping him off. Gavin is in fifth grade. This is his second day in Suspension and his second trip to this particular elementary slammer this year.

Gavin goes to his assigned seat, and I help Boyd and

Michael find the cubicles with their piles of school work. As I read the rules to them, Gavin starts drawing in a notebook smuggled in his backpack. I decide to deal with that after I get the Behavior Contracts from the other boys. Boyd produces his signed contract, but Michael looks past me and says he doesn't have his, that it must be at home.

I call the secretary, who says Michael's mother will have to return with the signed contract or take him home for the day. She tells me to keep Michael at his desk and make sure he gets to work. I realize I should have asked for the Behavior Contract in the office before I let the mothers slip away. I have made more work for the secretary and certainly more work for Michael's mother.

I tell the boys to begin their assignments, which are detailed in "to do" lists atop each of their piles. Gavin raises his hand and tells me that his list is from yesterday, and he had to finish all this work before he was allowed to leave school. On my way to Gavin's desk, I motion to Boyd and Michael to get to work.

I tell Gavin to put away his drawing and show me his completed work from yesterday. His irritation level rises with each question, but I feel it's necessary to have correct information before I call the office (again) and ask for assistance.

"I already *did* that paper, and that one, too!" Gavin shouts at me, tossing worksheets around his cubicle. "I turned in my work yesterday to Mr. Sullivan! I don't have it!" I order him to help me pick up the papers. He snottily rattles off answers to problems on the worksheet as he shoves the papers at me. The page numbers of the worksheets match those on his list of assignments for today. If he is blowing smoke, he is doing a great job of it. I call the secretary and describe the problem. Gavin is not the only person getting peeved. With an exasperated sigh, she says she will call his school and get some answers.

Michael and Boyd are now on the floor, playing with toys from their backpacks. Evidently I do not inspire even the teensiest amount of fear in the boys, because when I pause, frowning, with hands on my hips for emphasis, they throw preoccupied looks my way and keep playing. "What are you doing?" I bark. "Get back in your seats and get to work!"

"I don't know what to do," whines Michael.

"I don't get it. I don't know where to start," mutters Boyd.

Gavin surprises me by offering to help, describing how Mr. Sullivan lets him work with other kids when he's done with his assignments. I remind Gavin that he is not allowed to speak with the other students. He flings himself back into his chair with an angry snort, muttering about "stupid rules" and "stupid assignments." I'm not certain, but I think I also heard "stupid teacher," so I bellow, "Stop talking!" and glare at him. The room is very quiet.

I stop at Boyd's cubicle to check his progress. He seems unable to read his assignment page and find the correct book with its corresponding worksheet. He is in fourth grade. I assume he can read "Math, Social Studies, Daily Oral Language." I tell him to start with the first assignment listed at the top of the page. He appears truly stumped. I tell him to read the assignment out loud. He stumbles with the words, taking long pauses between each one. I ask him what he just read, and he shrugs. I stare at him as he slumps over his pile of work, already flummoxed and defeated. It's possible he has polished his ignorance act in order to get extra help or to be ignored, but what if he *isn't* playing me? How has he arrived in the fourth grade without these skills?

If I go back to my desk and let him flounder and fail, will I share the guilt of his failure? If he has to return to the Suspension Room tomorrow, will I have done all I can to help him? I can't bring myself to act as a detached overseer while a student needs my help. I worry it will be the first of many mistakes I'll make today.

"Which subject do you want to work on first?" I ask Boyd. He says he likes math, so I tell him to find his math book and the math worksheet. He perks up at the prospect of having a private tutor for the day. I scan the directions and get him started on the first block of problems. He begins work without any further protest.

Michael has been carefully observing my interaction with Boyd and has figured out the game. Books and papers are all as neatly stacked on Michael's desk as when he arrived, and he is playing with the pocket zippers on his jacket. I repeat the instructions to get the math book, find the worksheet, and get to work. Michael echoes Boyd's statement of "I don't know what to do," and I take the bait and help him get started.

The tone of the day is set, and on some level, the boys sense reprieve.

A knock on the door rattles me for a moment. The secretary appears with a pile of work that has been faxed from Gavin's school with a note from his teacher reminding him to complete all the work on his own. Gavin isn't happy about being told once again to put away his drawing and get to work.

A hush falls over the room. I open my book and read a couple of sentences before Gavin explodes.

"The idiots sent the same stuff! I can't believe they are so stupid! I already did this crap, and I'm not gonna do it again!" He pounds his right fist on the pile of papers, then crumples as many as he can get in his hands. I storm to Gavin's cubicle without taking time to think things through.

"Stop it, Gavin!" I holler with what I hope is conviction. "You're ruining all the worksheets! How can I see what they sent?" I look up from the mess and see tears of rage in his eyes. His frustration level matches mine, and I tell him I will get the problem fixed. He stomps to an unused cubicle in a corner and sits with his back to me, head on the desk.

Boyd and Michael have ceased working, of course, and are watching the drama.

Gavin is correct. The list of assignments and worksheets are duplicates of those he says he completed yesterday. I am going to have to call the secretary. Again.

While I am on the phone with her, Gavin uses up any sympathy points he may have earned from me by dragging a bin of interlocking plastic blocks from a covered shelf in the back of the room and dumping the contents all over the place. Michael and Boyd are on the floor in a heartbeat. The three boys look like an advertisement for playing nice as they collaboratively build towers and racetracks.

The secretary tells me she is going to hand the situation over to the principal. My compulsive Catholic training shifts into hyperdrive, and I examine my conscience for any and all substitute-teacher sins I may have committed. There are too many to mention, and I believe I will look like a spineless weenie when the principal shows up to see the kids playing.

I do an amazingly spot-on imitation of a woman on the brink of losing it.

"Pick up all the blocks! What are you doing?! How many more days do you want to spend in Suspension? PUT AWAY THE BLOCKS! The principal is on her way! Gavin, listen to me!" I am scooping up blocks, shouting, and leaning into their faces. The only thing missing is spittle flying from my mouth and a wire hanger in my hand.

Michael and Boyd pick up a few blocks, then retreat to their desks when they see Gavin refuse to help. Gavin argues that Mr. Sullivan lets them play with stuff when they are done with their work.

"No one here has done any work!" I snap as I put away the bin. "Sit down and be quiet!"

I am standing, arms crossed, looking like a prison guard, when the principal comes into the room. She is a tall woman with large eyes, very white teeth, and an irked expression on her face. She introduces herself and asks what is going on, and before I can manage even five words, Gavin starts blurting his version of the injustice dealt to him.

With the speed and precision of a laser, the principal silences Gavin. She focuses her now-even-larger eyes on him, leans forward, and uses a tone of voice I can only describe as cutting.

"Gavin! Sit down, and do not leave your seat unless you are told to do so. Do not speak unless the teacher asks you to speak.

You know the rules here, and you will follow the rules!" She is neither scolding nor shaking a finger at him, but the message is clear and precise. She then turns to me and says, "I will speak with Gavin's teacher and get this problem solved. I will let you know what we decide."

And she is gone. I expect to see a smoldering ash pile on Gavin's chair, but he has survived and waits for about thirty seconds before he puts his head into his folded arms on the desk top and moans about his terrible treatment. I make another mistake by ignoring his behavior, which clearly shows his disdain for me. Michael and Boyd drop the pretense of working after the principal strides out of the room. It must be bathroom break time, I decide, and we all troop to the boys' bathroom across the hall. I stand in the doorway just out of sight of the urinals and make sure they all wash their hands.

"No talking!" I snarl when words start sneaking out of their mouths. I march them back into the room.

Michael raises his hand and asks, "When do we get to go out for recess?"

I make an attempt to imitate the principal. "You don't get recess when you are in Suspension. I read the rules to you. You stay in this room all day except for bathroom breaks and when you go to get your lunch. You will eat your lunch in this room, and you may not talk." My delivery is crisp and authoritative.

"Mr. Sullivan lets us talk when we eat our lunch," challenges Gavin.

I am stunned. It's been less than ten minutes since the principal verbally smacked him down, and he wants to spar again.

"Gavin, what part of 'no talking' don't you understand?" I sputter. "I can call the principal and ask her to come right back if this is how you are going to follow the rules!"

"I don't have anything to do!" he shouts at me. "What am I supposed to do?"

"You will wait and be absolutely quiet until we hear from the principal!"

I know I should not have answered. He has stepped across the disciplinary line drawn in the sand. I should have picked up the phone and let him live with the consequences. Strike two.

The three boys are in their seats when the principal returns with Gavin's assignments. Her eyes are still shooting sparks, and I make a wild guess that the second trip to the Suspension Room was not in today's planner.

"Your teacher is sick today, Gavin, so your assignments were not taken to the office. This is the correct list, and I expect you to work very hard and get it all finished by the end of the school day." After a tiny pause, she adds three razor-sharp words. "Am I clear?"

Gavin's nod lacks conviction, but the principal allows no time for rebuttal and makes a quick, determined exit. Boyd and Michael need help moving to their next set of math problems. I mosey past Gavin's desk on the way back to mine and note that he is absorbed in his math worksheet.

For about twenty blissful minutes, the only sound in the room is the scratch of pencils on paper. I have a book open on the desk in front of me, but I can't read a word. I keep expecting more fireworks to go off any moment.

I give the boys five minutes' warning before we leave for

lunch. They close their books, and we march to the lunchroom. Only a few kids throw curious glances our way, which makes me realize that the Suspension Room must be occupied every day. The boys carry their trays back up the stairs to their bleak holding pen and begin eating. I have no idea when to take my lunch break, so I'm surprised when another teacher pops in and tells me she will cover while I "am away." I practically lope out of the room.

After I return from gagging down a sandwich in the staff workroom, the afternoon stretches out for what seems like eons. I must start making better lunches. It's the high point of my workday, but I am so sick of turkey and cheese on wheat bread.

I worry about the afternoon, because I know how elementary school kids, especially boys, live for their time on the playground during the lunch hour. I have watched the worst class cut-ups settle down and shush their classmates when I tell them no one is leaving for lunch and recess until the room is completely quiet.

The classroom feels depressive when I return. Any hope the kids harbor about getting out of work is gone. Michael and Boyd now understand they have two-and-a-half hours of hard labor left in their sentences. No recess. No "specials" to break the monotony of work. No distractions allowed. Having forgotten what they have done to warrant their punishment in the first place, they scowl and pout.

Gavin is slumped at his cubicle, head propped by one hand, scribbling in his notebook.

It's not long before Boyd and Michael stop making progress

on their assignments. Their whining kicks up a notch when I order them to start their fill-in-the-word social studies worksheets. It's obvious they were not listening when the lessons were originally covered, and they moan and groan about having to read a couple of paragraphs in their textbooks to look for the answers. I choose to act the part of drill sergeant so that they can learn how difficult and cold the world can be outside their regular classrooms. It's a luxury to see the boys think through their problems without having other kids braying the answers. They of course see it as slow torture, but I don't let them quit.

Gavin has pushed his work aside and is drawing in his notebook. I stand over him, scan his desk for completed worksheets, and tell him to get to work on his writing assignments. It's not a coincidence that all three boys chose math problems this morning when given the option. In my experience, most boys shy away from writing unless it involves descriptions of things. They tend to see anything that hints at feelings or relationships as "stupid" or "who cares?"

My son spent more time complaining about writing assignments than he spent actually writing, unless he was writing about science or technology, because he found safety in facts and logic. He was a good writer when he put some effort into it, but our family knew he was happiest with algebra equations and multiple computer screens. He was looking forward to physics and calculus.

True to boy form, Gavin starts rumbling about how much he hates writing. I order him to put away his markers and notebook and work on his assignments. I wait for him to comply. It takes about a minute before he grudgingly yanks a worksheet out of the pile of books and papers. He sloppily writes his name with a marker, despite the teacher's instructions to use a pencil. I order him to put it down and use the correct instrument. He hesitates for about ten seconds, then throws the marker into the corner of his cubicle and digs out a pencil. I then realize I've been holding my breath while glaring at him, so I let it out and return to my desk.

The tension in the room is palpable. Gavin's muttering gets louder, and I can't ignore it. I remind him of the principal's directives and add, "You don't want to spend another day in this room, Gavin. You need to get your work done."

"*You* need to get your work done!" he echoes with way too much attitude. "You get *your* work done! You don't tell *me* what to do!"

"Stop it, Gavin!" I roar.

"You better watch out! I might do something to you after school. . . ."

I don't wait for him to finish. I dial the principal's number and tell her Gavin is out of control.

She is at the classroom door as quickly as if she used the transporter from *Star Trek*. She tells Michael and Boyd to get to work and takes Gavin and me into the empty hall. Gavin is too angry to deny making a threat. He spins his side of the story while the principal listens carefully. She asks me a few questions, and I give brief answers.

"Yes, Gavin completed his math work."

"No, he has not done his remaining assignments."

"He said I better watch out, because he might do something to me after school."

I notice the expensive cut of her suit as she says, "Gavin, if you refuse to obey all the rules while you are in Suspension, you cannot stay here. I will have to call the police."

I figure she is talking about the School Resource Officer assigned to each school, but it still sounds frightening. Gavin's face shows outrage and frustration but no fear.

The principal starts to say, "If you cannot—" and then pauses for a second. "Never mind, Gavin, come with me." She puts her hand on his shoulder to guide him, and they walk down the hall. "I'll send someone to get his coat and backpack," she calls over her shoulder.

What I'm feeling isn't victory or smugness or relief. It feels more like failure.

Boyd and Michael wear questioning looks when I step back into the classroom. I know I cannot tell them what happened to Gavin specifically, but I sure as hell can let them know what happens to kids who test the system. We talk about what they did to get them suspended from their schools and what will happen if they don't change their ways. They are both counting on parental support to cushion any additional punishment, so they are shocked to learn that kids who keep breaking rules can be taken away from family and sent to juvenile detention centers. I let the news sink in, then remind them of the rule that states they have to finish their work or come back with a parent for a day two in Never-Again-Land.

They assure me they want to get their work done.

Michael is so antsy by midafternoon that he cannot sit still in his chair. Both boys get the giggles when Boyd starts to hiccup and cannot stop. I move Boyd's cubicle so that he cannot see Michael, but they are punchy, and everything sets them off.

"Michael, bring your papers to my desk, please," I say in desperation. As he stands by the desk, I let him wiggle, tap his feet, and sway in place as long as he is writing answers. He is supposed to write a poem, and I show my advanced age by giving an ancient example of alliteration. "Blue baby booties" sends him into spasms of laughter until he is nearly breathless. When he takes a breath, he repeats the phrase, and Boyd joins in the hysterical laughter.

I know I am not qualified or cut out for subbing in the Suspension Room when Michael says, "This was a fun day! I thought it would be a lot worse. I could come back tomorrow!"

I can't let them leave with that sentiment, so I tell the boys I won't be back in this school tomorrow, that the regular teacher, Mr. Sullivan, will be back, and he is a very, very tough teacher. I want to add something about bread and water, but I know they won't believe that.

Just before the dismissal bell, they stuff their books and papers into backpacks, and we trudge to the office for the official handoff to the parents. Boyd's mother is on the phone when we step into the office but quickly puts it away to hear my report. I tell her Boyd needs a lot of help to do his work, and she repeats her plan to have him tested for ADHD.

"He doesn't have to come to Suspension tomorrow?" she asks. I reply, "No," and she whisks him out the door.

Michael's mother arrives later, and it's clear that leaving work in the middle of the afternoon is a huge stressor. She nearly bursts through the school's front doors with no coat and her cardigan sweater flying open. She shoots quick glances at my face but avoids eye contact as I tell her that Michael is a very smart boy, but he has to read more and pay closer attention in class. She appears so relieved to learn he is no longer suspended that my message seems to evaporate.

I have very little classroom cleaning to do, and my notes to the teacher will be mostly about Gavin, since the others won't be back tomorrow. Did I do any favors for Michael and Boyd by bending the rules for them? Did I push a troubled child into dangerous behavior by trying to be conciliatory when I should have been consistent?

Winston Churchill supposedly said, "When you are going through hell, keep going." I sigh repeatedly on the drive home and pray for better work options.

Chapter 9

I SUB IN A RELATIVELY UNIQUE fourth-grade room on my next assignment, still early in December. The regular teacher is a man (most of the elementary teachers I've seen have been women) who has *not* covered every available inch of wall, window, and door space with decorative stuff. Cursive ABCs line the top of the whiteboard, printed names are taped to the lockers, and two of the bulletin boards have lists and photos. The room seems bare, as though students and teacher are in transition and shouldn't get too comfy, because a move is in the immediate future.

The desks are arranged in rows instead of "pods" (groups of four to six desks facing each other). I haven't seen the row arrangement since I started subbing, and I find it less stressful. I've struggled for months to capture and retain the children's attention when they are face-to-face and have determined I'm no match for the antics the pod setup inspires.

The teacher's lesson plan is spare and simple. Math is a worksheet, Social Studies covers an easy chapter on Native Americans, and PE and Music will be taught in different classrooms. There are twenty-three students in the class, but fourth graders are usually a decent bunch, fully versed on the consequences of bad behavior and not quite ready to risk it all for peer approval, as some fifth graders are. The wild card for the day will be the number of children in this classroom with special needs. By fourth grade, the kids who cannot read at or near grade level can be extremely disruptive. It's not only the constant traffic in and out of the room as they take their turns getting help from resource specialists throughout the day; it's also the acting up to reconnect with the other kids and prove they're not invisible. When they return from the resource rooms, they are supposed to read quietly or finish assignments, but that rarely happens. Instead, they often wander, chat, start arguments, or clown around for a laugh. I know that one child with learning problems will test my patience. Two or more can completely change the dynamics of the room.

The students arrive, and we slide into the morning routine without a glitch. My back and leg hurt, but I can ease the pain as I call on the kids by leaning against the whiteboard or perching on a stool at the front of the room. I'm on full alert in case the students in the back of the room take advantage of my stationary position and detach from the lesson. I do have to wander down an aisle once when I notice a knot of boys whispering, but they shape up as soon as I get close.

The weekly spelling test, usually a benign, gentle activity, exposes a problem that will rear its ugly head throughout the school day: some children do not have pencils.

I don't believe it when they tell me. A few seem embarrassed to admit it, but others say it as easily as "Here" when I call the roll. I have seen kids use all kinds of tactics to delay test-taking, but "no pencil" seems insulting even to a substitute. I scan the teacher's desk for extra supplies but come away empty-handed. I can't believe this class operates in such scarcity.

"What does your teacher do when students don't have pencils?" I ask incredulously when four kids ransack their desks in search of something to use. Others watch, slack-jawed and bored. This is a common occurrence.

"He says we should borrow one from somebody else," say several kids at once. I ask for a few Good Samaritans to step up, but it appears no one has a spare. We waste nearly twenty minutes digging in desks and discussing possible solutions. I find a half dozen colored pencils in one girl's desk and ask permission to sharpen and distribute them to the pencilless kids. She isn't happy with the request but shrugs her "yes," and the spelling test begins.

Teachers spend an average of four hundred dollars of their own money per school year for classroom supplies, and in some parts of the Sioux Falls school district, it's not nearly enough. Parent Teacher Associations hold fund-raisers, but the list of needs always exceeds the income. By the middle of the year, if parents aren't able to replace school supplies, kids and teachers just have to make do. Disbelief prompts me to make a mental note to pick up pencils on my next shopping trip. The purchase will nibble away at the whopping ninety-dollar-per-day salary I'm raking in, but I can't ignore what I see.

We limp along, sharing supplies for the rest of the day.

Everything takes longer than usual, so I bend the rules and allow some assignments to be completed with markers, which of course bleed through the paper and make smeary messes on the students' desks.

I rifle through cabinets during recess to see if the teacher has bundles of pencils stashed in hard-to-reach corners or hidden boxes, but I find none. Instead of piles and cartons of supplies, I find half-empty drawers and the bare minimum of manuals and books. It just feels wrong. South Dakota ranks last in teacher salaries, so maybe this teacher's income is stretched so thin that he simply can't cover one more student in need.

We are immersed in our social studies project in the early afternoon when the classroom door opens, and three students bearing half-filled grocery bags walk in. They set the bags on a table and shuffle out. I'm the only person who does more than glance in their direction. I open my mouth to voice my question but snap it shut when "the BackPack Program" pops into my head. This is the first time I've seen it in action.

Nearly 40 percent of Sioux Falls's elementary school children qualify for free or reduced-priced meals during the school week. That means many children and their families don't have enough to eat without help from people and programs in our community. About three years ago, teachers and other childcare professionals noticed how ravenously hungry certain children were on Monday morning and how they seemed to be eating extra or smuggling food out of the lunchroom on Friday. It was then that they decided to initiate a South Dakota chapter of the BackPack Program, a nationwide effort to make sure kids and their families are fed.

Funded completely by donations and operated solely by volunteers, the BackPack Program in Sioux Falls feeds nearly three thousand children and their families during the school year. The name came from (donated) backpacks that were packed with food items like cereal, oatmeal, juice, fresh fruit, granola bars, fruit cups, raisins, and nuts. When it finally hit Sioux Falls, the local newspaper, *The Argus Leader*, got wind of the story and picked up the banner. The newspaper took over the program's administration and printed the names of its many generous donors, which motivated even more people to help. The backpacks were abandoned after about a year. Now, the food is packed into disposable plastic grocery bags that are tied at the top, so the children can slip the donations into their backpacks. In some classrooms, half the kids participate in the BackPack Program, and there are still more on waiting lists.

I want to add "pencils" to the list of needed items. I know there are various programs and agencies in Sioux Falls that work to make sure children from low-income households start the school year on the same footing as others, with fresh supplies, new shoes, and haircuts. But shoes wear out, and supplies get used up. What then?

When I later tell people about the Great Pencil Shortage, their responses upset me. Most shake their heads, and some take off on tangents about "pouring millions of dollars into education, and that's what we get." Others are even less sympathetic.

"I'm tired of taking care of other people's children. I take care of my own kids. I shouldn't have to take care of someone else's."

"They'll just have to learn to make do, the way we did."

"It would be different if they acted as if they appreciate things, but they don't even take care of what they *do* have."

I learn to watch for pencils on the clearance shelves. I can get a pack for less than two dollars, which means there will be one less reason for these less-fortunate kids to wiggle out of spelling tests.

SNOW STARTS FALLING midmorning on December 8—white, fluffy feathers that float gently to the ground. I'm sure it's beautiful, but I'm in a kindergarten classroom without a single window, surrounded by twenty-three very busy children. I want to tell parents that it's simply not possible to provide much more than guided day care when there are so many children in one room, some with special needs. But no one asks, so I remain up to my elbows in five-year-olds, untied shoes, and snot.

I understand that parents have to send children to school before they're fully recovered from colds and flu. I realize that my aversion to seeing mucus smeared across a child's face is not shared by everyone. I know a kid's natural reaction to a drippy schnoz is to wipe it on his or her sleeve. Even so, my gag reflex activates when I see thick, green mucus from one or both nostrils ooze toward a child's open mouth.

Tissue boxes are everywhere, paired with bottles of hand sanitizer. We have barely begun the Morning Meeting rites when I call for a break. Many of the children still seated on the carpet are sniffling so frequently that it's only a matter of time before they drip. Phlegmy coughs bark from several throats.

Five kids head for tissue boxes, but only two make the return trip. I use my kindest pediatric nurse voice.

"On my goodness, it sounds as if a lot of K02 students have colds! Let's talk for a minute about what we should do when we have runny noses, okay?"

Their regular teacher has done an excellent job of drilling them on the importance of covering their mouths when they cough and using hand sanitizer after a nose wipe, but I'm certain the kids have not experienced my version of thorough nasal hygiene. I demonstrate the two-handed honk-and-wipe ("Good!") as well as the inefficient smear-and-toss that passes inspection for most five-year-olds ("Not good!"). I tell them it's a bad idea to sniff and swallow, because the mucus will go into their tummies and make them feel sick.

So many of the kids ask, "What's meew-cus?" that I capitulate and call it snot.

"Where does it go if you sniff?"

"That's why my brother is sick, 'cause he sniffs his snot."

The lesson seems to have landed. We finish Morning Meeting with many, many saturated tissues.

During one group activity later that morning, I overhear a boy telling the four children at his table that one of our local TV stations is able to track Santa Claus on its weather radar. "My mom says we'll be able to watch Santa on Christmas Eve!" he adds, so excited that he stops cutting and gluing.

One little girl, clearly the pessimist of the bunch, says, "What happens if Santa gets sick? Who will do his job?"

The boy glares at her. "Santa doesn't get sick! He never does, so he always brings toys!"

Miss Pessimist can't let it go. "But what if Santa Claus dies?! Then what happens?"

"Santa Claus can't *die!*" screams the boy. He jumps out of his chair, scissors in hand, near tears. The rest of the kids look scandalized and scared, so I tell them that Santa can't die and that they need to get back to work. I move Miss Doom-and-Gloom to another table.

The use of hand sanitizer is a good indicator of attention levels across the room. When the children lose interest in the book, song, or game meant to enthrall them, the levels of sanitizer go down. They linger at the bottles, playing with the pumps, soliciting reminders from me that only one squirt is allowed, and they must return to their places. After a while, it seems the whole class is finding tissues and sanitizing gel more riveting than colors and numbers, so I cut my losses and tell them it's snack time. We make it through the morning with only a few teary skirmishes about who gets to sit with whom, and I count it as a victory, because so many of my little soldiers are feeling under the weather.

Lunch approaches, and the teacher's instructions are clear about allowing enough time to get ready. These kindergartners put on their snow pants, boots, and coats before trooping to the lunchroom, leaving their coats open and their hats and mittens in their hoods. They eat first, then finish bundling up before heading outside for recess. It seems simple enough.

But I stop short of reading the teacher's instructions for handing out lunch cards. Thinking nothing of it, I do what makes sense at the time—I hand them out before the kids even start to get ready. By the time they're all half-bundled up, ready to walk to the lunchroom, I realize that most of their lunch cards have vanished. Some kids have exchanged cards with friends. Others look at me blankly when I ask where they put theirs.

We pay for my ignorance for fifteen minutes. I scour the room, the bathroom at the rear of the classroom, their pockets, and the wastebasket full of snotty tissues. A few kids get too warm, take off their coats, and wander to the play area before I can finally get cards into everyone's hand. I herd them back into line, lead a quick-march to the lunchroom, and hand them off to the teacher on duty.

If you don't learn a lesson the first time, it will be presented again and again until you do. I pummel this into myself as I disinfect my hands and arms. When I finally start eating my sandwich, I go back and study the teacher's instructions. There, bright and bold, is a highlighted warning about handing out lunch cards too soon.

If there were a remedial class for substitutes, I'd be first in line for it.

By the time the midday recess is over, snow is falling heavily, and the temperature is dropping. I can hardly distinguish my K02 kids from the snowy lines of little ones at the edge of the playground until I hear a high-pitched wail that gets louder as I step outside. Hetash, one of my little boys, is holding his hands out in front of his body, tears streaming down his face as he sobs in pain. Two of his classmates are supporting him, shouting over his wailing that he has frozen his hands. Hetash is a recent immigrant, and this is probably his first winter in South Dakota. He is wearing thin, single-layer gloves that are completely soaked and crusted in snow.

I put my arms around Hetash and lead him through the doors. As the rest of my students follow, I scan the area for an adult. How could this happen? Wasn't anyone on playground duty? A teacher saunters over and says the child was told not to play in the snow if he didn't want to get wet and cold. I'm still moving with the crying boy, and I'm too upset (and cowardly) to say what should be said. The teacher should have let the child come into the building as soon as he showed signs of distress. I can hear the reasons and excuses: recess was nearly over; it's December, and families should have learned by now how important it is to dress children for winter weather; kids need to learn that rules are rules. But what a punishing, cold-hearted way to enforce the rules!

I carefully remove the soaked, snowy gloves as we make our way back to the classroom. The child is trembling and crying. His hands show no sign of frostbite, and circulation is good, but he's scared and not hearing or understanding me. I fend off three classmates who bring paper towels "to wipe his hands off so they can get warm" and take him to the bathroom sink so I can gradually warm his hands in water. He's still crying, and I'm fully aware of the circus going on in the classroom. I see boots and mittens flying past the open door, but I'm not leaving this poor kid now. I call out the names of the two kids most apt to follow instructions and tell them to help everyone remove their outside gear and sit in the circle.

About ten minutes pass before the water yields positive results. I'm able to increase the temperature from lukewarm, and Hetash's pain and fear begin to subside. His crying tapers off to occasional whimpers, and the children in the classroom appear to be less stressed. They settle into chatty groups on the carpet.

I shed my coat as I bring Hetash back into the floor circle, cupping his hands in mine to keep them warm. I can't let this chance to teach an important winter weather lesson with a live subject pass us by. As Hetash's puffy eyes recover from crying, the rest of the class joins in an animated discussion of what we should do when someone is in trouble on the playground and what we must remember to do when our skin gets very cold. I continue to blot ("Never rub!") Hetash's hands gently with the paper towels to emphasize how carefully skin needs to be treated when it's too cold.

I have forced myself to ignore the piles of soaked coats, snow pants, caps, and mittens until now. Taking full advantage of every square inch of space on warm air vents, I shake out the wet clothing and place everything where it can dry. The kids seem fascinated by the process. One girl tells me they are supposed to put all their things in their numbered bins. I say that's a very good rule, but on snow days, we have to let things dry before we put them away. We take a bathroom and drink break before lining up for Art, and I tell the classroom skeptics to check the mittens warming on the heaters. They're astonished to find them still very wet.

I shepherd my class to the art room and head straight for the school office. I explain to the secretaries what happened and ask how and where can I find warm mittens or gloves for this child. (I am continually amazed that the women working in the school offices know the full name of each child on top of which teacher and classroom he or she is assigned to. Most of them also know the names of each child's siblings and parents!) With a very empathetic tone, one of the women explains that all of Hetash's outerwear, with the exception of his coat, came from the donated-clothing bin, which is now completely empty. She seems just as frustrated with the situation as I am. There is no solution today.

The end-of-the-day rituals of putting away toys, tidying up, and stuffing papers into backpacks seem to energize everyone. The kids marvel at their dry mittens and caps as I move from child to child to help zip up zippers, tie scarves, and put boots on the proper feet. I lean over to help Hetash, who has just learned his first lesson about South Dakota winters and snow. The suspenders on his snow pants have completely baffled him. One strap is wrapped around his upper thigh; the second is digging into his shoulder. It looks painful. As I ease him out of the jumble, I tell him to ask his mother for some warm mittens. His blank look tells me the message went in one ear and out the other.

It was much easier to leave work at the end of the day when all I had to do was pack my briefcase and turn out the lights of my corporate training rooms. I could roll my eyes and mutter about participants who refused to try new behaviors. I didn't lie awake at night wondering how I could find warm gloves for kindergartners.

2009 CANNOT END SOON ENOUGH. My daughter is coming home from college, and the ten-day Holiday Break (no longer known as Christmas Vacation) is in sight! I'm almost giddy as I start my last subbing assignment for the year. First grade, eighteen kids, school easy to find. God is good.

I wear my warmest winter coat, which my husband says makes me look like the Michelin tire guy, but the wind is raw, even for my overactive endocrine system. The homemade cookies in my lunchbox balance the boring sandwich, and I have a fantastic, thick book to read.

The secretary greets me so warmly that I almost feel . . . welcome. My smile is real, and my "Good morning" is heartfelt. The room key works so easily that I don't even have to drop everything I'm carrying—my purse, a canvas tote stocked with supplies, my boots, and an insulated BPA-free drink bottle loaded with ice and Diet Coke—to wrestle with the lock. The room temp is set on "sweaty," but it's easy to fix. The hall is chilly, certainly too cold for anyone without a heavy sweater, so I prop open the door, and voilà! Instant air conditioning.

The classroom is neat, clean, and cheerful without looking like a Timothy Leary acid trip in primary colors. I want to meet the teacher after reading her neatly typed instructions. She thanks me for subbing—in the first sentence! The phone extension of the behavior specialist is also in the opening paragraph, with encouragement to use it whenever needed. Not only is each subject carefully explained and each set of accompanying worksheets precisely placed on her worktable, but she has also written step-by-step directions for Morning Meeting and Calendar, two activities that vary from school to school and teacher to teacher, always giving me a fresh understanding of the origin of head-banging and cuticle shredding.

On her desk are adorable family photos of her three little boys, tanned and smiling in the summer sunshine.

The forms for attendance and lunch count are in the center of her organized worktable, erasable marker included. I'm scanning the list of names, puzzling over many, when someone in the office makes an announcement over the PA system telling us that the windchill is below zero, so the students will be allowed to wait indoors for the start of the school day. Hundreds of clomping, wet feet and chattering voices follow the announcement in a matter of seconds. They must have been pressed against the doors like sheep, trying to get out of the wind.

I take another swig of Diet Coke and head for the door so I can welcome my students, but I stop in my tracks when I hear, "First and second grade, line up against the wall and sit down!" It's not a happy voice. I peek into the hall, wondering if the kids are held in the sit-stay position until the teacher comes to take possession, or if their release is signaled by the electronic school bell. A few teachers are patrolling what looks like a mile of kids sitting against the walls. I timidly ask a teacher if I'm supposed to help. My status is evident, because she kindly explains that the kids stay in the hall until the first bell, and no, I'm not needed.

I scurry back into the classroom. There isn't enough time to get lost in my book, so I return to the attendance list and try some of the unfamiliar names. I feel woefully inadequate, because I don't know the gender of Ahok, Akol, Akou, Adeng, Deng, or Dut. I take a guess at Bentley, Hadley, and Yakim, but I can't be certain. Last month I stumbled through a whole day mixing up Ayden, Hayden, Kaden, and Avery, all girls.

A quick glance at the children's name badges taped to the

desk usually helps in pairing names with faces. However, I am SOL today, because their busy little fingers have pried off all traces of name tags. I reassure myself that I will learn the names of the standouts in the first fifteen minutes, and for all the others it'll just be a matter of repeating, "Stop that! Sit down!" until my tongue bleeds.

The bell rings, and my students stream into the room. I'm surprised when an irritated behavior counselor follows them in and crooks her finger at three boys and one girl, who immediately follow her back out into the hall. They're gone for almost ten minutes, so I introduce myself to the others as they shed coats, remove chairs from tabletops, and act as though I am not there.

The teacher's instructions say the children should be reading silently at their desks within five minutes of entering the room. For a split second, I wonder if I'm on *Candid Camera* or if I'm being punk'd. The children are dropping boots, gloves, and hats as they wander around the room, deep in conversations with one another. Backpacks lay near open locker doors. Two boys are playing tag. I clap my hands and shout, "Give me five!" Nothing. "First graders, what are you supposed to do now?" Eyes shift in my direction, but nothing changes.

The counselor returns with the four children whose names I will learn quickly. I don't know whether they've received a punishment or just a stern warning, but all four look chastised. The woman sizes up the situation and bellows, "103, get settled, and be quiet!" She is scaring me, but the kids don't react as I would expect. They move languidly to their desks, apparently at ease with her loud, angry voice and no-nonsense posture. The kids have to be called individually to return to the massive piles of clothing and search out their things to put away. She gives them a quick lecture about listening to the substitute and being good first graders, and she leaves with, "And I *will* be back to check on how things are going."

I get about ten minutes of curious attention as I take attendance. Adeng, Deng, and Dut are the three boys who started the day in the hall. Hadley, the girl, completes their ensemble. Before I can even finish taking attendance and lunch count, Adeng starts practicing his break dancing, to the other boys' delight. Two girls tell me that their tummies hurt, and they want to go to the office. A boy with a barking cough and red, watery eyes hands me a note that says he will get picked up by his dad shortly after 1:00 today. I ask him if he's going to a doctor's appointment, since he appears quite sick. The boy says he is going to see a doctor, but it's for his sister, who is getting her stitches "cut out."

If teachers have problems with drugs or alcohol, I can totally see how it happens.

In most classrooms, the kids get the message that something is awry when the teacher stands quietly, making eye contact with each child, using silence to draw their full attention. Those who are talking or otherwise flouting instructions usually get the message when the room gets very quiet.

It doesn't work today. If anything, the noise level increases. I realize the counselor has very good reasons for the drill sergeant behavior. I follow her lead and start barking orders.

"Adeng, sit in your chair!"

"No, Deng, we do not throw pencils!"

"Hadley, put your feet on the floor, and sit up!"

There are five children in the room who follow directions, answer questions, and quietly page through books when their work is done. I make sure they hear how well they are doing as often as possible, because if this is a typical school day, coming here must be frustrating for them. I spend so much time correcting and redirecting Adeng, Deng, Dut, and Hadley that each class activity takes three or four times longer than it should.

One of the girls is so persistent about her tummy problems that I send her to the office to have her temperature taken. On the note to the nurse, I say the child has had nothing to eat today, which may be contributing to her symptoms, and I ask if she can be fed something bland. She returns to the room with a "no fever" note. She looks worse after lunch, and I send her back to the office. Still no fever, but the poor kid looks so horrible that I let her put her head on the desk and rest.

Hadley argues with me when I repeat the principal's announcement that morning recess will have to be held indoors because of the windchill.

"Who says so? The flags in the hall are up! And what is 'wind shill' anyway?"

Even on a six-year-old, that attitude tests my patience. I ask her if she would argue like that with her regular teacher, and she takes a few seconds before answering, "I guess not." I try to explain windchill, but her attention span seems to be depleted for the day, and she plays with her hair, staring into space.

Adeng's hyperactivity is a constant distraction for most of the students. He draws my attention and makes it nearly impossible for others to do anything but listen to him and laugh. He has absolutely no self-control. If he thinks it, he says it. I hear his running commentary like the buzz of static. Deng seems annoyed as well, complaining that "Adeng says I have a big head. He won't stop talking to me." I make Adeng sit by himself in a corner chair, and he ups the ante by talking louder. I stand in front of him and stare at him as I explain the lesson, daring him to irk me. It is the only time he is silent.

When the counselor checks in with me during the lunch period, she says I should have called her, because the dynamics of the room will not improve until one or more instigators are removed. I agree, but the kids will soon be out for two afternoon specials, and then half the class leaves for ELL—English Language Learners. We'll be together for less than an hour before dismissal.

When the ELL students leave, the change is dramatic. The atmosphere allows each child a chance to ask questions. I don't make them raise their hands to speak, yet the conversation is relaxed. The kids are smiling.

I carefully watch the clock and follow the time line left for us by the teacher. I have a broken-down list of bus-riding kids who have to be ready first, kids who go to tutors after school, kids who walk home or are picked up by parents, and kids who are enrolled in after-school programs. Allowing what I think is plenty of time to put away books, put on coats and boots, and line up for dismissal, I give the order to "get ready to go home."

We are hopelessly behind schedule when the counselor pops into the room. I am struggling with a girl's coat zipper, which is resisting all efforts. Adeng, taking advantage of my focus on someone else, is leading a running game on one side of the room. The little girl with the stomach problems has collapsed on her desk, weeping. Deng and Dut are rolling on the floor, giggling.

I hand the girl and her impossible zipper to the counselor, who sputters more orders while fighting to close the coat. I wonder for a moment if the whole class is comfortable with complete chaos, but I see five kids waiting in line at the door, ready to go, and I realize it's not so. The counselor gives up on the stubborn coat zipper, says, "You'll just have to leave it open," and finally hollers at Adeng to get out to the bus. Then, she disappears. I'm quite certain she has an unfavorable impression of my substitute teaching abilities, and I don't blame her. If I had been the observer today, I would have drawn the same conclusion.

But 'tis the season for peace on earth and goodwill and yada yada. Even for subs.

Chapter 10

ALMOST TWENTY INCHES of snow falls on the Sioux Falls area during the Holiday Break of 2009. "No Travel Advised" rolls across television screens for days as the white stuff piles up. Plows growl up and down the streets as bleary-eyed city workers and private contractors attempt to open and maintain emergency routes. Anyone foolhardy enough to ignore the drifts in their driveway, thinking "I'll just wait for the storm to pass," spends hours chipping at wind-whipped swales too icy for the snowblower's bite. Digging out fire hydrants and mailboxes every twelve hours tests South Dakota's neighbors-help-neighbors Midwestern values.

Snow transforms our part of the world. Everything is covered, coated, hidden, and hazardous. Hardware stores sell out of roof rakes as homeowners audition for *American's Funniest Home Videos* by scraping tons of newly-fallen snow onto themselves. Cars creep into intersections with drivers peering past five- and six-foot-high piles left by plows. Snowblower chutes are cranked as high as possible, because there's nowhere left to throw the snow. Cold sets in, and the reality of winter hits like a shovel upside the head. Memories of brown Christmases and golf after Thanksgiving are erased. Winter has come to stay, and we are not amused.

School starts shortly after New Year's Day. Each school playground is buried in mountainous piles of scraped snow—the holy grail for kids with pent-up energy, sugar overloads, and too many hours of free time in overheated houses. Like fresh doughnuts rolled in sugar, the children arrive at the classroom door dipped in sparkly white stuff.

Today's assignment is a fourth-grade class at an older school with meandering halls, very limited staff parking, and many students who live at or below the poverty level. I have learned it can be either inspiring or sheer, discouraging drudgery to work with all the challenges presented at this school.

I arrive in plenty of time to trudge up and down stairs and find my classroom. I scope out the place for pencils, tissues, hand sanitizer, and instructions for the day. I score two out of four, locating pencils and lesson plans but nothing for noses and germs. *Jeez*, I think, hoping a student can tell me where things are hidden. Teachers often hide supplies, because some kids take everything offered and hoard or destroy it. Finding supplies can be a scavenger hunt.

Underneath the teacher's desk rests a large foam square with numbered slots for iPods. I then remember a news story I read about a pilot program in a few Sioux Falls schools that uses the iPod as teaching tools—for testing and as a reward for work done on time.

A quick scan of the attendance list reveals only a few names that will need clarification. I know Hassan is male, but I can only guess at Ajulo, Yar, and Sadiq. If they are quiet, I may say their names only once or twice anyway.

I write, "Good morning! I am Mrs. M." on the whiteboard.

As the minutes before the first bell tick away, I find myself standing in the middle of the classroom with a feeling of doom so dense it's almost palpable. It's not just the needy kids in today's classroom or the long hours for lousy pay and lack of adult camaraderie. It's January. I have been a substitute teacher for five months, and I still have no other job prospects. I also can no longer harbor my delusion that things will get better and that I'll soon step back into my old life. I may have to finish out the school year, weaving from classroom to classroom and school to school with nothing better on the horizon.

Corporate training sounds so crisp, professional, and smooth-talking: just plug in the PowerPoint, and wait for the aha's to roll from people's mouths! In reality, the work is far less glamorous. Participants are rarely happy to see you, because you are there to fix something. Leaders fix things in private, then hire trainers to make the fixes stick. I have dragged "fully portable," forty-pound flip charts through snow-clogged parking lots, cleaned meeting rooms, rearranged tables, and worked around wall-sized whiteboards filled with engineering schematics or company marketing plans with "SAVE" and "Do Not Erase" directives. I have trained in nonprofit organizations with hostile volunteers, churches with warring factions, and family-owned-and-operated businesses layered with melodrama and shock at high turnover. The few times when organizations assigned someone to help set up, I've fielded questions such as "Why are we doing this?" On the lucky days when someone also helped me clean up afterward, I tended to babble my appreciation. Participants evaluated and critiqued my abilities after every session. If the snacks were good and the room temperature was comfortable, I'd always get high scores. If participants were angry with the leadership, I'd be seen as the company shill, and the scores would show it. But every once in a while, everything clicked, and people left the training room with new ideas, new energy, greater understanding, and appreciation for the viewpoints of others. It felt as if I'd made a difference.

Today, I'm certain I'll be just another invisible substitute. The bell rings before I can descend any deeper into my self-pity sinkhole, and I hurry to collect my nineteen charges for the day. I make eye contact with a few red-cheeked faces and remind myself that I like fourth graders.

They're a chatty bunch, taking their time in the coat closet, leaving snow pants in wet piles on the floor, and flicking boots into corners. I try to make myself heard above the babble, pointing at the piles and shouting instructions to "Hang it up!" But my inability to match students with their correct clothing items gets me nothing but ignored.

"You'll lose recess time getting ready if you leave your stuff in a pile," I warn them before walking away. I've learned to turn down the volume of the obsessive-compulsive voice in my head and pick my battles. Making a big deal of it will just start the day on a negative note. And who knows? Maybe the regular teacher allows such messes to occur.

I introduce myself as the group gets settled. Each student has an assigned spot in the U-shaped table arrangement. It seems like an unusual configuration for elementary students—there is a pencil cup at each place and nothing more.

The kids need no reminder to get their iPods to check for the teacher's message of the day. The room quiets down as the screens light up. I'm impressed by the integration of electronics with curriculum. *It's long overdue*, I think, nodding and smiling as I wander around the room, giving them a few minutes to read, allowing for their various skill levels. Taking attendance and lunch count has never been so easy. They mumble their answers as though drugged. When some of them start plugging in ear phones and slumping into comfortable positions, I realize it's time to take a peek at what they're doing. Most have moved into games, their thumbs moving at a dizzying speeds.

The teacher's notes tell me it's time for the first subject of the day. The students are supposed to exchange iPods for laptops and work independently on a writing assignment.

"Aww, not yet!" is the predictable response when I announce it's time to write. I have to stand in front of several students while they take as much time as I allow to exit their games and put down their iPods. Some boys test my patience and keep playing with their devices under the table. Their classmates rat them out and tell me that the regular teacher takes away the iPods if students don't listen and obey. I must look grandmotherly and indulgent, because one boy keeps gaming after all others have begrudgingly quit. His iPod ends up in my pocket.

The other students are looking at me expectantly, so I ask one whose name the teacher has highlighted as "a good helper" whether we go to the computer lab to write. Honored and delighted to be asked, my helper points to the cart in the hall loaded with laptops and explains how I must allow only four students at a time to carefully unplug their designated machines and bring them to their desks. She explains which passwords are to be used to access assignments and describes the sites that can be used by the ELL students. Too bad she is so short. Dress her in khakis and a sweater set, and she could pass as a sub.

I am eager to see their writing without pencil smudges and misshapen letters. These fourth graders are the plugged-in, electronic-savvy worker bees of tomorrow.

The kids can either choose from a few different writing prompts (such as "My neighbor designed a time-travel machine and wants me to try it" or "For my birthday, I will get one special wish granted") or work on their own ideas.

I'm surprised to see just how much writing they have done on the laptops instead of on paper. All have at least one page written, and a few have multiple pages. The computer program points out misspelled words and run-on sentences and reads their stories back to them. As I watch the cursors move from word to word on their screens, it becomes apparent that their writing is . . . typical. A couple of kids write coherently and creatively, and they know how to spell the words they use. But the kids in ELL struggle with basic sentence composition (one child is unable to type in the password because of a learning barrier), and the rest of the students write like average fourth graders. Sigh. I was hoping to see something amazing.

I read over a boy's shoulder and see a full page of writing, single-spaced, no periods, commas, or any other form of punctuation. I casually ask him to read his story to me, which he does in a painfully slow manner. I ask him if he thinks the story should consist of one sentence. He shrugs. I point and suggest putting a period after one thought. When he follows my suggestion, I ask him to read the first part again. He struggles as if the copy is all new, and I worry that I'm not helping the situation. But I pat him on the shoulder and give the obligatory "Good work!" and tell him to keep writing.

After the first twenty minutes, the students grow restless. I read the teacher's instructions verbatim to "work quietly the entire time" and remind the children that I will make note of anyone who doesn't follow instructions.

I pick up my pace, no longer just strolling, because some of students who are stuck or bored with the assignment are clicking into games. It's clear they know the rules, but I'm a sub, and I must be tested. When I catch the gamers, I tell them they get one warning. After that, their names go on the list for the teacher. I remind them that I also have the power to make them read their stories out loud to the class (embarrassing!) or take away recess time (unthinkable!). This settles all of them but one—the boy whose iPod rests in my pocket. His focus has evaporated, and he can't sit still or stop talking.

One of the girls has trouble with her computer, and when the screen fades to black, I say, "I think it's kaput."

The boy-in-constant-motion says, "What did you say?"

I explain that kaput is a German word that means "broken, doesn't work."

"German! That means it's a Nazi word!" he says, his voice getting louder. I am a bit surprised at his vehemence and try to clear up any misconception.

"The Nazis are a very small part of German history. Not all Germans were Nazis."

He looks unconvinced.

After thirty minutes, about half the kids have disengaged from the writing assignment and are playing games, arguing, or roaming around the room. This is the part of subbing that is so disheartening. I can choose to ignore the behavior, or I can bark at them and make threats. If I knew the kids (and their names) a bit better, I could handpick partners and have them correct each other's work or write a new story together. If I knew which subjects needed more work (say, science or social studies), I could be creative and have them write two sentences about questions they might have or topics they find interesting.

My little schoolmarm-in-training has finished one story and started another. She is a positive influence on the kids around her. When I compliment her on being a good writer, the students on either side of her, anxious to hear praise, tell me about their stories. It makes me wish I could help *every* kid feel successful today.

While they are in PE, I get ready for the math lesson. So much of classroom work now involves teams, work groups, and kids learning in circles. The days of sitting at a desk, plowing through worksheets and struggling to listen to long lectures punctuated by screeching chalk-drawn illustrations are long gone.

I remember once overhearing a teacher explain to a parent,

"We're not teaching them *what* to learn any more. We're teaching them *how* to learn."

The math lesson starts off with confusion and arguing. I read aloud the teacher's instructions, which give the students three choices of division and multiplication games. The boys want to put together their own teams, but the girls shout just as loudly that their regular teacher never allows that, because they just get into trouble.

I try to listen to their bewildering explanation of the system the teacher uses to put kids into groups, but I can't even pretend to understand it.

"Listen up, everyone! I am putting the groups together," I bellow over their heads. Before their outrage can build, I stride around the room, pointing and barking, "You, you, you in the red shirt," until I have three groups of kids who barely look at each other. Their eyes connect with friends who are now separated by five or six feet, and they are devastated. I ignore any teeth that may be gnashing behind my back and tell them that everybody on the team should have a vote on which game to play. I realize it's a stupid thing to say, because of course the loudest kids coerce the rest of their team to vote for their choice. I harden my heart and assign each team a space in the room.

The games seem babyish for fourth graders, but the kids do play for a while, their noise level hovering between Barely-Acceptable and Quiet-Down-Before-We-Get-Busted. Their attention wanders after fifteen minutes, however, when arguments break out about the games' rules. All three groups merge into a mess of friends siding with friends.

I decide to let it go, because I'm seated near the front of the room, calling out equations for a couple of girls who have asked for "stuff that's harder to do." The girls are using legal-page-sized whiteboards so they can use the grouping method of figuring out multiplication and erase when need be, which seems to be quite often.

"Don't you think it would be easier to memorize the multiplication tables so each time you see a problem like six times seven, you can write the answer without having to figure it out?" I ask, trying to mask my exasperation.

"No, we do it this way," they respond, carefully grouping and dotting.

While I know I won't change the way they are learning, I sense an opportunity. I invite anyone who wants a change in games to join the whiteboard competition. I've learned that anything smacking of winning, being first, or bragging rights gets most kids' attention.

We gain a few new recruits. Some of the kids use their whiteboards to draw pictures, but most are hyped for the math competition. I throw out "seven times eight" to gauge their reactions. A few kids blurt out the answer while the others write it out. This of course starts another round of arguing.

"You're supposed to write it out!"

"Why should I write it when I know the answer?"

"You only know because you looked at my whiteboard!"

"No, it's because it's too easy. I'm not gonna do it."

"You aren't supposed to be here anyway. You're supposed to be playing the dice game!"

I start throwing out harder problems for some of the faster

kids and stick with the sevens and eights for the rest. After a few minutes, all the kids are working on different problems, but they seem to be busy. I'm betting they're quite used to working elbow-to-elbow with noisy, distracting classmates, so I smile when they finish their problems and show them to me for approval or correction. It seems to work. I speak in various accents to make them laugh and ask for more.

"So, you tell me 'nine times five' is forty-five?" I say in my Sergeant Schultz voice, cracking them up. "Excellent, my little scholars, you are correct!" I switch over to Mary Poppins and remind the girls to "write your answers neatly please, spit spot!"

A large boy suddenly points to the clock with a fearful look on his face, then shouts, "Isn't it time to go to lunch? We're supposed to be ready by now!"

Attempting to avert a stampede, I calmly give orders to put whiteboards and other games away. It is indeed time for lunch.

The afternoon drags a bit. The kids leave for Music, and when they return, they are supposed to finish various science and social studies projects. I am back to babysitting. The good students do their work after a few reminders; the others spend all their energy and imagination avoiding the assignments. By fourth grade, many kids are skilled at creating diversions. I wait these out and stand over them as they root around in carefully marked bins, arguing that they don't understand the assignment, didn't get the assignment, or have finished it and been given permission to spend time on their iPods.

It would be so easy to cave in and let them play. But I stand my ground.

When finally located, their smeary, messy, crumpled assignments tell different stories. Some kids don't understand the topic; others would rather take a poor grade than put forth an effort. A few have learning barriers and can barely string a sentence together. They need far more help than I can give. We have just an hour left.

I find that 2:40 p.m. is a magic time of the day. The "Get ready to go home" command transforms the room. Since most kids don't walk home, no one dawdles at the end of the day. Buses, day-care vans, rides home, after-school programs, and babysitters await. I take my post by the door (fourth graders need no escort out of the building) and wish each kid a good evening. The ones who liked me look up and smile as they clump and clatter out the door. The ones who were contentious and confrontational leave with frowns and downcast eyes.

Today was a mixture, so I sigh as I turn to clean the room. I want to sort and fold a pile of abandoned clothing in a corner of the coat closet, but it seems like a waste of time—it was there when the day started. It's hard for me to keep from judging the condition of some kids' clothing. I know they're tough on it, so it's not the holes or tears or broken coat zippers that bother me. It's the dirt. In some cases, filth. I would have to be a quadriplegic on a ventilator to send my kids to school in dirty clothes.

I remind myself to be compassionate. I have always had a washing machine and dryer, and I didn't have to drag myself and my family's laundry out of the house every week. I didn't have to struggle as a single parent to make ends meet, put food on the table, and keep kids safe.

As I start cleaning the room, my compassion for these parents falters. I spent my formative years with a mother who was obsessed with cleanliness. We washed everything often. The night before my mother was admitted to the hospital for the C-section birth of her tenth child, she spent most of the evening on her hands and knees, scrubbing and waxing a large floor (minimum of two coats for a good shine). I was only eight years old and couldn't yet be trusted to do a good job.

Unwashed clothes with ground-in dirt or kids smelling as if they spent the night in a cloud of cigarette smoke are hard to overlook. *If their hands and faces are unwashed, when was the last time they had a bath or shower?* I wonder. *Are we wasting time nattering on about photosynthesis when so many children's basic needs are not being met?*

I grumble my way around the room, picking up and putting away, talking myself into a thoroughly depressing outlook. Some corners are too messy and jumbled to touch without starting an avalanche of books and papers. I leave some freshly sharpened pencils on a table, because I feel guilty for being so judgmental and grossed out by the dusty disorder.

As I make one last inspection of the room, I see something wedged in a corner of a closet cupboard. I creakily bend over and dig out a child's insulated gray glove. It's a perfect match to a pair I bought for my son when he was in third or fourth grade and learning how to snowboard. He would come in covered with snow, glasses fogged, cheeks bright red.

I don't know how long I hold the glove, staring, remembering his beguiling grin and loud laugh. The faces of today's students dissolve in my mind until only my son's face remains.

I am subbing because he is gone. The work feels like an ongoing punishment.

When I finally come around, I quickly gather my things and leave for the day. I manage to get to my car before I start bawling, and I'm probably a traffic hazard as I drive home with tear-blurred vision. I spend the rest of the afternoon and evening crying. The dogs are so accustomed to my wailing that they no longer turn an ear as I stumble behind them on the walking path, wiping my nose and choking back the sobs when runners pass us. I have startled a few with the sounds of grief. It doesn't get better, as so many people have counseled. It just gets different.

Chapter 11

CERTAIN SCHOOLS are on the "no way" list for substitute teachers. Cramped classrooms, too many children who can't speak English, or staggering numbers of needy kids with heartbreaking stories and frightening behaviors make it easy for a sub to select "Prefer a different assignment" on the menu. The workday is so much simpler if you can work where you are comfortable.

"What am I supposed to do now?" a substitute asks me as I stroll down the hall of a school in central Sioux Falls. My students are safely deposited in the art room, and I must have made eye contact with her. The sub is holding a single glove over the heads of four students who are dressed for outdoor recess. Well, *almost* dressed. All of their hands are bare—no mittens, no gloves. She says, "I sent them to the office to get something from the Lost and Found, but all they came back with was this one glove!"

The kids are restless, probably getting too warm, embarrassed to be with subs who know so little. They look to be in third or fourth grade, so I pass on the South Dakota schools' tough love rule I've heard so many times from regular teachers.

"Guys, put your hands in your pockets, and don't play in the snow, understand?"

The children nod and head for the door. I shrug my shoulders, the sub exhales loudly and shakes her head, and we go back to our classrooms.

Compassion fatigue has set in. A few months ago, I would have felt more outrage at living in a small city where we send children out into cold weather without proper clothing. I would have commiserated with another substitute teacher and told her one of my It's-Hell-in-the-Trenches stories. I may have called a few friends later and asked them if they wanted to donate their kids' outgrown winter clothing. Today, however, I feel like Scarlett O'Hara. I'll think about it tomorrow.

Or maybe I'm just worn out, because my leg and back pain have been at the high end of the tolerance scale. I have an appointment with an orthotic specialist next week to develop custom inserts for my shoes, following up on a last-ditch referral from my physical therapist, who hasn't been able to ease the pain. Despite the huge athletic shoes I'll be forced to wear full-time, I have high hopes for relief. Maybe it will make this subbing job easier.

"Just do what you can, teach the kids who are here to learn, and call me if things get out of hand!" the young, tall, and slender principal instructs me as he walks me to my third-grade classroom. "It's a very tough group. They've had a substitute for the last two days, and it hasn't gone well." He tells me the regular teacher has worked very hard to gain the trust of the most disruptive child, Luol, a recent immigrant. Without her presence in this child's school day, he creates bedlam.

At least I've been warned. I delude myself and think the principal must believe I can handle the class, or he would . . . what? Call the substitute hotline and ask for a younger, beefier, buzz-cut disciplinarian who can get to the school in the next five minutes? I am his next-to-the-last option. Without me, he may have to spend the day in the classroom.

His description of the situation is accurate. I quickly learn that Luol is unable to listen, sit in a chair, follow simple directions, or stop talking. He is a tall, handsome kid with a loud voice. His partner in mayhem is Jack, a smart kid who has figured out how to avoid all work by egging Luol on to bigger and bigger disruptions.

"Luol, gimme that book! It's mine!" Jack taunts, so Luol shouts and throws the book. Jack laughs and tells me he can't follow the lesson, because Luol has his book. Luol jumps up and down, pounds on his desk, and shouts about false accusations.

They repeat the process every time I give a directive.

Add to the mix Deborah, a seemingly shy girl who wanders about the room, ignoring my invitations (and then commands) to sit at her desk. I don't know whether ADHD or fetal alcohol syndrome or autism is at play, but the other students eventually tell me that she is not expected to take part in the lessons.

There is another large boy, Alvin, who recites random facts to me about sharks while I'm struggling to hold the class's attention on the math lesson. Alvin's partner makes no effort to work with him, and when I ask why, the kid shrugs and tells me, "Alvin doesn't have to do math." Alvin tells me he wants to be a marine biologist when he grows up. Again, I don't know if I'm seeing autism or some other learning barrier, but I have no time to mull it over. Luol has written all over his desk and is tearing up his math paper with Jack's encouragement.

I want to make some phone calls. First, I want to call the parents of the ten or eleven kids whose time is being wasted in this class. I want to tell them to homeschool their kids or find a better classroom at another school in the system. I want to beg them to consider private school with fewer kids in each class, even if it means accepting financial aid. I will convince them that their kids are getting about ninety minutes per day of actual learning time after the time spent disciplining, correcting, and redirecting the problem students.

Second, I want to call all the South Dakota legislators, those who represent us in Pierre and those who fly off to Washington and try to make a difference on the national level. I want each legislator to work as a substitute teacher for two weeks, full-time and every day, in Sioux Falls's elementary schools. No reporters following their every move, no principals or superintendent to smooth the way and handpick classes that have been threatened with punishments for bad behavior. Just the legislator and the kids. Lesson plans would have to be followed. A positive learning environment would have to be maintained.

If children are truly our most precious resource and our

hope for the future, then our system for educating them is falling far short of where it should be. Why can't we treat each child as if he or she is extremely gifted or extremely challenged? The number of children in special classrooms is very small: six or eight kids with three or four adults. Some children are assigned an adult to be with them through the entire school day. But what about the ones who don't make the special cut, or the intelligent ones whose only option is to learn in classrooms rocked by disruption?

We would never dare treat adults the way we treat children. Picture yourself in a training environment, learning skills that are critical to your job. The room is packed with participants. You are elbow-to-elbow, and every movement of your neighbors shakes your workspace. Now imagine three, four, or maybe five other participants who are so disruptive that you cannot hear or see the trainer, and the lessons have to be repeated. The trainer cannot help you, because others are too needy. You get used to waiting and wasting time. You will be tested on what you're supposed to be learning.

Our education system makes learning a test of endurance and determination.

Too many of the children in my class today have learned to ignore directions and wait until the teacher has time to help individuals. For most of the day, I have no time to meet their expectations, so they follow me and repeat, "I don't get it," no matter how many times or ways I explain the directions. Some push aside the worksheets to color or doodle. One girl makes a trip to her locker every five minutes to reapply lip balm, which must not be working, because her lips remain cracked, and a circle of skin up to her nose and down to her chin is raw and red. It's a very eye-catching pattern.

Like a crazed juggler, I attempt to calm Luol, prod Jack to show some effort, and coax Deborah out of the corners. The ten or eleven kids whose parents expect them to learn have finished the assignment and are quietly reading. I've been instructed to take all twenty-seven kids for bathroom and drink breaks at the same time so that I can use zone defense to supervise them all at once. As I wait outside the boys' bathroom and remind them to wash hands *with* soap, another teacher and class approach. They wait quietly in line for my class to finish. I ask the teacher if her kids have mastered the lesson on hand-washing. She laughs and tells me about a boy who came up with a unique excuse. When stopped at the door and told to wash, he said, "I did-dint touch it, I just pointed it." She made him wash anyway.

I love the story. It makes me smile even as certain students act up while getting dressed for recess a few minutes later. I have cheerfully lost patience with the kids who ignore me, so when one group is ready, standing quietly at the door, I escort them out. (I can get away with this only because the classroom is very close to the outer door.) Luol leads the uproar that follows.

"No fair! They're supposed to wait for us!"

"They can't go outside without the whole class!"

"That's dumb! They get more recess time!"

I listen and calmly respond, "And you're *wasting* valuable recess time."

Luol and Jack blast toward the door, aiming to escape with no boots, no gloves, and jackets barely clenched in their hands. I step in to block them. Jack stops when he sees I am not yielding, but Luol throws a shoulder block and tries to run. I stand my ground and tell them to go back to their desks and wait; they will be the last students out of the room, and they will walk. When all the other drifty kids finally shuffle out, I lead Luol and Jack, making sure neither one bolts ahead of me. When we finally get outside, I watch them race across the playground to the football game in progress. The teacher on duty will have to deal with the fights they are certain to cause within the next five minutes.

The principal pops in to check on my progress and see if my sanity level is within the acceptable range. I describe how the day has gone so far, and he encourages me to send Luol either to him or to the behavior specialist if things don't improve. Apparently, Luol is used to spending large blocks of time each day with the counselor or principal.

Well, I certainly feel as if I just rolled off the turnip truck! Maybe Luol is simply trying to get out of the room because two substitute teachers in two days make him crazy. I wonder how Jack will behave with his diversion partner gone?

When I step outside to gather my students, I see Alvin, the big kid with the shark fascination, trying to throw his coat over his head and onto the school's roof. The coat catches by a sleeve, then falls into his arms. I bellow at him, and he barely glances my way. As I march up to him to threaten a behavior slip for his poor choice of activity, I wonder why he is wearing a red shirt when I am certain he was wearing a blue shirt the last time I saw him in the classroom. That thought rattles me, so he gets off with a warning.

"Get in line, Alvin, and don't do that again!" I order. He wanders away and joins the line of another third-grade class. But then I peer down my own line, and I magically see Alvin near the end of it, staring into the distance, coat open, blue shirt showing.

"Yes, they're twins, Alvin and Melvin," another third-grade teacher tells me when I ask about the boys' resemblance. "Both boys have learning disabilities, but they're nice kids," she adds after I tell her about my gaffe. I notice the kids from Melvin's classroom throwing Watch-Out-for-the-Freaky-Sub glances my way as they trudge back into the building. That's all right with me. I'll take a little healthy fear.

The last assignment of the day is to discuss the concept of citizenship, with its accompanying rights and responsibilities. The workbook's explanation is very basic:

> WE LIVE IN A FREE COUNTRY WITH A GOVERNMENT CHOSEN BY THE PEOPLE. WE SHOULD FOLLOW THE LAWS AND BE RESPONSIBLE CITIZENS.

I ask the children if they have heard of other countries where people are not free.

"Yeah, yeah, Iraq and those places around there!"

The discussion is a little loud, but the kids are engaged, so I don't shush all the blurted answers. We talk about voting when they are old enough to do so and following laws like speed limits and no littering. Luol and Jack have a private conversation going, but it's contained in their desk area, so I encourage the rest of the class to raise their hands and tell me their thoughts.

The little girl with the red, chapped ring around her mouth tells me, "I see police around the school all the time."

I tell her that's a good thing, because the police will stop the speeders who might hurt kids on their way to and from school.

"No," she adds. "The cops are there to make sure no one steals kids."

I am not about to argue with her, because by the end of her third-grade year, she will have attended several assemblies with her classmates to learn how to avoid stranger danger and how to fight off kidnappers.

I change the course of the conversation and tell the students to think about what it is like to live in a country where war is happening, where the kids can't go to school and learn, and where, in some places, girls can't go to school at all. The boys cheer and talk about shooting guns in the streets.

I call on another girl, who has been quiet and studious during the day. Her voice is so soft that it's a strain to hear her at first, but her story quiets the room.

"My uncle . . . he was, like, a soldier in the war. And he was with the other soldiers. And he, like, was walking down a street. And he, like, saw somebody he thought was a enemy, and he shot him. And, like, it was a little boy. But he didn't mean to. So, like, when he came home from being a soldier, like, my mom said he was really sad, like. And he shot himself, and he, like, is dead."

All the kids in the room, including Luol and Jack, hold her story for a few moments of silence.

"That is so sad, Kathleen . . . so sad for your whole family,"

I mumble, trying to say the right thing and honor the young man's suffering. "That is what happens in wars, and your uncle was a brave soldier." I can't believe how silly and pointless my words sound, but I have nothing else.

The school day mercifully ends with the getting-dressed, getting-ready-to-leave routines. My back is positively screaming, and I know I'll be limping and dragging my leg like Marty Feldman in *Young Frankenstein* for the rest of the evening. The resemblance would be uncanny if I had a hump and a hood.

I'm hobbling around the room in cleanup mode, thinking about my future clown shoes, when I notice a bulletin board with the headline "Star of the Week" in large, glittery letters. The central photo is of a smiling Luol, taken at the start of the school year. The photo that holds my attention is in a corner, like a last-minute addition. Luol and what I assume is his family are posing outside some sort of small building, all standing on a woven rug that looks like an island in a sea of packed dirt. Luol looks to be three or four years younger than he is now. I don't know if the building is the family home in a village or if it's part of a refugee camp. It's definitely not something I would see anywhere in America. There are other photos of Luol and a large family, taken in an apartment setting. The woman (Luol's mother?), looks unhappy in every single photo. Even so, I can see Luol change from the scared little boy in the photo from Africa to the happy, grinning kid in his school picture.

Is his out-of-control behavior a result of what happened before he and his family came to Sioux Falls? How does he act at home, where his face is not the only black one in the room?

Is his behavior a diversionary tactic intended to keep me from finding out some scary truth, like perhaps he can't keep up with the other kids in class?

I'm staring at the photo when the principal shows up. His head is slightly tilted to his left, and his eyebrows are raised—it's body language for an imminent plea.

"The teacher you're subbing for is taking another day of leave," he says. "Would you ever consider subbing for one more day so that the students don't have to adjust to another new teacher?" He explains that two specials, PE and Music, are scheduled, and I would not be required to take the regular teacher's early morning playground duty. I would really be helping them out, and it would be in the best interest of the kids.

Since I did all right today, despite my back pain, I say yes, but I tell him in great detail how Jack and Luol make the job very difficult. The principal thanks me profusely, promising more help if I need it. I wonder if I can get stronger pain medicine from my doctor before tomorrow.

THE KIDS START THE FOLLOWING DAY with an eyeball-to-eyeball stern talk from the young principal. He stands in front of the classroom and makes his expectations very clear. Luol is the only kid fidgeting, and it earns him a drill sergeant–like bark to "sit down and pay attention!" The principal follows up his order with a steely stare and a step toward Luol. It works! The room is quiet.

He pulls a chair close to the first group of desks and sits.

His head is high enough to see all the kids in the classroom, and his face is quite close to Luol and Jack.

"Not only will Mrs. M. call me if there is any disrespectful behavior, but all the other teachers in this wing will be watching and reporting to me." Wow. That's powerful. The normal teachers are here forever, and they'll be able to report any shenanigans long after the subs leave. His lecture may be overkill for the good kids, but they too are in danger of being sent to the stocks if order is not maintained.

The first assignment is to use a prompt to tell a story in the students' writing journals. If they finish the story, they can illustrate it. Most of the class moves right into the assignment, which is to describe an especially good time they had. I ask a few rhetorical questions to help the kids who seem unsure of what constitutes a good time.

"Have you gone to a fun birthday party? Maybe you went to a sleepover that was fun? Maybe you went camping or fishing and had a great time? Do you like to play sports or watch them on TV? How about going on a trip to see relatives or going to a special place like a water park?"

Each time I mention a possible source of fun, another head turns toward the paper. Soon, all the students are writing. Almost.

Luol and Jack are wandering around the room in search of paper. When I tell them they're supposed to write in their notebooks, Luol becomes argumentative.

"I don't have a writing journal notebook! I have to use a piece of paper, and I can't find one!"

Meanwhile, Jack is picking the lead out of a pencil he just sharpened.

I tell both boys to join me at the worktable in the front of the room. I find paper and pencils for both. "Write," I tell them, maintaining strong eye contact. I'm leaning forward on my elbows, holding them at the table by sheer willpower.

"I don't know what to write!" they say in unison, as though scripted.

"What do you do to have fun?" I ask. They stall and squirm, and I prompt and nudge. After about ten minutes, I get a description of a fun day both of them spent with Jack's dad attending a semipro ball game. They don't know how to start the story, so I help them with, "I had a lot of fun when . . ."

The rest of the kids have finished writing, and I tell them they must show me their work before they move on to do the illustrations. They form a line to my place at the table, which creates just the type of diversion Luol and Jack count on to avoid schoolwork. Neither boy has finished a sentence.

"Boys, you will not be able to go out for morning recess unless this assignment is finished," I order. "Get to work!" I turn to check the other kids' writing, and I end up sending half of them back to their desks with instructions to write more than one sentence.

"At least three sentences! You can do it! You're good writers!" I say, laying the praise on thick. Even the shy kids respond when I tell them their story is great. They return to their desks to write more.

Jack and Luol have abandoned the assignment. Jack is drawing a cartoon character on his paper, and Luol is laughing, criticizing the creature. I watch them and decide not to punish myself any further by keeping them in the classroom for recess.

"Jack, Luol, you are going to the principal's office, and I don't want you to return to this classroom until you are ready to listen to my instructions and do the work."

Feeling as if I have made a sound decision, I head for the phone and dial the number.

"What? What did we do? We didn't do nothing! I'm not going to the office!" Luol shouts. Jack is silent, slumped in his chair. Luol stomps the floor, pounds the table, and flings his arms in the air.

I tell them they should leave now, that they don't want to keep the principal waiting, or worse, make him come to the classroom to get them. Any doubt that I made the right decision evaporates when Luol sweeps his arms across the worktable, throwing books, papers, and teaching supplies around the room. Knowing he has earned everyone's attention, he storms out of the room, protesting about unfair treatment. Jack follows, eyes on the floor.

The rest of the day goes so easily that I feel relaxed. We are able to spend as much time as the children need to understand the math lesson about rounding numbers. I don't have to act the part of the prison warden, because a gentle "Settle down, please, third graders" is all that is needed to recapture wandering attention.

The principal brings Luol and Jack into the classroom about ten minutes before dismissal. In his presence and with downcast eyes, they apologize for being disrespectful to me. Luol seems genuinely upset, while Jack appears to be going through the motions.

When I leave the building late in the afternoon, I'm ready

to collapse. Despite the principal's reassurance that my actions were correct, I feel as if I've failed in something important. Is it right to sacrifice one or two students for the benefit of the rest? If I had been able to work with each boy one-on-one, I know I could have made a connection. Kudos to Luol's regular teacher for finding a way to motivate him. My fatigue is due not only to the physical nature of teaching but also to the fact that I'm barely getting by in the job. I can't shrug off the sense of failure any longer. What if the kids have picked up on that? I'm so glad I won't have to face them all tomorrow.

Chapter 12

February is a cruel month. Another foot of snow falls, and the wind keeps blowing. My son's birthday is February 24. He would be seventeen, a junior in high school. As the day creeps closer, I compulsively look for his features and mannerisms in the boys at school—in my classes and in the halls. It is exhausting, this "constant vigilance" that Mad-Eye Moody demanded in the Harry Potter books. I want so much to hear another boy talk like Ian or see a hint of resemblance, even though I know I'll be overwhelmed by grief if it happens. The gray daylight drains my energy further. I have to pretend to be competent.

The little faces blur together, and I can't remember which line of kids waiting by the playground is my responsibility. I try to pick out the face of the most disruptive child of the day, but it's no use. There are times when I can't recall the classroom number *or* the name of the teacher for whom I am substituting, so, like a person hiding her inability to read, I have to ask vague questions to cover.

"Am I at the correct door for second grade?" Or I squint and ask, "I can't tell with all the blowing snow—which line is mine?" I quickly cover my ignorance with a statement that elicits immediate sympathy: "I've been at three different schools in the last two weeks, so I get confused."

One afternoon, as I stand guard in the hall during a bathroom break with my third graders, a male teacher strides out of his classroom and makes a quick turn directly into the boys' bathroom. Some of my students are in there, and for a moment, I wonder if I am in trouble. Am I letting them stay in there too long? Is the teacher after one of my students or one of his? I shush the kids in line just to cover some bases.

I have a questioning look on my face when the teacher reappears less than sixty seconds later. He straightens his tie and explains, "Just checking to make sure they aren't peeing all over. For some strange reason, they do that when they have a sub. It's just the third graders, and we don't know why."

All I can manage is, "Really?" before he takes off. The boys are all back in line, luckily, or I would have popped into their bathroom to make sure their aim was true. I have to smother a laugh, because the kids are watching my reaction.

We stroll back to the classroom so I can read a couple chapters of *The Boxcar Children* to them. I loved that book as a kid and enjoyed reading it (and its many sequels) to my own children. The thought of setting up a cozy home in an abandoned boxcar, drinking cold water from the stream and eating blueberries picked by an enterprising big sister was so appealing.

But it sure isn't appealing for my class today. By the second paragraph, most of the kids are squirming and looking for distractions. The story isn't holding up.

I am a good reader. I vary my tone and speed. I use voices for characters and can make almost any copy interesting. Not so that day. I can't blame the kids. Even I'm getting impatient with the slow pace of the story. How long does it take to get three kids and a dog into a boxcar when a storm blows in? Didn't anyone think about the germs the kids were exposed to as they dug through crap in a junkyard to find dishes? As for washing their cups off in the stream before they ate, what about *E. coli*? Are we encouraging kids to run away from home with this story?

With relief, I close the book and instruct the class to line up for Music. During the five minutes it takes for the kids to stop talking, I feel sulky and irritable. I hate to admit that the whiny kids who complained, "This book is boring!" might have been right. Or am I peeved because I wasn't able to work my magic with them?

THE LESSONS IN PATIENCE and compassion keep coming. I'm standing in a second-grade classroom one morning, trying to slow my breathing and assume the persona of Mother Theresa, whom I believe to be an excellent role model, aside from the dish towel she wore on her head. Maybe she wasn't *always* so patient and kind. Maybe she moved slowly because she was old as dirt and couldn't go any faster. Maybe as a young person she had learned that all you get when you hurry is sweaty, so she decided to take her time and listen.

As usual, it's taking way too much time for the kids to get ready for Morning Meeting. I smile tiredly as I remind them to hang up their things, put away their backpacks, and blah, blah, blah.

A very pale boy is seated near the lockers, his coat on the floor. He unzips his snow pants and yanks at one suspender, then slumps back. I lean over and ask if he is feeling sick. The question is enough to trigger a spasm of vomiting, which I dance to avoid before rushing to the trash can. I neatly catch spasms number two and number three with the receptacle and, with all the diagnostic skills of Marcus Welby, MD, decide the child is sick and will have to go home.

I call the office so that the secretary can begin the process of finding a parent for pickup. The other students are awed by the volume of vomit in the trash can and on the floor. I arrange them in a circle on a clean part of the floor and ask them if they can do the daily greeting (Good grief, don't they know each other's names by now?!) and suggest they take turns telling each other about a time when they were sick. They love the topic. I hope it will last until I return.

The poor little puker looks wasted, so I don't hurry him as we head for the office. I carry his coat and backpack and try to comfort him as he clumps along in his heavy boots. I want to give him and his family the benefit of the doubt and not entertain the possibility that he barfed at home and had been sent to school anyway. Lack of childcare options can make parents do stupid things. It's possible that his symptoms were mild early this morning or that he had used "I have a tummy ache" too often. He certainly had eaten a hearty breakfast. But tally together the lack of paid sick leave, no money for a sitter, and no one at home to act as a nurse, and it can add up to a child spending hours on a bench in the office.

I picture the pampering my kids enjoyed when they were home sick: favorite blanket and pillow on the sofa, all the kids' movies they wanted, a TV tray with ice chips, crackers, juice, and choice of Jell-O, and constant monitoring by me.

"I hope you feel better when you get home and lie down," I say in my motherly voice. "Do you get to lie on the couch and watch TV when you're sick?"

He miserably shakes his head and answers so softly that I can hardly catch his words.

"No, I have to be quiet, so I can't watch TV."

I wonder whether there is a new baby in the house or if one of the adults works the night shift.

"Oh, someone sleeps during the day?" I ask. It's a long way to the office, and his pace has slowed. He trails his hand along the wall.

"Yeah, my mom's friend. And he gets mad if there's noise, so I have to be quiet."

I sense there is more of this story that needs to be told, but I don't want to spook him.

"So you have to read books and lie on your bed when you go home?" I ask.

"I hide under the bed 'cause I'm scared," he answers.

"Are you scared of him?"

"Yeah," he whispers.

I don't know what to say or how to comfort him. We finish our trip in silence.

The office is full of sick kids and scurrying adults. I hand the boy over to the school nurse, then give myself shin splints by race walking back to the classroom, imagining the worst. No one is bleeding or naked, but two kids are crying, and a few boys are demonstrating their running karate kicks for the enjoyment of the rest. I don't know their names, but I know enough to shout and threaten them with a trip to the office. It's not the best way to start the school day, but it's effective. For the moment.

Feeling the pressure of the clock, I forget one of the most important lessons I have learned this school year: *Stop the manic energy before it consumes the room. Ignore the lesson plan and take ten minutes to set expectations.*

The school day goes downhill at warp speed. Two boys with loud voices talk over me, argue with each other, then ask to go to the bathroom every five minutes. The girls react to the chaos by conducting whispered meetings in groups of three or four. It slowly dawns on me why the teachers in the neighboring classrooms didn't intervene when I took the sick boy to the office. This classroom is always ridiculously noisy, so unless they hear glass breaking or sonic booms, it's a typical day.

Most second graders can't tell time and depend on the teachers to keep them on schedule. The order of the day, since it changes with specials, is listed on a board at the front of the room, duly updated before the children arrive. The kids may not know that lunch period starts at 11:30, but they know Morning Meeting, Math, Social Studies, Language Arts, and recess must all happen before they go to lunch.

Just as I manage to corral these kids and force them to sit

in one place and listen to directions, one of the leaders yells, "It's recess time! We're missing recess!"

They stampede like cattle spooked by a rattlesnake. Children who need fifteen to twenty minutes to find their desks in the morning now have snow pants, boots, and jackets on before I can brace myself in front of the door and bellow the bad news: it is *not* time for recess. Most of the kids grumble and moan as they take their time putting away their winter clothing, but the performances by the leader boys are worthy of Oscar nominations. Their show of suffering at the unfairness of school, teachers, and life in general is so full of pathos that their audience is mesmerized. They throw their boots on the floor, kick their locker doors, fling their arms, and do pretty good imitations of crying. I should let them keep going, because at least it's passing time.

"If everyone is *not* in their seats by the time I count to ten, you will all miss recess!" I don't know where that threat came from, and I don't know how I can enforce it, but they buy it and scramble for their seats. I draw the count out just a bit, because one girl's leg is caught in her snow pants, and she looks as panicked as Little Nell tied to the railroad tracks with a train racing toward her. Miraculously, she gets to her seat in time. We muddle through the morning schedule with few bright spots. The regular teacher must have needed time away, and she chose a good day for it.

The afternoon schedule requires little more than adult supervision. When the kids return from lunch, they are supposed to spend about half an hour reading. While a few of them actually do, about a third thumb through picture books or dig through book baskets until I stand over them and force a choice. I can understand why the ELL students can't read at second-grade level, but why so many of the others? Are we losing that many kids along the way?

Junior Achievement graduation is next, and I have to remind myself to put on a smiley face. My kids went through the program when they were in elementary school. Sioux Falls business leaders want children to understand the basics of the economy—how people pay for goods and services, how communities . . . whatever. I shrugged it off when my kids brought home the papers and when my husband taught the course one year. It seemed like a diversion at best, maybe a bit of a time waster.

Today, the children parrot the phrase "Human Resources" with a great deal of prompting. When they are asked, "What can a business use to help it grow?" I try to resist shaking my head, succeeding only when I shift my focus to see if any of my kids are being noisy. They know the volunteer instructors brought cupcakes to celebrate graduation, and I warned them earlier that disrespectful behavior will land them in the hall. I'm wondering how much longer the irrelevant review of terminology will take when the women turn on a disc player and chant along with a rap song written just for Junior Achievement. It's awkward, to say the least, watching two blonde white women rapping about "keeping money in the community and helping the economy grow."

Each child gets a certificate of completion and handshakes from the volunteers, who work at a local bank.

"When do we get cupcakes?" the kids ask over and over.

I've given up attempting to quiet them. Who wants a piece of paper and a handshake when a tray of heavily-frosted cupcakes is calling? With huge smiles, the women hand a decorated cupcake to each child and tell him or her how great it was to work together. Before the women can quickly gather their purses, disc player, and extra cupcakes, the boys who have gobbled their treats start begging for seconds. The women look to me for direction, and I tell them to leave, that I have things under control. I have to catch grabbing hands as the women whisk the cupcakes toward the exit. The mess in the room makes me grind my teeth. Cupcake wrappers litter the floor, frosting is smeared on faces and desktops, and crumbs are scattered from one end of the room to the other.

Really? I want to say to the people who spend time and money organizing Junior Achievement. *With all the needs in our elementary schools, this is what you decide to do? How about making sure the kids see a dentist once before they move to middle school? Or get eye exams and glasses so they don't have to sit twelve inches from the whiteboard and still squint?*

We have ten minutes to clean up before the class has to be in the gym for an assembly. Some children are still eating, and the wild boys are bothering them for bites. I press the boys into service and make them carry trash cans down the aisles. I send a quiet girl to the bathroom to get paper towels so we can wipe up the worst of the frosting globs. I figure I'll end up spending a minimum of half an hour cleaning desks before I settle down to write my note to the teacher at the end of the day.

After a quick side trip to the bathroom to wash hands, the class joins the boiling, babbling mass of first and second graders in the gym. There must be a couple hundred kids seated on the floor, eagerly waiting for the show to begin. Teachers have pulled up chairs so they can maintain control, but the end of the school day is in sight, and the room is abuzz with excited voices. The beloved School Resource Officer, a veteran police officer assigned to this elementary school, is going to demonstrate another way for kids to stay safe. Several thick gymnastics mats are on the floor at the center of the gym. I know firefighters teach "Stop, drop, and roll!" so I'm curious about today's lesson.

When Officer Kirchofner enters the gym, the kids roar their welcome. He is their hero and, for many of the kids, one of the few men they see almost every day, other than the principal and custodians.

Officer Kirchofner is wearing his navy blue uniform—pants and shirt filled with badges and a big, black belt minus his gun. I can see he has a bulletproof vest underneath his shirt and sturdy, black shoes for chasing the bad guys. A couple of boys break away from the crowd and run up to give the office a high five. The rest of the room pulses with excitement—Officer Kirchofner is these kids' version of action and entertainment. The teachers are having a hard time quieting everyone. They use raised voices and drag the hyperactive instigators to the penalty zones—the areas around each teacher's chair.

"Everybody, give me five!" hollers the officer with his right hand raised above his head. Most kids quietly comply, but there is still a buzz in the back rows. We scramble to shush the offenders and reposition groups so that the chattiest kids will be separated from their peeps.

"Today, I'm going to talk about something very, very important, first and second graders, so you have to be quiet and listen very carefully," the officer says, making eye contact as he moves around the front of the room. "I'm going to talk about staying safe and what you should do if you are kidnapped. Then I'm going to show you what to do to get away. This is very important, boys and girls, so you have to listen, okay?"

The kids are bouncing with eagerness, and the teachers are calmly reining them in. I make a mental note to ask my daughter whether her School Resource Officer ever showed her class how to evade kidnappers. Maybe that's why she had so many nightmares in elementary school! Yes, I knew the kids learned about Stranger Danger, Don't Go Anywhere Alone, yada yada. But giving pointers on how to foil a child abduction seems too frightening for kids at these young ages.

Officer Kirchofner eases into a review before he starts the new material.

"What should you do if you are walking home alone and a stranger tries to talk to you? And what should you do if you see a stranger watching you while you are playing?"

He calls on the kids who are staying seated and are raising hands. The answers come quickly and are all pretty accurate. They know this stuff so well that some of the second-grade boys in a knot near me start laughing and talking out loud.

"Do you think this is funny? Is that why you're not listening?" the officer barks at the boys, pointing at them. All the other little heads turn in amazement at their blatant disrespect.

"Do you know what can happen to you? You can be kidnapped and killed! Now stop talking and listen! Do you hear me?" Maybe it's because the room is warm and his vest is raising his body temperature, but Officer Kirchofner is now red in the face, far less jolly than when he started. The boys lower their heads, but it's too late to blend into the crowd. Their teacher has already swooped down upon them, and I can see "You Will Lose Recess for This" written on her face. She moves them into the penalty zone.

"All voices off!" he reminds them. "Now I am going to show you how to get away from an adult who is trying to kidnap you. I need a volunteer." Half the kids surge forward, hands in the air, whispering, "Oh, me! Oh, pick me!"

The next thirty minutes pass in a flash as Officer Kirchofner shows the kids how to wriggle and fight their way to safety. "Stick your fingers in his eyes!" He encourages them. "Scratch his face, bite him, kick him as hard as you can!" The kids love it. He tells his little volunteers to fight him as hard as they can and to use the techniques he has shown them. Of course, each child is able to fight off his attacks and run to safety with cheers and applause from the audience. The officer is no spring chicken and probably regrets his last choice of volunteers. He calls on a tall, chubby girl who, when lifted into the air, causes his knees to buckle. She hardly has to wiggle, and he lets her go.

Officer Kirchofner wraps up the safety assembly with instructions on how to attract attention if your kidnapper sticks you in the trunk of a car.

"Stay safe, kids! See you later!" and he is out the door.

I have ten minutes to get my kids back to the classroom, dressed in winter gear, and sorted into groups of bus riders, walkers, after-school-program participants, and ones who stay for tutoring. I spend almost an hour cleaning the room and writing notes before limping down the halls to pick up my paperwork. The sky is overcast, promising more snow tomorrow, but the cold wind feels good as I step outside. I think about the safety demonstration all the way home, musing about the need to teach first and second graders about a topic that never crossed a parent's radar when I was growing up.

It's only when I'm climbing into bed that I remember the sick boy's confession about his mom's "friend." I can't believe I didn't say something to the principal before I left the school! And right after such a grisly safety lesson to boot. There I had been sitting, wondering how necessary it all was, when one of those kids was facing the reality of returning to an abusive home for the night. I can't believe I let the ball drop on this.

The next morning, I call the principal and relay my conversation with the boy as closely as I can remember.

There. His safety is in another person's hands. I hope that person will respond faster than I did.

A FEW DAYS LATER, ever closer to Ian's birthday, I accept a job in a Cluster Classroom with a shrug. The six students are fourth and fifth graders, all able to walk without assistance, and a few return my smiles as the day starts.

The two EAs are middle-aged women who treat the kids like favored grandchildren, giving help whenever necessary and prodding them to do as much as possible for themselves. I feel myself relax. No one will take a swing at me today, and I won't have to help students in the bathroom.

Morning Meeting is full of songs and clapping along to images on the SMART Board. The students sit in a row facing me, with the EAs positioned between ones who need reminders to pay attention. The lessons are set at preschool or kindergarten level, and I allow myself to be animated, even playful. The kids are a little shy at first, so I let them choose the story they want me to read. They listen so carefully to *The Little Red Hen* that I don't want the story to end. The magic of getting lost in stories is something I fully understand, something I wish I could provide for every child.

We color and glue our own version of the story until it's time for recess. Some of the students dawdle, and the EAs get surprisingly stern.

"Marcie, you know how to put on your boots! You don't have to wait for help!"

"Calvin, it's time to get dressed to go outside! Stand up!"

I can understand why the kids aren't fired up about recess. When saddled with playground duty, I've seen the Cluster Classroom kids tightly grouped around the EAs, slowly making their way around the playground. They rarely interact with other kids. At some level, they know they are different.

I get many opportunities to converse with the children during the day, particularly when they are taken in pairs for bathroom breaks. One boy is unable to speak, but the other five are chatty and want to talk about their families, pets, and favorite movies.

As we wait for two boys and an EA to return from the bathroom, the other EA asks me about how long I've been a substitute, if I've worked in a Cluster Classroom before, and where I'm from.

I know the next question. I can feel it coming.

"Do you have children?"

I launch into a monologue about our daughter and her first year in college, trying to fill the space. When the kids and the EA haven't returned, and I am running out of breath, she asks, "Is she your only child?"

Should I tell the truth, cry, and make the other person feel sorry she asked? Or should I lie and hate myself for dishonoring Ian's memory?

I choke out the truth with tears in my eyes and a tightness in my throat. "Our son, Ian, was thirteen years old when he died from heart failure in November 2006." It is the first time I've been asked about Ian during the school year. By the time the kids are settled and lessons resume, my eyes are red, and the tissue box is noticeably lighter. But the afternoon passes quickly with gentle laughter and more stories.

We all trek to the outside doors at the end of the day, and I get hugs from a couple of the kids. The EAs tell me it's difficult to get substitutes for their classroom, so they were glad I showed up.

"You are so good with the kids," they say. "You make it fun for them!"

I hold the compliment in my heart and remind them that they are the heroes in this story, because they show up every day.

"We don't do it for the pay," they laugh. "You just have to love the kids and do your best, then go home."

They are so kind that I manage to reach my car before breaking down into sobs. If there is some sort of Big Holy Plan for Who Goes and Who Stays, for why is my son gone? Why are some children burdened with a long life of violence or disability? It's a good thing I'm not subbing tomorrow, because I cry so much during the evening that my eyelids swell nearly closed, and my voice grows muffled by a blocked-up nose.

Chapter 13

I AM NOT TOO PROUD to work at a tough job or a boring job that has very little chance of improving. Nurse Assistant at a skilled-care nursing home on the night shift? Check. Waitress at a Chinese restaurant during the late shift, when all the bars close? Check. Employment counselor trying to place clerical support people for a fee during an economic slump? Check. Taco and burrito slinger at Taco Bell for minimum wage? Check. For heaven's sake, I worked in banking for five years! I have paid my dues.

Like Sisyphus pushing that damned boulder up the mountainside each morning, I keep answering the phone and accepting substitute teaching jobs.

"Why don't you do something else?" my friends ask when I spin the stories and discuss my deteriorating physical condition. Despite the crappy economy, it's possible that I could find another job that pays slightly more. But whenever I consider it, I realize I'd have to give up the one benefit of subbing: the freedom to choose which days of the week I will work. I am too tired on my days off to think about job hunting, so I keep pushing the boulder.

In mid-February, I accept a job at one of the schools mentioned in whispers by other subs. The school has a gold-plated list of retired teachers who happily fill in whenever they're needed, because it's so much easier to teach in a familiar spot. The teachers know they won't have to face the effects of extreme poverty, the lack of English, the daunting emotional problems, or the physical challenges of students in many of Sioux Falls's other elementary schools. So, I am surprised to find myself pulling into a well-cleared parking lot.

One of the second-grade classrooms is mine for the day. The teacher's absence was planned, so her notes are descriptive and thorough. The room is in meticulous order. Each basket of books is clearly marked—I won't find Junie B. Jones creeping into Amelia Bedelia's basket.

As the kids file into the room, I smile and scan each face, saying "Good morning!" while trying to relax and keep from transmitting any performance anxiety. I would like to do a good job today, if for no other reason than to prove to myself that I can teach under normal circumstances.

The students need very few reminders to put away their winter things and begin the assignment written on the SMART Board. They've carefully lined up their boots in the hall and put their mittens, gloves, hats, and scarves in the proper lockers. Each child has shoes, so no one will be schlumping around in boots all day, trailing in melting snow, or asking to go to the office to dig through the Lost and Found bins for footwear.

Taking attendance is simple, because no student is still eating breakfast in the cafeteria. All arrived clean, well fed, dressed for the weather, and ready to learn. The day's schedule is loaded with specials, so I will have plenty of time to read. For once I might get to live out the substitute teaching myth that it's a slough-off job where you don't have to use your brain and you get to go home early. But I have earned this assignment, and I'm going to savor it.

I go to the classroom door as the children line up for Music.

"You don't have to go with us," says one of the very bright little leader girls. "We go on our own."

I am stunned. My brain cannot process the message! Allow second graders to march through the halls without adult supervision and expect them to arrive at the designated destination on time, all students accounted for? No frickin' way!

Forming a perfect line, the children stare at me, waiting for me to step aside and let them leave. My mouth hangs open in amazement as I scan each little face for a sign that I am being conned.

I let them go. For ten minutes I sit at the teacher's desk, watching the phone, which I'm certain will ring. The secretary will tell me that some of my students are playing beer pong in the hall and that the others have locked themselves in the computer lab, making large purchases on the Home Shopping Network website with the school's credit card. I'll be properly punished for my grievous error.

The phone is silent.

I try to read my book but can't concentrate. The kids return on time with smiles on their faces, singing the song they're learning. They loosen up just enough while going through a reading and writing assignment that I'm able to suspend my suspicions that they're all little cyborgs from *Star Trek*—half human, half computer. A boy with Harry Potter glasses can't sit still or refrain from blurting out nonsensical answers, and a little blonde girl with wispy hair wanders around the room as much as I allow, hopping out of her chair as soon as I turn my back.

That's more like it! I know what to do now!

As the kids gear up for recess, I find myself shaking my head in wonder at their clean, matching coats and snow pants, their warm, well-fitting boots, and their hats of all colors and designs. Nothing is ragged or torn, no holes or ground-in dirt. Before this year, I had no idea how many children in our community were growing up in poverty.

When the last period of the day rolls around, I ready myself for the arguments and misbehaving that bubble to the surface when the end is in sight. My adrenaline rush fizzles out as the kids politely divide themselves into teams and play math games. My sole responsibility is to type in the correct codes for the SMART Board, a task that I prepared for when they were in PE. It's anticlimactic. I'm hardly needed.

My ego takes another hit when I go to the office and hear one of the secretaries tell a student teacher that each school's PTA supplies the classrooms with pencils and paper, as much as is needed for the year. My Joan of Arc campaign to rally everyone I know to buy pencils for the poor suddenly seems theatrical and sort of silly.

I slink out the door to my car, recalling the movie *Out of Africa*, when Meryl Streep's character says, "When the gods want to punish you, they give you what you ask for." Or something like that. Her Danish accent was beautifully distracting.

My next assignment bounces me back into the real world of subbing: a small, crowded classroom in an older school, crammed with desks for twenty-three second graders. I'm surprised when I realize it's a classroom where I subbed last fall. I thought I would be banned for life after a well-meaning but evidently life-endangering mistake.

The kids had been so good all morning, listening well and following directions. I told them how pleased I was to see their good behavior. I laid it on thick. "Your teacher will be so happy when she comes back tomorrow and reads my notes! I am going to tell her that she has the best second graders in the whole school, maybe the whole city of Sioux Falls!"

One little boy, a future union negotiator or attorney, raised his hand and asked if there were any rewards for being so good.

"If we are good students for the rest of the day, what do we get? Candy?"

"No," I said. "No candy." I was sensing my error of giving overblown praise, so I offered, "How about extra time for reading or drawing?" But they wrinkled their noses. "Board games?" No takers.

After much discussion, they said what they wanted most was to get out of school early. I was a new sub, and I wanted to please everyone, a fault that follows me like dog doo on a shoe. I'd listened to many adults who would happily go to great lengths to earn the privilege of leaving the workplace early, so I had empathy for anyone craving some room to run.

The kids agreed to be good and follow the rules for the rest of the day if they could leave five minutes early. Using peer pressure to prod slackers and silence the chatty ones, they quickly became model students.

I actually didn't think they could pull it off, but what did I know? I was negotiating with second graders.

After tiptoeing to the door precisely five minutes prior to the dismissal bell, I gave the kids who had to wait for a sibling or a ride home strict instructions to stay on the playground. I walked the rest of the children down the hall to the gym, where the after-school care program was held.

The first hint of my severe breach of protocol wafted my way when I tried to send my kids into the gym for a few minutes of extra play time. The care program employees were standing in a group near the sign-in desk, casually talking about personal matters. I smiled as I told them how good the students had been all day, earning them an early dismissal.

Using good old-fashioned Midwestern passive-aggressive behavior, the leader didn't say anything to me, just barked at the kids.

"You guys get back here!" she shouted. "Sit on the floor against the wall. You're not supposed to be here until the bell rings. We're not responsible for you until then!"

I looked at the clock. It was less than two minutes to the bell.

The employees' body language spoke volumes about my

unspeakable blunder. Arms crossed, eyes averted, backs turned away from me, they closed ranks. I apologized to my kids, who were lined up like convicts on the floor, then walked back to the classroom.

The bell rang one minute after I walked through the door. Any residue of the good feeling I had when the kids earned five minutes of freedom evaporated when the principal appeared in the doorway.

Her message was clear, concise, and complete. What I had done was never, *ever* going to happen again. "The children's safety has been compromised, and it was very serious! The parents have shared this important responsibility with us, and *it cannot be ignored*!"

I gave myself whiplash agreeing with her on every point while at the same time apologizing profusely. My face was burning, and I hadn't felt so incompetent since I plopped my youngest sister on a bouncing horse that was riding unsecured on a wagon. I pulled the darling little two-year-old up and down the street before I took a turn too quickly and tipped her out, face-first, onto a gravel driveway. She still has a scar on her forehead.

Now, I'm back in the same classroom, but the kids are no longer the hardworking, cooperative little angels I could have once clasped to my bosom if I were the clasping kind. When I stop to answer one child's questions, the rest of the room erupts in chatter. I take a moment to attempt contact with a boy who is doing nothing but make origami stars out of pink paper, and two boys try to leave the room without permission, provoking shrieks of indignation from the students who are upset because they didn't think of it first.

It's not just the disrespectful rule-breaking behavior that frustrates me. So many of the kids simply seem to need one-on-one attention. They aren't acting up as much as acting out. They talk out of turn like kindergarten kids, begging for my attention. The room is so noisy that I have to give instructions over and over, squeezing between desks to make sure the kids in the corners hear what they need to do. The noise level acts as a cover for the boys who are answering the call to entertain.

One boy ends up in the Time Away chair because he won't stop singing. Another boy is so disruptive that I put him in the hall and tell him he'll have to stay there until he can calm himself. The banishment must meet his needs, because he spends all of math time rolling around on the floor by the door, shouting answers to the problems I put on the board. His answers are all correct.

Head coverings of all kinds are banned except for Muslim head scarves, so I am surprised when one of the girls pulls the hood of her coat up over and over throughout the day in what appears to be direct defiance of my repeated order to remove it.

"Sherry, if you can't keep your hood off, the coat will have to go in your locker," I say with a sigh. "Why do you keep putting it up when I turn my back?"

"I'm cold," she mumbles so softly that I can't understand, even after three repeats. The kid seated next to her has to say it for her. I find her excuse hard to believe, since the room is stifling and she is wearing a turtleneck shirt and a sweater underneath the down-filled coat.

The hood-on-hood-off game continues until the last recess of the day, when another little girl enlightens me. When I hear that Sherry is covering her head because the boy seated behind her says her hair is ugly and he doesn't want to sit behind her, I let him know the meaning of "unacceptable." Taking him into the hall, I give him no opportunity to explain why he acted like a bully.

"Corey, did you say something today about Sherry's hair?" I ask him in my best prosecutor's furrowed-brow tone. I look fierce. He decides not to lie.

"Yeah," he says, busted.

"The only reason you would say something about another person and use the word 'ugly' is to hurt that person. That is not allowed, and you know that, right?" I'm on an avenging roll, and Corey senses I should not be stopped.

"You will apologize to Sherry, and I will tell your teacher what happened so that if you do anything like this again, you will have to talk with the principal. Do you understand?"

He is blushing, slumping, trying to avoid my stare.

"Yeah, okay," he says.

I call Sherry into the hall, the apology is made, and the three of us reenter the hushed classroom. Sherry's friends have rallied around her; it's obvious the news has zipped through the room while we were in the hall. We finish the day subdued. No one gives me a high five as they leave. I hope I don't have to face this group again before the end of the year.

ON MY NEXT SUBBING JOB, I land in a classroom marked "Third Grade," but I wonder if the sign is correct when I scan the crowd. Three of the kids are my height, five foot four, and are close to my weight. I notice it when I turn from my carefully written instructions and find myself eyeball-to-eyeball with two students. I make a mental note to avoid any direct confrontations. There are a few small girls present, but most of the other students look like junior East German swimmers-in-training.

The morning passes quickly despite indoor recess (due to strong winds and a nasty windchill). I don't have to promise God that I will stop swearing and never take another drink if I can please, please go home. We get a few things done on the lesson plan, and I never once have to jerk my thumb toward the door like a baseball ump and say, "Sit down and be quiet, or you are *out of here!*"

But the day *does* present one big challenge.

In certain Sioux Falls elementary schools, students move to other classrooms for certain subjects. I don't know if it is done to get the kids used to switching classrooms in preparation for middle school or whether it's due to certain teachers' specialized training. I know only that the arrangement drops the day to a deeper, hotter level of Substitute Purgatory. Can't remember twenty-six kids' names from taking morning attendance? Tough. A fresh flock will come pouring through the door anyway, and you'll stumble through the next lesson, calling on "the girl with the green shirt" or "the boy without a book."

The room-swapping challenge happens in the afternoon. My kids head across the hall for Science, and another twenty-six third graders roll into my room for Health. The lesson plan sounds so simple: give a short quiz on personal safety, have the students switch papers with a classmate while we correct them, then read four pages in the book and discuss.

"Piece of cake," I think. They know how to stay safe around strangers, even kidnappers. I wonder if I can send them back to their teacher early if we run out of material to discuss. Or will she make me stand in the hall with her students just to see us squirm? Finishing early becomes a moot point after we have read one page in the textbook. Their questions illustrate a couple of unsettling discoveries: their little eight- or nine-year-old brains can hold the basic Stranger Danger lesson but cannot make adjustments for "nice" strangers. They perceive their lives as much more dangerous than I perceived mine at that age. In third grade, I just wanted to be popular *and* nice and holy so I could be chosen to crown Mary during a special ceremony in church. It proved to be oxymoronic. Only very, very nice and quiet girls got chosen for that honor. I don't think I was even in the running.

With worried looks on their faces, my third graders ask how to save themselves and younger siblings if someone tries to break into their home while they are there.

"Should you throw things at the bad guy?"

"What if he has a mean dog? Should you try to hit the dog, or should you just run out the back door?"

"What if the burglar breaks down the door with a tank?"

"How can I call 911 if my mom is gone and she has the phone when the burglar comes?"

I try patiently to wind through the questions while four boys conduct their own lesson on the side, laughing at the questions and telling tales of their own little-boy bravery.

"I'd shoot him with a rocket launcher!"

"I'd take my dad's gun and shoot him in the head!"

We get off on a tangent when one girl asks how to return dishes to people who have given you food.

"Can you wait until an adult comes home?" I ask, confused.

I try to maintain control during a convoluted discussion about shift work and family responsibilities, but I can no longer ignore the four boys' behavior. I tell them their regular teacher will have to come by after class to hear how they acted. It settles them down immediately.

We are minutes away from the end of the class period when a shy little girl who has barely moved asks something that must be bothering her.

"What should you do when you give food to someone, and then he comes back and wants to give *you* some food?"

She looks scared.

'He comes back when your parents aren't home?" I ask, stalling for an answer.

"Yes" she whispers. I picture her crouched behind a door, too frightened to call for help.

"You don't open the door. Even if you know him, you wait for your mother or dad to be home, okay?"

She seems satisfied with my firm answer and nods okay. It's apparent that these kids spend a great deal of time unsupervised at home. Their tough talk is all whistling in the wind.

My students arrive at the classroom door, shuffling and rustling papers, so it's time to send these students back to their teacher. As the kids make their way to their desks, I wonder if I helped anyone feel safer today.

During the afternoon recess, I'm correcting papers when a

teacher enters my classroom, trailing four boys. I smile at first, because I have no idea who they are or why they're here. I don't recognize anyone until the teacher says, "These boys all have something to say to you about their behavior in Health class today."

Ahhhh. The four young comedians who took advantage of my cluelessness and disrupted the classroom. I picture their classmates burning rubber in the hall, rushing to tattle, embellishing the list of crimes. It's possible that the boys have been acting up in her class as well, because the teacher exhibits a high level of pisstivity, and the boys look quite contrite. Their consequence must include the most painful punishment of all—loss of recess. Two of the boys have tears in their eyes and are sniffling.

At a nod from the teacher, one boy steps forward, hands me a note, and says with a shaking voice, "I am very sorry for my behavior in your class today."

I read his written apology and thank him.

"You won't do that again, will you?" I ask, mentally kicking myself for such a stupid, rhetorical question. Of course he will say yes with his teacher hovering over him! I know it's important to correct disrespectful behavior, and the boys did take advantage of me, but my heart goes out to them as we stand face-to-face.

Each boy takes his turn at humiliation. I thank them individually, then include the teacher. They leave as I shake my head, feeling sorry for the boys and for myself. How could I have contributed to a different outcome? Am I ignoring bad behavior when I try to connect with the kids who seem interested in the lesson? I applaud the teacher's quick follow-up and firm stance. She is apparently okay with being the tough cop. I just hate to be the tough cop all the time. Outside of subbing, I'm the type of person to connect with kids through silliness, laughter, and imagination. But being this jack-booted disciplinarian? It's not my forte. Deep down, I want these kids to like me.

Chapter 14

As I turn the calendar page into March, I feel a bit more competent and relaxed. I've survived so many difficult, heart-wrenching assignments that I should be proud of my hard-earned skills. Or maybe I'm just being cocky and deserve to get whittled down a few notches.

I still like kids. Given my druthers, I prefer to sub in second-, third-, or fourth-grade classrooms. Oh, I won't turn down work in kindergarten, first-, or fifth-grade classrooms, because novice subs can't be choosy. Kindergartners are endearing in small groups. But a herd of them in a classroom can make me question any sanity I might have left—and that's *before* lunchtime. First graders still need a lot of help with everything. Fifth graders can be funny and interesting, but their total preoccupation with their peers wears thin after a couple of hours.

Kids between the ages of seven and ten have figured out the school rules, and they still seem interested in learning. Like blobs of Play-Doh, they are open to all possibilities.

Smiling, ready to "Make a Difference in the Life of a Child," (teachers get all kinds of gifts with pseudoinspiring sayings like that; on almost every desk and shelf I see mugs, apple-shaped tablets and photo frames, and figurines of droopy-eyed puppies, kittens, and adorable children—but I think they would rather have gift cards to their favorite stores), I show up in a third-grade classroom just before the teacher has to leave to pick up her own sick child and head home. The school is known for extra large class sizes, but what the hey, it's third grade. I like third grade.

"I have to warn you," the teacher says as she packs her stuff. "I've been a teacher for almost twenty years, and this is the worst class I have ever had!"

I creak my neck around. Desks cover just about every square inch of floor space.

"Yes, having twenty-eight kids complicates everything, but this group has some really needy kids along with some severe behavior problems," she says, watching me scan the room. "Don't let them get away with anything. Be tough right away, or they will walk all over you!"

I'm not smiling as she apologizes repeatedly for leaving me to face her students, and then she is out the door.

Well, crap. Double crap.

The bell rings as I'm scanning the lesson plans for the day. I join the parade of teachers shuffling down the hall to the pickup point.

"You're subbing for Daphne today?" asks a teacher, narrowing her eyes and raising her brows. I nod, and she says, "Don't try to be nice. You are gonna have to ride herd on them, or they will take control!"

I mentally debate whether it's better to be warned that you're sailing into a hurricane of horse manure or whether ignorance is bliss.

The kids are big. Eight- and nine-year-olds are supposed to be small and cuddly, or have stick-skinny arms and legs. They're not supposed to be surly, pimply hulks with huge, untied shoes. Two of the boys have hair down to their shoulders. Many of the girls have discovered Victoria's Secret. I'm shocked they're not in middle school.

During the long walk to the classroom, I thumb through my mental catalogue of mistakes I've made this year. Trying to be friendly when faced with blatant bad behavior tops the list. I have just been handed the opportunity to regain some lost yardage. Game on. For once, I don't feel guilty about being the tough cop.

I give clear instructions and follow up immediately with reprimands. The wanderers, the comedians, the chatterboxes, and the never-listen-the-first-timers get one generic warning. At the second offense, I threaten them with a trip to the office, saying, "It's a waste of your time and mine if you don't want to follow instructions. Your choice." I am calm, unwavering, showing no irritation. Like a jailer, I am prepared for any and all rule-breaking behavior.

They get to work. I patrol and squelch the slightest hint of rebellion. The kids are sly, avoiding eye contact when corrected, denying any intent to break the rules. It takes a great deal of energy to stay in the combat-readiness mode. When the kids leave for Music and PE, I collapse into the teacher's chair.

The mission of the Sioux Falls school district is "to educate and prepare each student to succeed in a changing world." I guess the definition of "educate" is wide-open to interpretation. Do we mean "Do the best you can under impossible conditions?" How about "Whatever was good enough for me when I was a kid?" My personal favorite is "You can't just keep throwing money at the problems!" as if South Dakota schools have been irresponsible with tax dollars. All the surrounding states spend more per pupil than we do. Our teachers' salaries rank lowest in the nation. Go ahead, look it up. What a claim to shame!

"Our children are our future." Yah, sure, you betcha. We are expecting teachers and school professionals not only to teach children but to nurture them, build their characters and self-esteem, and provide a safe haven in which they can grow. It's not only for the immigrant children, the homeless kids, the kids with severe emotional problems, or the kids who are victims of abuse and neglect. I've now realized that it's for *all* kids. Somehow there's an expectation that we can squeeze large numbers of students through the system like sausage. But sausage-making is messy.

Today, I spend about half an hour actually teaching or explaining new concepts. Most of the time, I troll the classroom with my arms crossed, jaw set firmly, and lips pressed together. All I'm missing is a tan polyester uniform stretched to the breaking point, a couple of hairy moles on my cheek, and a nightstick in my belt. Otherwise, the prison-matron is complete.

The kids are quiet and quick to leave at the end of the day. I am sitting at the teacher's desk, wondering whether it's worth my time to write four pages of notes and tell the teacher what she already knows. I notice a small boy lingering at his locker, taking his time with his backpack and coat. He'd been silent around the other students and had kept his head down to avoid drawing attention.

After making sure all the other kids have left, the boy turns in the doorway and says, "I feel sorry for substitute teachers, because some kids are so mean." I tell him that he's a good student, and he should just ignore the kids who make school so difficult. "I like school," he says. "I actually don't like summer vacation, because I miss school." I tell him to hang in there, because once he gets to high school, some of his classes will be full of smart kids like him, and they will fly through the lessons, and it will actually be fun. He gives me a sad smile and slowly heads down the hall.

I have joined the ranks of Adults Who Say Stupid, Unbelievable Things to Kids.

MY SENTENCE IS ANOTHER DAY in kindergarten at a tough school. The classroom is roasting when I arrive at 7:30 a.m., and I know I'll melt before morning recess unless I find some way to lower the temperature. The thermostat is useless, locked at a cozy seventy-two degrees, so I attempt to open a window. I spend ten minutes moving boxes of games, books, and who-knows-what but still cannot reach the latch or the window sill.

The thick layer of dust on everything tells me that the boxes haven't been moved since school started. What is going on in this classroom? Is the teacher a kindly-but-compulsive hoarder? Is her room used as a lending library for the other teachers? Is she so overwhelmed that she just closes her door at the end of the day and applies (and then reapplies) for jobs as an ice road trucker?

A student teacher recently told me that everything in a classroom, with the exception of textbooks and workbooks, has to be provided by the teacher. The baskets of books, the games and toys, and the charts and posters must be purchased by the teacher with personal funds. Some teachers scavenge through garage sales and write grants so they can buy things that will help kids learn.

I should feel more empathy for this teacher. However, the only spaces not buried under piles of crap are the children's work tables, which are placed close together because, yes, the piles of crap are threatening to overtake them.

I don't dare move anything on her desk, because I haven't found her lesson plans yet. C'mon, it's kindergarten. How hard can it be to copy the same plan you used last year and paste it into the three-ring binder? My OCD is in hyper-drive—fingers twitching with the need to clean and sort, sweat dripping down the sides of my face.

I find a class list. Twenty-seven kids. The day will be punishing. I should have taken more pain medication. I won't be anywhere near a chair until the wee darlings are at lunch, happily sucking ketchup straight from packets and poking each other with sticks from their corn dogs. I wonder if the principal will give the standard "We don't hide the sticks from our corn dogs in our coats so we can play swords at recess, boys and girls!" speech. I rather enjoy that one when it's delivered with lots of animation and hand gestures.

Still no lesson plan. I move a pile of papers and watch another stack cascade to the floor. Near tears, I scoop and grab. I don't care if some of the papers are crumpled. I find a sheet of handwritten notes with the correct date and stop sniffling. I scan the morning agenda. We have something in the gym for the first hour of the day, then Music and Art. It's survivable.

I take attendance with the help of two little girls. They shout, "Brittany, are you having hot lunch today?! How about you, Andrew?" and tell me who is absent. They find my questions surprisingly novel, because their teacher "doesn't do that." Of course their teacher would know which kids aren't there right off the bat, then probably subtract the number of cold lunch containers from the total in a perfectly seamless fashion.

Of course, I'm also the only person in the room who doesn't know why the students are supposed to go to the gym right away.

"We're supposed to bring our information papers, too!" add the two helpers who are acting a bit superior because I know so little. The girls show me their papers, but I'm still confused. Name, address, phone number, and parents' names and work locations are listed. Huh?

My class joins meandering lines of two more kindergarten

classes in the hall. I decide to pump another teacher for information since all I can get from my kids is "We go and tell somebody the stuff on our papers."

The gym has about thirty adults seated at tables around the room. In front of each table is a student reciting . . . something. The only adults I recognize are three police officers (because of their uniforms) and a couple of local businesspeople.

I get the scoop from another teacher as we wait with our kids in the hall, trying to maintain some sense of order.

"This is the final part of an exercise to help the children learn their basic personal information like name, address, and phone number," she explains. "We got volunteers from the community to come and quiz the kids. That puts a stronger focus on knowing the information. The kids were supposed to study with Mom or Dad at home for about two weeks, so today's the day!"

I can't get too huffy about spending school time on things that parents should be teaching at home. We had moved many times before our daughter was enrolled in kindergarten. With a disapproving look, her teacher told us it was time to stop moving and stay in one place, that our child didn't know where home was and didn't feel safe. I want to ask why these kids' parents aren't involved, but I decide to shut up and let the exercise eat up an hour.

The kindergartners are a bit intimidated by some of the adults, so other teachers help pair them with people who won't make them cry. My job is to prevent the little lambs from wandering off while they wait, a task that increases in difficulty as more classes arrive at the gym door. Even if I had spent a couple of hours with my students, I would be hard-pressed to recognize all of them in a crowd like this. Having spent less than thirty minutes with them, I can positively identify two, maybe three, only because they have wild hair or are wearing unusual clothing—like the girl in a ballet leotard with full-length tutu. But the other teachers and the principal seem to know who goes where. Eventually, I'm reunited with my flock and sent back to the classroom.

The day proceeds as a typical kindergarten day should, but where two of me are needed and only one showed up.

"Gabriel looked at my butt when I was in the bathroom, and that is private, and he's not supposed to look at my butt!" shouts a very indignant, red-faced boy leaving the bathroom, pulling up his pants. I have given the directive to join me in the circle, but it has fallen on deaf ears. Kids are milling about the room, and I see no male child who is near the bathroom or looks guilty. The accuser points Gabriel out. "There he is! He does this all the time! He looks at private places!"

Gabriel is a cute little boy with huge dark eyes and a disarming smile. I crook my finger at him, and we go into a corner for a discreet discussion.

"Gabriel, Keith says you looked at his butt. You know you're not supposed to peek into the bathroom and look at other kids' private parts, right?" I ask calmly, making sure I don't act disgusted or dump a load of shame on behavior that is common at this age.

Gabriel nods slowly and looks away.

"You're not going to do that anymore in school, right?"

No response.

"Gabriel, I need to hear you say you won't do that anymore in school."

A tiny squeak of "Yes" comes out. That's all I need for now. If he's a pervert in the making, his regular teacher will have to deal with it. If she can find him under all the piles of crap in this room.

I follow the line leader as we travel to the art room, wondering how the immigrant kids from other cultures deal with privacy and private-parts issues. If they came from a hot climate, they may not have had to wear a lot of clothing and may not have had access to bathrooms. Using the great outdoors when needed may have meant other kids saw butts and everything else. I know—our country, our rules. But I'm sure it makes life confusing for those small children.

While my students are politely following the art teacher's directions, I attack the overheated-classroom problem. The teacher in a nearby room says the temperature is set in a central facilities management office, and there is nothing we can do to change it. I get a hot flash just listening to her. I have thirty minutes to get a window open, and I use my time well.

There is a far corner of the window ledge that is not covered in boxes and other junk. I start my climb in the corner and crawl about ten feet to a window in the center of the wall, a location that should provide the best air flow if I keep the door open. The window latch hasn't been moved in a very long time, so I have to wrench it open. Success! Houston, we have air! I have to replace all the books, boxes, and figurines that I displaced in my quest, then make the crawl backward to dismount.

I am covered with dust and sweat, but who will notice? I

tidy up in the bathroom and nearly skip to the art room. I get a thrill thinking that I have outsmarted the system, sort of like my days in boarding school when we pulled off a good kitchen raid.

Between the time when I pick up my students, who are standing in a quiet row, and the time we arrive in the classroom, they morph. Not even five minutes have passed, and they are whining, arguing, and trying to play with games and toys reserved for indoor recess. I know this because the kids not playing the games are shouting at me, hoping I will punish the others with something humiliating. Two boys are running around the room playing Gotcha Last.

I'm trying to get their attention by clapping, calling "Give me five!" and putting my hand on the shoulder of the game-playing ringleader—and I'm about to start shouting—when we get a visitor. Was this on the daily schedule? An older man, nicely dressed in khakis and a sweater, steps into the room and says he is here to read a story "to the good kindergartners who are ready to listen." He must be real, because he is wearing the proper visitor badge and a picture ID badge. He tells me that he comes to this school to read to students once a week. *Yeah*, I think, *easy gig. Read and go home and pour yourself a tall one.*

Good grief, I can be judgmental! I should be thankful that this person has volunteered his time and energy to help make a difference. What a snot I can be.

The kids find their chairs and stare at him. He has a New York accent, so he's a bit of an oddity, enough to hold their attention for a few minutes. The kids seated farthest away from him lose interest first and twist in their chairs, making noise so others can't hear the story. By the time our volunteer reader has finished, most of the room has tuned him out. His wonderful age-appropriate story about a rabbit and a kangaroo does not hold up to the distractions of classmates giggling and kicking each other under the tables, a child hopping around the room "like the bunny," and a little girl who is crying, saying, "I just wanna go home!" *Yes*, I think. *I want to go home, too.*

The reader leaves. I am the only one who notices.

Throughout the morning, I've heard the intermittent noise of a child wailing. I peek into the hall and see a teacher with crossed arms calmly standing over a child who is thrashing about on the floor, red-faced, snot flying, kicking at the teacher and the walls. "He gets like that a lot," says one of my students, shrugging. The screeching continues for another thirty minutes or so, and the teacher doesn't try to say anything. I don't have a student like that, so I count myself lucky.

We muddle through the rest of the morning, cutting and gluing numbers onto colored sheets of paper. That's what is supposed to happen, anyway. Half the class is engaged, but the rest do what kindergartners do when they are not closely supervised: they cut paper into pieces and glue it to themselves, they cry and refuse to do anything, or they fight with the other kids they haven't liked since the first week of school in August. After making sure no one is bleeding, I make them keep the noise level down and try to ignore the kids who are staring into space or rolling little balls of glue pellets.

I nearly weep for joy when 11:30 rolls around.

Kindergarten teachers in this school are expected to stay in the lunch line with their students until the kids have their trays, so there will be no simple handoff at the lunchroom door.

"Bobby, did you tell your mother you need lunch money?" asks the woman taking lunch cards. One of my little ones stops and stares as though trying to remember anything prior to this morning.

"Huh-uh."

"Well, you're behind in lunch money, so you don't get a tray," the woman says without a trace of empathy.

"Does he go without lunch?" I whisper to the woman.

"No, he gets a cheese sandwich until he brings lunch money for his account," she says as she takes cards from the rest of the class.

Two slices of white bread and one slice of processed cheese stuffed into a sandwich wrapper. It is disgusting, but Bobby takes it and wanders to his table.

His family is not one of the 40 percent on a subsidized lunch plan in the Sioux Falls school district, so he will eat that slop until his parents remember to write a check. A reminder has already been sent home with Bobby, but it could still be lurking in the bowels of his backpack. If Bobby is their first child in the school system, the parents have much to learn.

Returning to my classroom, I find that the open window has brought the room to a bearable temperature range. It doesn't get cold, because heat continues to pour from the ducts. What a frickin' waste of energy! Why are thermostats set at 72 degrees in a public building? I'm not advocating cold rooms and widespread suffering, but couldn't they trim energy costs instead of salaries?

During the afternoon, while walking with the class to the music room, one of my students demonstrates how easily the school's security system can be breached. We pass by a set of glass double doors that are locked from the inside. A very large man is standing outside the doors, tapping on the glass, asking to come in. I step between the students and the door and loudly tell him to go to the office and register as a visitor.

"No one is in the office. It's locked," he answers. I doubt that and make no move to the doors.

"I can't let you in here," I say. "Go to the office."

"I came to pick up my daughter," he shouts, getting a bit worked up.

Before I can repeat my directions, one of my girls darts around me and opens the door for him, saying, "He is Ariel's dad. She's in K03."

I take a step in front of him and tell him he has to go to the office and get a visitor's pass. He starts up the stairs without answering me.

I hustle my kids to Music and trot to the office to report. I'm a bit traumatized, because he could be a noncustodial parent, and I'm responsible for letting him in. But the secretary mobilizes forces, dispatching the principal to lay down the law with Ariel's father, and we avert a crisis.

At the end of the day, I make a big deal out of the incident in my notes to the teacher so she can reinforce the rules to her kids. The man got through the locked doors and was on his way up the stairs in a matter of seconds. If he had been armed or dangerous in any way, my kids and I would have been first in harm's way. I'm still shaken when I stagger back to the office before departing.

"What could have been done differently to make the day go better for you?" the secretary asks. I am stunned. I've been subbing for seven months and have landed in about twenty schools. This is the first time I've been asked such a question. I hardly know what to say other than the usual "class size is too large to get anything done." She is writing my response when she notices a mother and son standing in a corner of the foyer.

When invited to come to the secretary's desk, the mother, wearing a Muslim hijab, pulls her son by his coat sleeve to stand in front of the secretary. He looks as though he's in first or second grade and would rather be anywhere else.

"Can I help you?" the secretary asks politely.

"He says he is gay. What is this gay?!" the mother asks, fearful and upset.

I gather my things. Trying to avoid looking obvious, I continue to put away my papers and put on my coat, but I move slowly. The room is very still.

With a neutral expression on her face, the secretary looks at the little boy, then the mother whose fingers are locked on his sleeve. I get the feeling that he would run if she loosened her grip.

"Let me call the principal. I know he will want to talk with you about this," she says as she punches the numbers. I can almost hear her thinking, *There is no way I am going to try explain "gay" to this poor woman!*

I am dressed and ready to go and have lost my reason to linger. I leave with a suppressed smile, wishing I could hear how the principal handles the situation and realizing that even the best and brightest education professionals can't handle everything perfectly. Maybe the best thing about the job is the stories that follow people home.

Chapter 15

LATER IN THE MONTH, I spend an afternoon at one of the newer schools in Sioux Falls and get to watch how a talented teacher maintains order and calm while taking care of the emotional needs of her little first graders. The teacher, Mrs. Revling, introduces me to her class before she leaves. There are twenty-four faces tuned to her every gesture, listening carefully as she tells them her expectations. I don't sense fear in their silence; it appears they are as calm as their teacher.

However, as they line up for lunch, a few disagreements pop up.

"Mrs. Revling, Harrington pinched me!"

"Are you okay?" she asks without raising an eyebrow but still conveying concern.

"Yes," answers the injured.

"Please take your place in line then," is all she says. No whining follows. No muttering about revenge. I can't believe my eyes and ears. Yes, her demeanor is worthy of high praise, but it's also apparent that something is missing: the impaired children, the extremely needy kids who are growing up in poverty. She is able to spend most of her time actually teaching.

When the children are safely in the lunchroom, I ask Mrs. Revling if the kids always listen so well. She looks at me as if I have drool coming from my mouth and says most of the kids are quick to obey, except for Harrington, who will "push your buttons." She asks me to document Harrington's behavior, because she will be meeting with his parents soon.

Yesterday, we enjoyed a freakishly warm spring day with a high temperature of fifty-five degrees. Water ran from the melting snow hills, and the playgrounds were muddy messes. Winter returned today with below-freezing temps. Many parents were fooled, and their kids got out the door with sweatshirts or light jackets instead of coats, caps, and mittens or gloves. Of course I have recess duty.

"No, you may not throw chunks of ice! Stop that!" I shout, but I'm distracted by the large numbers of kids who are wearing little more than sweaters. The wind is nasty, swirling around the barren field, spinning dust devils. I tell the girls who are huddled in a clump to run and play Tag, so they can warm up. They look at the ground and hop from foot to foot like sparrows, shivering. I find out later that Tag is a forbidden game, because it can get too rough and turn into shoving or slapping.

There are so many pieces of ice all over the playground

that I capitulate and look the other way when kids start kicking them around. At least the kicking means they're moving.

When the bell mercifully rings, everyone hustles to line up by the door. Well, almost everyone. Harrington lazily strolls across the pavement, ignoring my shouts to hurry up. I am chilled to the bone, so I know for certain that the kids are freezing. Harrington makes sure he is the last person to enter the building. I stand, holding the door for him. I can barely hold my temper in check, but I remember his teacher's air of calm and tell him that his behavior will be included in my note for Mrs. Revling. He shrugs. I take a wild guess that his behavior at home is seen as precious, precocious, and too-darling-for-words. His mommy probably gets the video camera and records every amazing step he takes.

Mrs. Revling has her other students so well trained that the rest of the afternoon slides by without much effort on my part.

I read a story. They listen, sitting quietly.

I give them instructions for a math worksheet. They work without a murmur.

After they copy their spelling words into their notebooks, they're allowed to draw or write for the remaining fifteen minutes of the school day. Little heads bow over their papers as they share bins of crayons. Writing on the whiteboard, a highly-coveted prize, is reserved for the two names on the Special Helpers chart.

Harrington is the only kid who decides to act like a little fart. He drapes himself across his desk and moans, "I am so bored! I don't wanna write or draw!" I ignore him at first, because his voice is quiet, and the other kids are paying no attention. He repeats the whine a second time, and then a third. Finally, it creates a stir.

But "Don't wanna" isn't an option in Mrs. Revling's class.

"Harrington, if you don't write or draw, you will put your head down on your desk and rest until it's time to get ready to go home," I tell him, standing over him, blocking his view of the audience.

"I don't wanna!" he whines.

"Then you get some new choices," I carefully say. "Sit in the hall until it's time to get ready to go, put your head down and be quiet, or come with me to the office and tell the principal why you won't follow directions."

Some of the little girls gasp. First graders don't get sent to the office! Not at this school!

I will feel pretty stupid if I have to send him to the office with ten minutes of school time left, but I will follow through. Harrington weighs his options. He sulkily slumps onto his desk, muttering to himself.

My attitude needs a thorough adjustment. Why am I frustrated with normal behavior from children who are so much better-off than those in the schools near the city's center? Why do I feel compelled to tell them how good their lives are compared to kids who are homeless and hungry, to children whose families can't afford school supplies or winter clothing? I can almost see and hear my mother telling us, "There are children in India/Africa/South America who would love to have your life! You are acting like spoiled rotten brats!"

I hold my tongue, but the kids aren't fooled. I know my

clashing with Harington was stressful for them, because they leave at the end of the day without a single high five or hug or fist bump. I don't feel particularly good about myself either. I try to make excuses, rationalizing that I'm a bit of an adrenaline junkie. As a nurse, I craved the excitement of the emergency room over the predictability of seeing patients in the daytime clinic setting. Maybe I just like stirring up trouble myself! However, I could also just be blowing smoke up my own . . . skirt.

THE PENDULUM SWINGS in a huge arc the other way as the calendar creeps toward the end of March. I accept a teaching assignment in a Cluster Classroom, fully aware that the day could be unsettling. I remind myself that there is a huge difference between being a regular EA in a Cluster Classroom and being a clueless sub in the same room. Often, the subs barely have to do anything, because they're clueless about particular day-to-day operations.

Spring is whispering to me as I walk from my car to the school building. The sun is warming the air, beating back my seasonal affective disorder. I feel lighter and maybe even a touch happy.

One of the administrative assistants, the principal, and a young woman are deep in conversation when I sign in at the office. I catch a few phrases like "legal liability" and "according to the contract." It's no concern of mine until the administrative assistant says, "Oh, Peggy is here!"

The principal turns to me and explains how my services are needed only in a supervisory capacity today. The Cluster

Classroom teacher is ill, but her student teacher, the young woman involved in the earlier conversation, is fully capable of flying solo as the teacher of the day. They need me only because the teachers' contract specifically states that student teachers must be supervised at all times.

I feel a bit relieved, but I'm stung by her dismissive tone at the same time. The burden of being in charge, however, lifts from my shoulders and lands on those of the petite, attractive student teacher. I will get paid for my "only supervisory" role today, and Molly, the student teacher, will do all the work.

"Just tell me how I can help," I tell her, trying to let her know I have every intention of being useful. With poise and maturity, she lets me know my help will be appreciated, especially with a couple of the smaller children. Molly tells me she will be in charge of a tall, strong boy with autism who can be "very disruptive and very active," and with the help of the two EAs, we will get through the day just fine.

All six of the children are ambulatory—no wheelchairs. We collect them from buses as hundreds of other students pour through the school doors. I take the hand of an adorable little boy, age six or seven, with big dark eyes and the scissoring gait of cerebral palsy.

His name is Barry, and he steals my heart even before we get to the classroom. I don't know if his physical limitations are the only reason for his presence in a Cluster Classroom, but he seems cheerful as he greets the other kids and adults. My second little charmer, Burton, about the same age, has a distant stare and a tendency to echo whatever is said to him. I guess autism, but of course I can't be sure.

"Hi, Burton, how are you today?" he repeats back to me, word for word, with the exact inflection and tone of my voice. He sways back and forth as I help him remove his coat, then waits to be told to sit at his desk.

Molly and her student, Paxton, arrive at the classroom door later than the rest of us. Paxton, the tall, strong boy with autism, looks older than any fifth grader I've ever seen. Maybe Cluster Classroom kids are not automatically sent to middle school after fifth grade?

The whole school heard them coming. Paxton communicates by howling. He sounds like an out-of-control adult roaring in wordless anger. Something apparently upset Paxton in the hall, which led to his flailing arms and shrieks. Molly helped him lie face down on the floor and sat over him, holding his shoulders, until he found some measure of control. She is short of breath and sporting a fresh floor burn on her elbow. Paxton gets hustled to a stationary bicycle in the middle of the classroom, which he rides at high speed, howling at intervals.

"Are you okay?" I ask Molly as she straightens her clothing while keeping an eye on Paxton.

"It's just a bruise," she remarks casually. "I've been hit much harder." Paxton is taller than Molly and probably outweighs her by twenty-five pounds. When I ask how they discovered that the exercise bike helped settle Paxton, Molly tells me it was pure coincidence. Someone donated the bike, and Paxton took to it immediately. The exercise helps calm him and burn up some of his explosive energy. She tells me that the scene in the hall could have been brought on by Paxton's frustration with having a favored teacher replaced by a stranger—me.

Paxton rides the bike through Morning Meeting with minor growling. Barry wants to sit on my lap and give me kisses, but I have to disengage from him to keep Burton from wandering away. The EAs are busy with Rowan, a tall, slim boy who sucks on his sweater sleeves, grabs his hair, and shrieks when excited. The only girl, Mayella, has to be held by the hand to keep from wandering the room and bouncing off tables and chairs like a pinball. A pretty little girl, she appears to be talking nonstop, but her sounds are pure gibberish. She is about six or seven years old and is wearing a diaper. Our group is completed by William, a higher-functioning boy with autism, who is about eight or nine years old.

Molly announces to the class that we will be attending the school's spring program, which involves all the third and fourth graders singing and dancing in the gym. None of the children react, but the EAs seem very surprised.

"We usually don't get to go to the school programs," one woman explains. "The kids are too disruptive, we're told, so this is a big deal!" I imagine us crammed in a corner of the gym, far away from the risers and stage.

Paxton has picked up on the excitement and lets out a roar, which Molly quickly quiets by counting back from three to zero, showing corresponding fingers. I can hardly believe it works.

When we arrive at the gym doors, the other students are already seated on the floor, and the bleachers are full of parents and other guests. We teachers are told to sit on the floor with our students. Apart from being unsure whether I'll be able to get up afterward without help from paramedics and a front-end loader, I'm unsettled by our assigned location. We are right in front of bleachers full of people who probably don't know about Cluster Classrooms and severely impaired children. *If you have kids who might be disruptive, is it really wise to place them in full view of the audience?* I wonder.

The kids are so enthralled with the props, costumes, and performances that they sit still, except for Rowan, who has shown his excitement by chewing on his wrists and squealing. The staff has found that music is a powerful motivator for him, and usually, it's used as a reward for completing tasks and following instructions. The excitement proves to be too much this morning, so they have to take him into the hall to calm down.

During the program, I notice a row of children in wheelchairs along one wall. Some of them sit slumped and motionless. Others shift restlessly, heads bobbing. I wonder how their parents cope and how much the kids understand.

I have to roll to my knees and use my hands to push off the floor after ninety minutes of sitting. My butt is numb, and my lower back is shooting pain messages down my legs. I limp back to the classroom with my little guys, who seem dazed by the experience.

After bathroom breaks, we tackle the morning's lessons. Each child has a specific set designed to improve communication skills and teach numbers, letters, and colors. Repetition is the key, it appears. Sign language always follows the instructions, Molly tells me, because while the kids may not be able to communicate verbally, they *can* learn some basic signing.

Molly goes to work with Paxton while I take my little guys to another table. Barry is still more intent on climbing into my lap to give me hugs and kisses than on learning his lesson on colors and shapes. Burton sits quietly and matches letters on cards. Before too long, I find myself chanting along with Molly's directions, which she repeats every ten seconds, accompanied with signing.

"Paxton, watch me. Find the number. Paxton, watch me. Find the number."

I've learned from my reading that children with autism often have difficulty making eye contact with other people. Molly at times has to touch Paxton's chin and turn his face toward hers. Paxton complies for about ten minutes, then blows spit and shows he's had enough by howling and swinging his arms. He goes back on the exercise bike.

The morning snack is Goldfish crackers and water doled out two ounces per cup. I start to ask why so little water when Rowan flings his across the room. Molly smiles at me and shrugs.

"They can have refills as often as they ask, but only in small amounts for that very reason," she explains. When I ask whether Rowan should be corrected for tossing his cup, she says, "No, we're working on correcting other behaviors, so we're ignoring that one for now."

While I wipe the floor, Mayella drinks straight from the pitcher. For a split second, her gibberish disappears, and I hear her distinctly say, "Delicious!" Her little face lights up as she smiles at her own joke. I reach for the pitcher, and she reverts to her nonsense language, and her eyes make no more contact.

When the EAs take the children to the lunchroom, I ask Molly how long Paxton has been in this classroom.

"He came to the program as a five-year-old," she says. "He had the roaring, out-of-control behaviors he still shows now. It took months of trying to find something that would grab and hold his attention for any amount of time."

"Little pieces of candy turned out to be the key," she says. "At first, he would stop howling for one second if he got a candy. Then two seconds. What you see is the result of years of work."

My heart goes out to his family. How must they manage him at home?

"I don't know how his mother is able to cope," says Molly, as if reading my mind. "She is a single parent, so she doesn't have help! If I have a rough day with him, I can go home and forget about it. His mother never gets a break!"

An elderly woman appears at the classroom door later that afternoon. She is carrying a few large picture books and says she is a volunteer from the library. In this school, the Cluster Classroom kids don't get taken to the library, an aide tells me, because they are so disruptive and because they put things in their mouths. Everything they touch has to be disinfected because of the germs in their saliva, so the library sends someone to the classroom to read.

Two more adults with clipboards follow the library lady into the room. As everyone gets settled on chairs around a large table, I ask the visitors whether they are teachers observing the class or administrators observing the staff. The noise level in the room is high, because the kids seem afraid of all the strangers. I think I hear, "We're just here to observe a child," but I can't follow up on the conversation to ask which one, because Paxton is kicking and flailing his arms and has to be quieted with a beanbag chair. Molly helps him to the floor, then presses the beanbag onto him. It soothes him, just as being swaddled soothes a baby, and he rejoins the group.

Our little library volunteer is at least seventy years old with snow-white hair, a warm turtleneck sweater and vest, elastic-waist pants, and sturdy shoes (like mine). She has books about jungle animals—a topic that appeals to every kid. As she starts reading, the excitement level in the room climbs. Rowan grabs his hair and shrieks, Mayella bounces and shouts her peculiar stream of sounds, and Paxton blows spit across the table, howling. The volunteer gamely reads on without missing a beat until Burton's echolalia kicks in.

Burton has been sitting quietly, staring off into space, when the reader says, "That lion is the biggest one!" with emphasis and expression. Before she can take a breath, Burton repeats her statement with perfect pitch and tone. She glances at him for a second, then turns the page and reads on. Burton waits for her to pause, then echoes her next sentence. It is uncanny and amazing. The brave volunteer reads on.

We don't finish the book, because something sets Paxton off, and it takes two adults to calm him down. The library lady says she will come back "some other day," and the two observers hustle out of the classroom without a backward glance.

Individual lessons continue, and I'm again amazed at the staff. They have patience with behaviors that may never change. Barry still wants to do nothing more than sit on my lap, wrap his arms around my neck, and give me kisses. But I can think of many, many worse ways to spend an afternoon.

"You are so good with the kids," an EA says. "We don't have subs very often. One sub left after ten minutes!" She adds, "Thanks for staying."

I feel humbled.

The "We have problems getting subs at our school" complaint takes me to another school later that week. That it's accompanied by the "And we *really* have trouble getting kindergarten subs!" follow-up makes me certain it's going to be a stressful day.

At least half the class is foreign-born and still struggling with English. A couple of the boys are so tiny that they could pass for three-year-olds. Their writing assignment is to write their first name three times, then fill the page with any other words they know. One of the tiny boys writes "ass, ass, ass" on half of his page. I ask him if he can read that word for me, and he just smiles.

Two little blonde girls tell me they are sisters but that they don't live together. They bear no resemblance to each other and pay no attention to the rest of us. They cling to each other like zoo monkeys and giggle.

A couple of the immigrant boys are so antagonistic toward each other that I have to keep them on opposite sides of the room. They shout, refuse to share crayons, and scribble on each other's paper if they get close enough. I ask one of the other kindergarten teachers about it, and she says, "It's been a problem all year. We think the kids are from warring tribes, and there doesn't seem to be anything we can do except keep them separate."

I ask about the tiny boys, and she says the families they live with are just guessing at birthdates. The boys were born in refugee camps, and their birth parents are deceased. She says they do seem young and probably will have to repeat kindergarten.

When the kids go out for recess, I offer up a prayer of thanksgiving for my blessings. No wonder this school has trouble getting substitutes!

A quick trip to the teacher's lounge for ice makes me laugh out loud. Someone has written on a whiteboard asking for amusing things that have happened around the school.

One boy said, "I just wet-farted and need to change my underwear!"

Another little boy got in trouble on the playground for yelling, "Jack S., Jack S.!" It turns out there are two Jacks in the kid's classroom, so last name initials are used. He was just calling for his friend.

"You have really big boobs, Mrs. XXX!" one first grader said. I bet everyone else was thinking the same thing.

The room is a mess by the time the kids leave. I revert to cleaning when I am frustrated, a pattern I've had since childhood. I barely make a dent in the piles, but I have only sympathy for the teacher. Day after day facing way too many kids who have moderate-to-severe problems and many parents who are just barely coping with their new lives—this teacher deserves a whole bunch of medals.

I want to do more, but my lower back muscles are in spasm, and the gray skies—which seem to have made the promise of spring vanish—are weighing me down. I limp out the door and shake my head. Working in a situation where I cannot make a difference is almost physically painful for me. I don't want to maintain the status quo—I want to move things toward excellence. It's something I simply cannot do being the sub who is there one day, gone the next.

Chapter 16

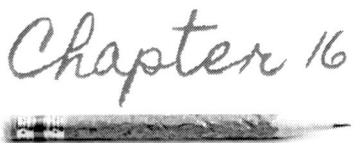

My sister Kay tells me to "relax and just go with it" when I complain about the trials and tribulations of being a substitute teacher in elementary schools. She says, "Everything happens for a reason, and there must be a lesson you need to learn from this. Just step back and take it all in." As New Agey as it sounds, it helps.

I still get frustrated with the kids' behavior, but I don't take it personally. I try to laugh at least once a day and remind myself that subs rarely are able to replace the regular teacher, get all the work done, and maintain order. That is what a dear friend tells me when I ask for help. She has been teaching first and second grade for the thirty-plus years since we graduated from college.

"Just do whatever you need to do to get through the day," she says. "I think you're very brave to sub! I couldn't do it!"

I soon get a third-grade class that has lost most of its kids to the Dark Side. The secretary warns me that it's their second day with a sub, so I know I won't get any pity at the end of the day if I accept it. *Turn around and run! Now!* says the alarm sounding in my brain, but I'm too spineless to ask for another assignment. I'm not even sure if that would be kosher.

The principal strides into my classroom just as the kids are getting settled, while I take attendance and get the count for hot lunch. He barks at the kids, and they sit quietly. Hidden in their little brains must be a tiny trace of fear, because they listen (a few actually look embarrassed) as he expresses his "concern" about yesterday's behavior and outlines the consequences of any complaints that might come from me today. The room is silent as he leaves. I let his threat sink in for about thirty seconds as they size me up.

I scan the students. My combat-honed sense of survival tells me which kids will act like untrained stray dogs if I take my eyes off them for even a second, and which kids have been sent to school wrapped in parental hope of learning something new each day.

We don't get too far into the math lesson before the leaders begin to laugh and chatter in nonsense conversations, ignoring everything I say. I remind them of the principal's message and ask who is ready to visit his office. It shuts them up for a few minutes. In this school, as in many, there are so many children with learning and behavior problems. By third grade, these kids are extremely skilled at drawing the teacher's attention away from their deficits, so it seems quite useless, especially for a substitute teacher, to keep them in the classroom while trying to teach everyone else.

I put them in Time Away corners or make them sit in the doorway of the room on the hard tile floor. Anything to get them away from their audience! I warn them that the next infraction will put their name on the list for the principal, which means at least one lost recess. What happened to children being concerned about notes going home to their parents if they got in trouble?

We're off to the art room, so I remind my class that the hall is a Quiet Zone, and I will continue to add names to the list. They are so loud and out-of-control that another teacher comes out of her room with fire in her eyes.

"302! You are being extremely disrespectful, and this behavior stops now!" She watched them misbehave with the sub yesterday, she says, and has decided they need a strong punishment to capture their attention. She revokes their noon recess!

"You will sit at your tables in the lunchroom after you have eaten and, instead of going outside for recess, you will go back to the classroom, put your heads down, and think about how you are going to behave for the rest of the day!"

That's a gutsy move. Yeah for her!

"And, 302, remember that some of you will be in my class next year! I won't forget how you have acted this week." She delivers her threat with conviction, and I have no doubt she will follow through.

I open the windows in the classroom before I scrub up and have my lunch. It's a beautiful spring day with vivid green grass shoots and snippets of tree buds. What a shame that my class won't see it until 2:45.

The children are slightly subdued when they trudge into the classroom after lunch. Shouts from the playground drift through the open windows and remind them what their disobedience caused them to miss. I put the class to work on a social studies worksheet that directs them to match the type of shelter with the correct Native American tribe. Really? Kids who can hardly read and add two numbers correctly are spending time matching tipis with Plains Indians? Really? Okay, maybe it's just busy work, but what a waste! I patrol the room and, like the Dog Whisperer, I stop bad behavior before my charges can get too far out of control.

We get a break in midafternoon from the drudgery of the classroom. Several classes from this school have been chosen to take part in an Arbor Day presentation that will be held at a new park in Sioux Falls. Volunteers from the city are putting the event together. The mayor, some dignitaries, and the local media will all attend. For their training, the kids sit cross-legged on the floor of a different classroom that usually holds about twenty-five students. We have twice as many as that crammed into the space today—plus teachers and volunteers.

The main speaker is a retired teacher who still knows how to silence children with her daggerlike stare. She tells them to listen, because their job at the event is very important. They will help dig the holes and plant some saplings, all under the watchful eyes of the news media and the mayor.

Two boys from my classroom are sitting near a girl from another room, and I can see them laughing at something, pointing at the girl's back. I lean forward and see that the girl's low-waist jeans have slipped down so that her butt crack is on full display. Why do parents let little girls wear things to school that make them targets for teasing, like low-waist pants, short skirts without tights or leggings, and shoes with high heels that restrict their ability to run and play?

I touch the shoulders of the snickering boys and glare at them. They stop for a couple of minutes. The presentation drags on. The giggling and pointing resumes.

"You! What is your name?" the retired teacher yells, pointing at one of my boys.

He mumbles, "Aaron," eyes downcast. His buddy inches away.

"Well, Aaron, I know all about kids like you, and I want you to know something. I don't take any of that crap! If you don't listen to the rest of what I have to say, your teacher can take you back to your room! We don't need that kind of behavior. Am I clear?"

The room is silent. Not only has a visitor raised her voice in anger, but she said "crap," one of the all-time bad words! They will talk about this day for the rest of the year.

As the rest of the afternoon progresses, we cover no more than four pages of the much-longer lesson plan. The office staff apologizes for the students' behavior, but I tell them, "This wasn't the worst class I've worked with, not by far!" It is the truth, and it seems to make them feel better.

IT IS SO DIFFICULT FOR ME to refrain from judging other people. When first graders come to school tardy without having eaten breakfast, I want to call their parents and rag on them for not accepting their responsibilities. When I ask another teacher what to do with the hungry kids, she rolls her eyes and says, "Send them to the lunchroom. Breakfast is over, but at least they can have milk and cereal."

I once made the observation that all the children in the room were having hot lunch. I thought it was odd that not even one child had brought cold lunch.

"I hope you don't think the parents of these kids would pack a lunch!" was the other person's sarcastic reply.

In many classrooms, certain kids are tardy so often that when I call names for attendance, the rest of the class will tell me, "Oh, she's always late," or "He doesn't ever come on time." I think teachers send notes home to the parents if the child is always late, but the notes must be too tame, because the kids keep missing their first hour of school.

EVERY ONCE IN A WHILE, I get a chance to actually teach a lesson. If I do a good job, I savor the moment for weeks. On one particular spring day, I use a few of the students to illustrate the rotation of the earth, which causes day, night, and the seasons. I put little blonde Maryann in the middle of the circle for the sun. Derek and Jared volunteer to be the earth and the moon.

"Derek's nose is where we are in Sioux Falls, South Dakota, everyone," I tell them. "Watch his nose! See when his nose turns away from the sun. That's when we have night."

The little moon has trouble keeping up with Derek, but

the lesson lands. I hope some kid, someday, says, "That substitute teacher we had in first grade showed me how the earth rotates." Yeah. I know. Delusions of grandeur.

MARCH IS ONE OF THE MONTHS of testing in the school system. No Child Left Behind has put pressure on teachers to deliver improved scores even if many of the students are impaired or struggling with the English language. It is ridiculous to compare the scores of all third graders in Sioux Falls. There are too many variables, and politicians will never understand that until they face today's classroom realities firsthand.

Today I will be administering the Dakota Step Reading Test to third graders in one of the newer schools in Sioux Falls. The kids took the math test yesterday, so they know they have to put folders up around their desks to make it difficult for wandering eyes to find answers. The folders put each child into a cubicle. They call them their "offices."

I read the directions out loud to them when they are ready. Two boys are engrossed in coloring, ignoring me. I ask a spokesperson student why Larry and Darryl aren't getting ready to take the test.

"Oh, they don't have to take any tests," Cindy informs me. "They will be going to Resource pretty soon anyway. They don't have to do the work."

She is correct. I begin the test, and Larry and Darryl wander off about ten minutes later. When the kids finish and it's time for recess, Larry and Darryl return, and we all march outside. I would love to take some time and ask teachers how they measure the progress of children who are unable to complete kindergarten-level work. Will they ever improve? Will these children be passed from grade to grade until they age out of the school system?

LATER THAT WEEK, I sub for a fourth-grade teacher who warns me in her notes "to be firm." When that phrase pops up in the first paragraph, I know it's a rough class.

A group of three boys tests me first, talking over me as I give instructions. They are laughing at Murray, the leader, who mutters something under his breath when I tell him to stop talking. I tell him to take a break and get himself under control. He slouches to the chair in the corner, muttering some more.

I start the lesson. Murray throws a paper airplane over my head. Laughter erupts. I tell Murray that he is on his second strike. He mutters.

Ten minutes later, when the kids are working on math problems, I ask Murray if he is ready to work.

"Yeah, I suppose," he answers.

"Okay," I say. "Then you can return to your desk and get to work."

He gets out a pencil, decides it needs to be sharpened, strolls to the pencil sharpener, and grinds on the pencil until I tell him to return to his seat. His buddies smirk at him, clearly knowing his typical pattern of behavior.

I don't know whether Murray makes conscious choices or if he just goes with the first impulse that comes to mind. He certainly isn't afraid of consequences, because he flips his math paper on the floor and says, "I'm not doing no math today."

I point at the classroom door and say, "Murray, go to the office! I will call and let them know you are coming."

He saunters in a pretty fair imitation of a gangsta walk to the back of the room, grabs his crotch, puts his other hand in the air, and yells, "So long, suckas!" He leaves to laughter and applause.

I believe Murray is salvageable, but it will take a great deal of someone else's time and energy. Whatever he needs, he isn't getting it at home, so the school system putters along, trying to help him.

A FEW DAYS LATER, I take an assignment as a resource room teacher just to see how the students and teacher interact in that setting. It's much more relaxed than in a regular classroom. Every twenty minutes, children show up at the door. Some of the kids come to my table; others head for the other teacher in her corner of the room. The kids know exactly how each lesson proceeds.

"You're supposed to help us with our math now," says a little girl who writes everything backward. One of her classmates has such trouble shutting out the distractions in the room that she has to sit in a corner, shielded by bookcases, in order to do her work.

Next, I get a group of boys who need a little individual

attention as they finish their papers. Sitting face-to-face with a teacher discourages goofing around and showboating. I could get used to this!

The other teacher has children who are severely impaired, so it's noisy in her corner. One little boy has set up camp under her table, refusing to sit on a chair and work on the lesson. The teacher coaxes him for a few minutes, then has to crawl under the table to retrieve him.

The kids who show up right after lunch are fourth and fifth graders: three girls and one boy. They are supposed to take turns reading out loud from a book written at a second- or third-grade level. I don't know if the girls are madly in love with the boy, Luke, who looks old enough to be in middle school, or if there is bad blood between the sexes. They snipe at each other after each sentence, and it takes almost ten minutes to cover a single paragraph.

"All right, guys, this bickering stops now," I say, leaning forward to make eye contact and appear in charge. "No one talks unless I call on you, got it?"

I point to Lorraine, who flips her hair back and begins to read, stumbling painfully with "about" and "around." Luke snorts when she makes a mistake. I glare at him. When it is his turn to read, he flips the book shut and says, "I don't feel like reading today." He crosses his arms, leans back in the chair, and smirks at the girls.

I give him an opportunity to change his mind. He tilts his chair back so he is balancing on two legs. I point at the door and say, "You are out of here! Go to the office!"

So much for my new relaxed attitude.

"I didn't do nothin'!" he protests.

"Go!" I lean into his space, practically daring him to challenge me. He slaps his book and paper onto the floor, throws an ugly glare my way, and stomps out. The other teacher is watching the proceedings just as I have watched her kids' behavior while I teach.

When I am cleaning up for the day, I ask her if Luke is usually well behaved and if my sub-ness provoked the behavior. "He can be difficult at times," she says in a noncommittal way, which makes me think she disagrees with how I handled things. Maybe I didn't try hard enough to reach him. I should have expected some push-back from a boy his age; he was just showing off for the girls, after all. But what *should* I have said or done?

My run of tough assignments continues. I land in a first-grade classroom, which, by this time of year, should be a piece of cake. With less than two months left in the school year, kids have been molded into model students, fully aware of the consequences of poor choices and ready to feel the release of summer vacation.

As I read through the day's instructions, I see a clipboard with "Emmet" written on the top of the page. Oh crap. Clipboards are never good. Clipboards mean a child is so out of control that his or her behavior has to be monitored every minute of the day. I will have to ride herd on this one all day *and* make notations—not the easiest thing to do while maintaining order with the rest of the students!

Emmet's day is broken into four time periods. I'm instructed to give him either a star (good) or a check (bad) during each period for the following behaviors:

- I CAN STAY IN MY AREA AND KEEP MY HANDS AND FEET TO MYSELF.
- I WALK IN LINE AND KEEP MY HANDS AND FEET TO MYSELF.
- I FINISH MY WORK AND STAY ON TASK.
- I WILL NOT TALK WHEN THE TEACHER IS TALKING.

Too many checks, and he loses recess. Stars allow him to choose between going out for recess or playing a board game with the counselor.

The clipboard is to accompany Emmet to Art, PE, and the lunchroom so that other adults can write reports. It reminds me of a similar practice followed in the workplace by supervisors who document an employee's behavior so they can justify discipline or termination. Some companies simply move the Emmets of the real world to other departments and supervisors. But what can a school system do with kids like him, who keep getting checks?

Emmet's behavior isn't the worst in the room today. Another boy, Benjamin, seems even more hyper and out of control. He has brought a gold chain necklace to school and plays with it whenever he thinks I'm not watching.

"Put it away, Benjamin, or I'll take it and keep it until the end of the school day," I warn him.

"He's not supposed to have that in school anyway," blurts a classmate. "Mrs. Hagel would take it away!"

"Okay, then, Benjamin," I say. "Put it in your backpack so you won't be tempted to play with it."

He takes a leisurely stroll to the lockers, sifting the necklace back and forth through his fingers. I have to turn away when Emmet starts a disruption around his desk, and when I turn back to glance at Benjamin, I see him slip the necklace into his jeans pocket. I put Emmet in a Time Away chair and walk Benjamin to his locker so I can observe him putting the necklace into the backpack.

I start the reading lesson again, but in no time, Benjamin asks to go to the bathroom. I give him my permission, but he retrieves the necklace on his way.

When he returns, I let him get back to his desk before reaching my hand out and saying, "Give it to me. It's mine for the rest of the day."

"What! I didn't do nothin'!" he answers.

"Give it to me now, or go to the principal's office!"

He's in first grade, for pity's sake! How has he learned to lie and stand up to adults and act unjustly accused by the age of six or seven?

Confiscating the necklace proves to be more of a punishment for me than for Benjamin. I put it on the teacher's desk.

Like clockwork, he asks me every ten minutes if he can have it back. I keep my cool for the first two or three times he asks.

"No, Benjamin, you will not get it back until the end of the day."

"No, Benjamin, you may not have the necklace. Don't ask again."

"Stop asking, Benjamin! You won't get it back until 2:45!"

Meanwhile, Emmet's behavior is earning him all checks, and the rest of the class isn't following directions. So when Benjamin asks me for the necklace right before recess, I whirl around and stare at him. It gives me a few seconds to regain control. I imagine myself screeching at him, spittle flying from my mouth and hands rattling his shoulders, telling him what happens to children who drive their teachers into madness.

With icy calm, I say, "No, Benjamin. No. Ask me one more time, and you and I will go to the principal's office, and you can ask *her* for the necklace!" I know my eyes are bugging out and that I look fierce. He studies me, then stomps his foot and gets in line, muttering under his breath.

I wonder about the circumstances in his life that provoked and perfected this infuriating behavior. Maybe a parent or adult ignored him when he asked for something. Maybe then his behavior escalated past annoying, and he was shouted at, then ignored again. Maybe he kept asking and demanding. Maybe he got punished, because persistence was his strong suit. Maybe he didn't give up. Maybe he won.

Repeat scenarios like that a few times, and the behavior becomes ingrained. With Benjamin, it seems he gets what he wants as long as he is willing to put up with unpleasantness along the way. We applaud that type of persistence in an adult, probably even reward it. At the end of the day, I wonder if his teachers might someday find a way to channel that strength of character into something that will benefit him.

I CLOSE OUT THE MONTH in a second-grade classroom at a school that has difficulty getting substitute teachers. The regular teacher has been called for jury duty, and after a couple of hours with her kids, I wouldn't blame her for begging the attorneys to keep her in the courtroom for the duration of the case.

It is the second day at this school for a little boy whose family has just moved from Washington. He falls asleep on the carpet during Morning Meeting, snoring slightly, impervious to the class's giggling. I let him catch up on his sleep, because he is the only student who isn't blurting or arguing or shoving a classmate. Little blonde Martha Jane is the first kid sent to the Time Away chair. She looks outraged as she stomps to her corner.

I raise my voice to correct and redirect students multiple times before we even get to morning recess. It's a frustrating start to the day. When I collect them from the playground, Martha Jane hurries to the front of the line to tell me one of her classmates, Katie, was very bad.

"She showed me the bad finger!" tattles Martha Jane. I ask her to show me which finger is bad, and sure enough, she shows me the bird but shields her hand with her coat sleeve.

"Katie!" I call. "Come here please."

Martha Jane slips behind me so she can observe justice being done.

"Katie, did you show someone the bad finger?" I ask, expecting denial.

Katie nods, holding the offending finger.

"Do you know that means something bad?" I ask, hoping she is mimicking what she has seen elsewhere.

"Yes, it means a bad word," she admits.

I weasel out of the whole situation by saying, "You must not do that again, and I will write a note to Mrs. Pryzyk and tell her what you did. She will talk to you about it, understand?"

She nods.

Will she remember what she did when the teacher returns? Should I have sent her to the office? Are most second graders familiar with flipping the bird? I was under the impression that most kids in our wonderful, small, Midwestern city were growing up sheltered, cared for, and protected from ugly influences. What in the world was I smoking?

Chapter 17

In most schools, when I leave students at the door of the lunchroom, I sigh with relief, because I have about half an hour to forty-five minutes without any responsibilities. But sometimes I stay for a few minutes and listen to the amazing work being done by a few dedicated educators.

Almost all schools use whistles, clapping, or just shouting to get the kids' attention, and it's a constant battle. The children twist around and face other tables, stand up, and toss food onto the floor or across the table, all while arguing, laughing, and conversing in loud voices.

"Second graders, you are too noisy!" the teachers on duty say. "Use inside voices, or you will have to sit in silence to finish your lunch!"

Some teachers call the children "my friends." I think it's because children know they treat friends in a special, nice way, and the adults want the kids to treat everyone like that. The problem? It means they see adults yelling at their so-called friends.

"My friends, it's too noisy in here! Everyone will stop talking for two minutes. I don't want to hear any talking until I give the signal!"

Kids who test the adult's mettle end up at a separate table, often called the Naughty Table, in isolation. They can't leave until talked to and dismissed by the teacher or administrator.

After twenty minutes, when most are done eating and milk cartons and paper scraps are collected on trays, the children are dismissed in groups. They take their trays to a custodian, who stands over two huge trash cans. The trays banging on the side of the cans followed by their clanking into a pile sounds like drums being played with a four-four count: "Boom! Crash! Boom! Crash!" in perfect time as the kids throw away mountains of food. EAs and lunchroom helpers scurry to clean the tables and sweep up the chunks before the next wave of kids flows into the room. Some schools repeat the process four or five times.

I find lunchroom rituals fascinating, because when I was in elementary school, our teachers sat at the table with us. Yes, classes were smaller, and teachers were (mostly) nuns. The whole school, first grade through eighth, ate at the same time. The mere presence of the teachers was enough to maintain control. Even tiny first graders could be brought back in line with a simple look from the teacher. Noise levels were never a problem. I'm certain eating with us was more of a punishment for the nuns, but then again, they were into that type of thing.

In one particular Sioux Falls school, administrators have decided to teach children how to eat at a table, face one another, use manners, and engage in conversation. It is an illuminating commentary: basic social skills now have to be taught in school. Using a microphone and PA system, a teacher or administrator speaks in conversational tones at each table, noting what is being done well, and asking the children to remember the rules.

In fairness, by the time I witness this calm, structured approach to maintaining order at lunchtime, the school year is nearly over, so the rules have been enforced for months, and the kids are well trained. The early months may have been rough and messy, but the end result is wonderful to see.

The administrator gives the children a few suggested topics of conversation.

"Ask the people at your table if they have pets, and if they do, ask what kind of pet they have. If you don't have a pet, tell the people at your table what kind of pet you would like to have."

As the kids talk, she reminds them of basic manners.

"Please use your napkins, children. Thank you!" Or: "We don't want to see the food in your mouth as you chew, so please do not talk when you are chewing."

When the conversations get a bit too animated, she diverts the kids and tosses out another topic, all the while moving around the room, giving positive feedback whenever possible.

"Oh, table four, you are doing such a good job of staying seated and making sure everyone at your table gets a chance to talk! That's awesome!"

When it's time to clean up and head outside for recess, the

administrator goes from table to table, inspecting, asking for the behavior she wants.

"Table five, please pick up all the wrappers around your places and make sure everyone closes their milk cartons before standing up."

The "Boom! Crash! Boom! Crash!" soundtrack is the same, but there is very little mess to clean up before the next shift arrives, because the kids have done such a good job policing their areas. They'll remember the skills taught here just as they'll remember addition, subtraction, and the names of their first best friends.

April is so full of promise. After the miserable winter, buds and shoots replace the crusty snow, and there's a bit more sunshine each day. I can see the end of the school year on the calendar, and, like a barn-sour horse, I'm ready for the release of summer.

My journey isn't quite over, however. Near the end of the month, I have to sub in a fifth-grade classroom at one of the tough schools. The teacher is retiring at the end of the year, and I'm one of the lucky subs who gets to see why.

"I know this is the worst class in our school, but I also think it's the worst class in the district!" says one of the administrators as I try to get my bearings for the day. Another teacher pops in and reaffirms how bad the class is and tells me I should just send for the behavior specialist and ask him to sit in as much as possible during the school day. She tells me about Winston, a boy with severe ADHD, whose parents are unable to afford his medication.

"He finds it difficult to sit still. Just ignore his behavior as much as you can. He gets worse if you yell at him."

Oh crap. Double-triple crap on a stick.

The arrangement of the room speaks volumes. One student's desk has been moved to one end and hemmed in by file cabinets on either side. Another desk is nose-to-nose with the teacher's. A third desk has been dragged to the front of the room so that it's touching the whiteboard.

The teacher's notes warn me about a boy who "has temper-control problems" and should be sent to the office if he starts to misbehave.

The kids file in, sizing me up, trash-talking loud enough for me to hear every word about "how stupid this school is." The bigger boys are also already picking on the smaller boys. My heart is beating fast, and we haven't even started yet.

Taking attendance is a battle. After each name I call, I have to shush the kid so I can hear his or her lunch choice. The teacher's notes didn't tell me anything about Ramona, a skinny girl with either ADHD or a finely honed behavior pattern so irritating that it makes me grind my teeth. Ramona is seated at the desk that butts up against the teacher's desk. I'm about to find out why.

She talks nonstop, cannot stay seated for more than sixty seconds, ignores my orders to sit and zip her lips, and works on a notebook full of drawings no matter what subject the rest of the class is pretending to work on.

"Ramona, sit down. Stop talking. Get out your math book. Sit down. I don't want to hear another word from you unless I call on you."

"Ramona, where are you going? Get back to your seat!"

"Ramona, put your drawings away and get out your math book. No, you may not go to the bathroom. Stop talking, and listen to directions."

"No, Ramona! You may not go get a drink. Sit down!"

When she hears me say, "Ramona, you are on my last nerve!" she collapses on her desk and wails, "You're picking on me!"

Ramona's drama is not the only thing going on in the room. Winston, the boy who should be on medication, is so full of unfocused energy that I can almost see an electric, crackling aura around him. "Can't sit still" is such an understatement. I can hardly keep him in the room, much less in his seat! He also babbles nonstop while shredding paper and thumbing through picture books. He is mesmerizing, but I can't afford the luxury of watching him.

The boy whose desk is shoved against the whiteboard is also high-maintenance. When I tell him to sit down while I take attendance, he launches into a loud, monotone presentation of the schedule of his day: what time he goes to the resource room, what time he's to be excused for extra math tutoring, what time he does everything else. I read "Dale" on his desk as he stands at my side, avoiding eye contact, taking me step-by-agonizing-step through his schedule. I move away from him; he follows. The more I try to avoid him, the closer he sticks to me. When he finishes with "and then I go home," I sigh with relief and tell Winston to get up off the floor, where he is showing his classmates how to swim. Dale takes this as a sign that I am not listening and repeats his schedule, starting with what he does when he gets to school.

The boy with the temper-control problems is absent today. Thank you, God, for small favors.

There are two other problematic kids in the room who demand attention. Dixon, a little dark-haired boy, is also a nonstop talker. I don't know when he takes time to breathe, because he talks extremely fast without a hint of breaking for oxygen.

And then there's Adrienne, whom I'm sure has been voted Most Obnoxious by the class. Slouched as low as possible in her chair, she is totally absorbed in making yarn bracelets. I tell her to get out her math book. She ignores me. I stand over her and repeat the order. She makes no move to obey. "Put away the yarn or give it right to me, and get out your book," I say, trying to look menacing. No response. I reach for the yarn, which she gathers and stuffs in her desk. I continue to stand over her while she casually digs in her desk for her math book.

When she slams it onto her desktop, I turn to walk back to the front of the room, and she mutters, "Retard!"

I spin around and say, "What did you say? Not only is that disrespectful to me, but it's an insult to people who have learning disabilities! Go to the office!" She doesn't move from her chair. I go to the phone and dial the office number, which is, of course, busy.

She says, "I'm not going to the office! I didn't do nothing!"

"Out!" I say, pointing at the door, staring at her. The room is fairly quiet, so I figure Adrienne has pulled this crap before. "Go, Adrienne. You are not staying in this classroom!"

She saunters out the door, and while I watch, I wonder if I can work the rest of the day. I am so tempted to call the office (but who would answer the phone?) and tell them I'm going home. Ramona is on the move, Winston is pawing through a locker I hope is his, and Dixon is yapping like a clown on crack. The other students are casually talking among themselves, so I know this is business as usual. Is this how they spend their days?!

We crawl through the math lesson and pretend to discuss social studies questions. When one of the kids returns from a bathroom trip, he informs the class that Adrienne is just standing in the hall. When I confront her, she strolls back into the classroom and tells us that she didn't go to the office because "she didn't do nothing wrong." I try to call the office again as the kids get ready for recess, but the line is still busy. Adrienne looks at me with a snotty "I won" face, and I worry she's right.

While the kids are at recess, I take a breath and try to come up with a plan. If the rest of the day is like the first couple of hours, I will have to leave. Another fifth-grade teacher pops her head into the room and asks how it's going. All I can do is shake my head, wide-eyed, and say, "I can't believe this! This is the worst class I've ever had, and I'm not going to put up with their behavior for the rest of the day!"

"I will send Mr. Hoover in. He's the behavior specialist. Hang in there." And then she is gone.

I think of my first fifth-grade class and how I was overwhelmed by their disrespectful behavior and rule-breaking antics. They were a piece of cake compared to this perfect storm of kids.

When the class returns from recess, I let them know that Mr. Hoover has been called and will join us today.

"Oh, you had to call for help!" Adrienne remarks, which inspires her followers to titter and guffaw like donkeys.

"Yes I did, Adrienne, and I will be telling him about your behavior first," I answer calmly. She rolls her eyes and gets out her yarn. I walk over to her desk with my hand out, but she quickly puts it away. Game on.

Winston leaves the room for help with math, and I feel a stab of sympathy for the teacher who has to work with him for the next hour. Dale informs me that he has work to complete from the resource teacher, so I gladly give him permission to do it. Two major distractions neutralized.

Dixon is still in his hypertalking mode, but I can get him to stop if I stand over him. However, that leaves Ramona free to trot around the room in search of art supplies while also visiting with classmates, working the room like an insurance salesperson. I divide my time between the two and find that Dixon can be left without direct supervision for five minutes at a time. Ramona cannot, so I stand over her and physically block her attempt to get up. She is hemmed in by bookshelves on her left side and by me on her right.

"But I need to get some markers for my homework," she says as I stand so close to her that she cannot get out of her chair.

"Ramona, we are studying science right now. Get out your science book."

"But I—"

"No! Science!"

She throws a hissy fit, knocking her notebook and pencils to the floor, jerking open her desk, digging around in the mess of papers, and slamming the lid while yelling, "I don't have a science book!"

I make her turn around and share a classmate's book. The lesson is something about the earth's atmosphere, but it's hard to believe anyone is learning anything.

I send them off to lunch without a smile. I'm exhausted, and my back and leg are letting me know it's time to lie down with painkillers and a heating pad. It's only 11:30 in the morning.

I eat my lunch in a corner of the room, trying desperately to lose myself in the book I've brought. It doesn't work.

When the kids return and Mr. Hoover has not arrived, I feel myself panic. Winston is back, and he is so cranked-up that he can't sit. Ramona is refreshed, on the move, and ready for another room circuit. Adrienne is smirking at me so defiantly that I want to send her to the office just for being a snot.

I tell the students to get out a book and read silently for the next thirty minutes. "That's what the lesson plan says," I bellow. "You all know what to do! Get your books out!" Of course they ignore me. But it's a good thing I don't give up, because a few minutes later, a very big man appears in the doorway carrying a dinner tray.

"I am Mr. Hoover," says the mountain in a polo shirt and khakis, "and if it's all right with you, I will spend the afternoon in this classroom."

"I'm glad you're here," I tell him. "We've had a very tough morning, and I need your help." I feel a bit of shame at having to be rescued, but soon I'm just relieved. The room is already quieter, and there is less movement. Dixon's medication must have kicked in, because he is sound asleep on his desk, drooling a bit.

Mr. Hoover puts his tray on a table at the back of the room and settles in. When Ramona leaves her desk and heads for some unknown destination, Mr. Hoover lets her know the game is over.

"What are you doing?" he roars, stopping Ramona in her tracks. "Get back to your seat, and don't leave it unless you have permission!"

"But I need—"

"Get back to your seat! If you leave it again without permission, you will be in detention with me after school!"

Ramona spins on her heels and makes a show of stomping back to her desk. Winston's desk is just a few feet in front of Mr. Hoover's table, so I am not surprised when the next shouted correction is directed at him.

"Are you supposed to be reading right now? Then sit down and read! Don't make me tell you again, or you will join me in detention!"

Winston blinks, twitches a shoulder, and slides back into his chair. I almost feel sorry for him, because his behavior is out of his control.

I let Mr. Hoover finish his lunch before I speak to him about Adrienne's flagrantly disrespectful behavior. "I'm not surprised," he says. "She is a frequent flyer in the detention room." He turns to the little devil herself. "Adrienne, you have detention after school with me."

She slumps and snarls something under her breath.

"Do you have something you want to say to me?" Mr. Hoover says in a pretty good Dirty Harry voice. All that's missing is the "Do you, punk?" part.

I hope like crazy that the afternoon will go well now that Mr. Hoover is in the room—free of stress and rotten behavior. But it doesn't. He yells at the kids far more than I did and is quite threatening. He uses athletic coach language like, "Shut up and sit your butt down!" and, "Who told you that you could do that? No one! Sit down!" and, "You must think you're pretty special and you don't have to listen! Well, you're not, so do as you're told!" They don't listen much better to him. Five kids end up with detention. The mood in the room is angry and rebellious.

The best part of the whole day is seeing the last kid walking out the door. I know right then that I couldn't make up a worse subbing experience if I tried.

When the assistant principal comes by to thank me for staying for the whole day, I get the feeling that other subs have left before the dismissal bell. I tell him how I felt nothing but sympathy for the regular teacher. "I know why she's retiring! No one could continue after a year with this group!" I say, neither mincing words nor trying to sound detached and professional. He thanks me again and leaves. As I clean up the room, I wonder how these kids will handle next year's tighter discipline in middle school, where sheer numbers dictate stronger enforcement of rules. What a waste of time for the teacher and the six or seven kids who have developed lousy study habits due to the circus they learn in.

As I drive to my next assignment in the rain, I dwell on the fact that it's almost the end of the school year, and the kids will be wild. After I arrive at my school, I'm trying to think positive thoughts when the secretary tells me I'll be subbing in kindergarten for another sub who "got sick yesterday while teaching and had to go home." The regular teacher is on maternity leave.

Oh, my sweet sainted Aunt Agnes, I must have been a prison guard who tortured inmates and small animals in a past life. Is this my karma?

As I walk with my kindergartners from the door to the classroom, I notice what seems to be a huge disparity in height. About half the class is so tall that they could easily blend in with first or second graders. The others look tiny and fragile. I try to encourage the little ones to hang up their backpacks and take off their coats, but they just sit on the carpet and watch the big kids run around the room and shout as if they are on the playground.

I hate to start the day yelling at kindergartners. They are probably still shell-shocked from having a sub yesterday, and I'm just another stranger to them. The noise from our classroom must reach the ears of the principal, because he enters just as the Indy-500-racer kids are taking a curve toward the door. I'm trying to block their way so they don't step on the fingers of the little ones, but they jump over a little blonde girl and keep on running. The principal barks an order to come to the carpet for a Come-to-Jesus Morning Meeting.

"Kindergartners, I am very disappointed to see how you behave with a substitute teacher! Stop running and sit down!"

I know I'm in for a tough day when some of the bigger kids show no concern. They take their time getting to the circle on the carpet as the principal waits with hands on his hips and a frown on his face.

He warns them that Mrs. Appert, their regular teacher, wants to hear a good report, and she won't get one if they keep acting as they were when he came in. But he might as well be playing the kazoo with his nose, because the kids just keep squirming and whispering to each other.

I enlist the help of the big kids to get through the indoor-recess day. Later, when it's time for the kids to work on school-provided laptop computers, Sefton, a tall boy in a yellow sweatshirt, is a huge help. As we hand them out, I compliment him on being so supportive and smart. He beams a bright smile. When another tall boy (Lyndon, one of the ringleaders in the racing game) shows me his excellent printing skills, I make a big deal of it and ask if he likes math, our next subject. He grins and tells me it's his favorite part of the day. I ask if he will help me with the smaller children, and he nods, grinning.

There are two tiny boys who don't seem ready for first grade, or even another year of kindergarten. Shane has a marked stutter that keeps him from saying more than a couple of words at a time, a mouthful of black stubs for teeth, and an inability to write his name in a recognizable way. Blaine, just as small and toddlerlike, simply sits in his chair and stares at the other children unless I put a paper in front of him. If I don't give him a pencil or crayon, he twists his hands in his lap and blows spit bubbles.

One of the bright spots in the day is a tall girl, Patrice, who completes each assignment on time, hands it in, and raises her hand to answer questions. I want to clone her. Her mother picks her up about an hour before dismissal. Keeping an eye on the rest of the flock, I congratulate the mother for having such a good student. Holding the hand of a toddler and balancing a baby on her hip, she tells me that her little girl "is going to be a doctor." I agree and tell her, "Patrice is the smartest in the class! She will be a great doctor!" I want to give this mother all the reinforcement I can.

I have end-of-the-day playground duty, which means I will stand in the rain and make sure each child gets to the proper bus, day-care van, or parental vehicle or gets paired with a sibling or friend for the walk home. Yup—it's a great task for a sub who can barely identify her twenty-five students, much less the hundreds of other kids in the school. Teachers are expected to cover a certain number of recesses or before- and after-school playground duties. If they volunteer to do more, they get paid extra. If a sub is covering a teacher's classroom for the day, he or she has to cover these duties but for no extra pay. It causes a bit of resentment in people who tend to keep track of indignities. Against my will, I'm one of those people.

Standing in the rain after an exhausting day, I'm feeling very sorry for myself. My shoes and slacks are wet, and just as I'm getting ready to go back into the school, I realize I'm the only teacher outside, and my ID badge won't let me in the door. I'm going to have to walk all the way around the school, in the rain, to the front door. I start wallowing even more in my self-pity but stop when I notice stuttering little Shane standing alone by a tree on the edge of the playground. I figure I should probably check on him, so I amble over.

"Who are you waiting for, Shane? Does your mom pick you up?"

He shakes his head.

"Do you walk home? Does someone walk with you?"

That seems to stump him. He scuffs his shoe against the tree trunk. I'm beginning to worry that he's been left. A few other soaked kids come to the tree and say Shane usually goes home with them, but their ride hasn't come yet. A teacher who has seen our little group comes out to tell us that since it is after 3:00, the children have to come to the office and wait for their ride. And I'm lucky—she has a badge that lets us back into the school. We squelch down the halls to the office, and I leave Shane and the others in the office, dripping on the carpet.

Should children be in school when they are unable to remember how they get to and from school every day? After eight months? I go back to the classroom and sort books for half an hour, trying to savor the few satisfying moments of the day, like when Sefton responded so nicely to my request for help and when Lyndon turned from being naughty to good just because of my praise. Maybe I'm not a great teacher, but I know I'm a great mother, and maybe it's extra mothering that I can offer these kids. Something tells me I can't go wrong with that.

Chapter 18

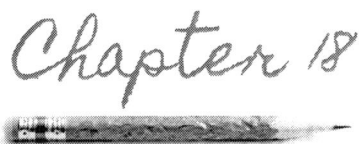

I SHOULD BE FAR MORE CONCERNED about summer employment than I am. All I can think about as I finish each subbing assignment is getting through the day. I don't know if there is a need for summer school teachers, because I don't even know if there *is* such a thing as elementary summer school. If there is, I'm certainly not signing up to sub.

Pining for a change of pace, I pick up a unique assignment in late April.

I administer the Dakota Step Test to a fourth grader named Isaiah who is serving an out-of-school Suspension. It's the easiest job I've had in a long time. Comfortably settled in a small office, I read the directions to Isaiah and pull out my book while he takes the test. I don't have to be hypervigilant, because he has no one to cheat from. We're scheduled to do this the whole school day, but he's a very smart kid and whips through all the sections of the test before noon. He goes back into Suspension, and I go home. The principal apologizes for not having more work to do, but I'm thrilled to be released, even though I'll be paid for only the half-day. I go to the library and browse the New Fiction aisle. I have always found refuge in make-believe.

NEXT, I SUB FOR A HALF-DAY with fourth graders after their teacher has a family emergency. She has left detailed instructions. The students will leave the classroom for thirty minutes of art. Take another twenty minutes off the afternoon for recess, and it's a cushy day.

When I meet the kids on the playground after their noon recess, they are arguing and upset. It seems to be boys against girls. There is a lot of "You said" and "No, *you* said." I can hardly get them to line up and come into the building. Four girls, in a tight knot of outrage, approach me as the class is filing in.

"Michael and Ryan and Colton called us 'lesbians,' and we want to go talk to the counselor!" says the spokeswoman. Their faces are flushed, their jaws set. "Okay, go to the counselor's office," I say, glad I won't have to handle this one.

The boys are talking in small bunches as I try to get the students to take their seats. They've taken sides and started testing each other's loyalties. Will they stick together or hang the perpetrators out to dry?

We're working on Celsius and Fahrenheit when a woman appears at the door and asks for Michael, Ryan, and Colton.

Since I'm very intelligent, I assume she is the counselor. The boys slink out, heads down, eyes averted.

With seven kids out of the room and the rest subdued, worried about their classmates, we cover the lesson and move on to Teacher Read-Aloud. They are working on a book about the adventures of two girls who always get into silly situations, sort of a Lucy-and-Ethel story for kids. I think it's too babyish for fourth graders, and I'm sure the boys don't find it compelling. The highlight of Teacher Read-Aloud is a very loud fart (not mine) that reduces the kids to hiccupping laughter. All I can do is wait them out.

When the accusers and the accused return, the boys look sheepish and angry. The girls look triumphant. I am so glad that I won't be here tomorrow, because I'm certain that I have seen only the first skirmish between the two sides, and retribution won't be far behind.

NIGHT PASSES; THE SUN RISES. Until today, I have rejected assignments at one particular elementary school, because it operates differently than all the others, and I'm pretty sure I can't sub there. I'm still getting a handle on the "normal" school day even after eight months, so how can I sub in an out-of-the-ordinary school?

Jane Addams All City Elementary was established almost thirty-five years ago with a different name, located in another school building. Their website says, "This school has the belief that children benefit most when their parents or guardians are actively involved in their education." I know the bit about parental involvement at Jane Addams, but I have no idea what it means. I arrive at the school and pick up my fifth-grade assignment. I've barely entered the room when three parents show up, say "Hello," and get settled at a table near the back. I appreciate any help in the classroom, but I am clueless about their roles, and no one is volunteering information.

The day's lesson plans are pretty simple and straightforward, except for math, of course. Prime numbers. I know prime numbers exist, but I don't know how to find them or who the hell cares where they are. Good thing I have a smart student and the instructor's manual with the answers. By fifth grade, there's always at least one smart kid who can go to the board and show how he or she got the right answer.

The TV program *Are You Smarter Than a 5th Grader?* will not be calling me.

The kids chatter among themselves but settle pretty quickly when I ask for their attention. The feeling of being thrown alone to the wolves is completely absent. The presence of three more adults in the room evens the odds and stabilizes the energy. We present the lessons, and discussion follows. Students complete the work, and those who need a bit more instruction can ask me or the parents for help. Parents correct the worksheets while I introduce the next lesson. The kids get to see their mistakes and correct them before they leave for the day! What's even more amazing is that the parents take recess duty! Jane Addams, where have you been all this year?

Near the end of the morning, most of my students leave the classroom for "family time." This must be what the website meant when it said, "Multiage activities are built into daily activities." A seemingly random selection of children from differing grades wanders into the room, and my instructions say to divide them into four groups, each with varying ages. The remaining fifth graders sort out the younger kids, so within a minute or two, four groups are ready. I am supposed to give each group the name of a pet—for example, a cat, dog, hamster, iguana. Their assignment is to brainstorm why their pet is the best and how the pets are alike.

Whaaat? I have no idea what that means.

The kids are used to this strange activity, however, and the room gets noisy very quickly. I shut the door and stroll around the room, listening. The little kids are the loudest, but the discussion is pretty well controlled by the fourth and fifth graders. I act enthused to hear their predictable answers, thank them for their ideas, and send the little ones on their way once the clock mandates it.

There is no lunchroom, so the kids eat at their desks. Because it is Wednesday, their lunch period is shortened, as the school day ends at 1:00 p.m. to allow for teacher collaboration. Every week! I happily endure stomach rumblings, knowing I will be on my way home by 1:30, paid for a full day.

The website also says parents and guardians have to volunteer a minimum of one half school day per week, per child, and they are responsible for transporting their children to and from school. I visit with one of the parents before he leaves. "The obvious benefits of being immersed in your child's education far outweigh the inconveniences," he tells me.

I'm so curious about this environment. "By looking at the kids," I say, "I'm guessing that no one in this class comes from a low-income household or has severe disadvantages. Am I right?"

"That's true," he answers. "Most of the kids in this school have parents or guardians who have the flexibility to work here each week." His fifth grader is the third child that he and his wife have shepherded through Jane Addams School, he goes on to say, and they have nothing but praise for the system.

This school serves another very important purpose in our community. One wing is dedicated to provide children who do not speak English with a year of immersion in our language before they are sent to a neighborhood public school. For the rest of the day, every time I'm in the halls, I see adults seated at desks with a little, scared-looking kids practicing the alphabet or working on reading skills. I pass long lines of wide-eyed, darker-skinned children as I make my way to the office. I'm ashamed to admit I wouldn't be able to listen to the stories of what their families have endured to come here. I take so much for granted in my life. But I'm happy to see that these kids are at least getting a fair shot at education by learning English.

A FEW DAYS LATER, I find myself back in a regular school with twenty-one third graders. No matter what I do or say, about a third of them rebel. Putting the troublemakers in the Time Away corner is useless. They just talk louder. And the children who might have listened and learned something under different circumstances simply join in the melee.

"Cyril, sit down!" I shout at one boy as he prances around

the room. I try to get as close to his moving face as possible, but it seems useless—I've been correcting him since he came through the door at 8:00 a.m. "I don't have to!" he shouts back. I know that if I follow him, he will run faster, and it will turn into a game.

"You are going to the Buddy Room *now!*" I tell him, marching him to the door. The Buddy Room system allows cooperating teachers to send a student to another classroom to settle down. The student calms quickly when removed from his or her audience. Cyril is a bit less animated by the time we get to room 301. I have learned that Buddy Room teachers share plans of how to discipline frequent flyers. I don't have to say a thing when I hand Cyril over. The teacher nods and says, "Cyril, you know where to sit. Go, and do not talk!" With a tight smile that tells me she will do some attitude adjustment, she waves me off.

The classroom phone is ringing when I return. A voice tells me to send a girl named Penny to the resource room immediately. I hang up and relay the message, but Penny ignores me and continues shredding paper.

"I'm not going to Resource," she says. "I don't want to go today."

I may have treated the situation with a bit more sympathy if Penny wasn't one of the kids making me wish for old Sister Basil's unique form of discipline: smacking upside the head with a book.

"Penny, it's not a choice. You go to Resource now!" I order.

She ignores me until I pick up the phone, tell her I am calling the principal, and begin a countdown. She hangs in there until "four . . . three . . ." before she bolts out the door with a furious look.

By the end of the day, I'm nearing a full-blown rant. "I feel as if all I did was shout at them," I tell the teacher who pops in to see if I survived.

"That's the effect of poverty," she tells me. "I've been a teacher at this school for about twenty years. This used to be a great neighborhood school with involved parents and great kids. But so much has changed. We have so many apartment kids with single parents. The kids are used to being yelled at, and they are used to chaos. That's what we have to work with," she says, shaking her head. "It's hard, and we all wonder if we're making a difference."

THE NEXT ASSIGNMENT renews my hope in the school system. I go to one of the newer schools where the classrooms are a bit larger and the class sizes more manageable. It's a second-grade classroom, and I still like second graders. They're talkative, but they listen when it's time to work or move to another activity. I have recess duty, so I get to watch a group of my girls practice a cheer they have made up and stand near another group of girls and boys who are playing house "like the pioneers." They like my reminders to keep the baby away from the river and the fireplace. The little boy playing the father is busy fighting off bears and skinning the moose he shot. He tells me he loves me when I suggest he buy some horses for his farm so he can plow the fields and grow corn. I return his hug and kiss the top of his head.

"I'm never gonna wash my head!" he tells his classmates as they line up after recess.

It's such a radical change from so many previous assignments that I leave the building smiling and find myself singing on the way home.

I HAVE READ NEWS STORIES about the mentor program in the school system, so it's interesting to be in a classroom when a mentor shows up. Mentors are volunteers who pass background checks and agree to spend time each week during the school year with children assigned to them. Kids who are most in need of a stable, caring adult are chosen by teachers and administrators and matched with mentors. There are never, ever enough mentors.

One of the first things that children tell me when I enter the classroom is whether their mentors are coming today. The child gets to eat lunch with his or her mentor in a quiet place, which can mean the classroom or a table set up outside the library. The expressions on kids' faces when their mentors show up in the doorway are always priceless. For thirty minutes, they will have an adult's full attention, which for certain children is a rarity. Even if the kids dump their lunchroom trays and spend the time proudly reading to their mentors, they return energized, smiling, and pleased with themselves. Kids who have been nothing more than irritants to the class get to play board games and talk about "guy stuff" or "girl stuff" with their mentors, who listen while the dice roll.

"Mrs. M., my mentor said I'm getting real good at reading, and she's gonna bring a book for me next time!"

"Mrs. M., I beat my mentor at the game, and he says I'm really good at numbers!"

I see an older man seated at a table in the hall, surrounded by ten little boys who are all talking at the same time as they chomp down their lunches. I raise my eyebrows and ask, "Are they all yours?" He smiles over the racket, saying he's a retired custodian, and he knows how important it is for the kids. I agree heartily and head back to my classroom for lunch.

Fifth graders make me nervous in general. Fifth graders at the end of the school year fill me with foreboding. They are so close to making the leap to middle school that I can almost hear their cocoons cracking and splitting, as if they are about to be moths (butterflies emerge from chrysalises, my daughter would remind me, and fifth-grade boys never quite strike me as butterflies). Subs hardly make a blip on their radar screens.

On my next assignment, there are twenty-eight large desks crammed into a classroom made for fewer, smaller children. Piles of books under each chair tell me that the desks designed when I was in grade school cannot hold everything a student needs today. The teacher is leaving for a meeting, so when I arrive early, I get to watch her in action for a few minutes. She's petite, almost dainty. Most of her students are bigger than she is, but this doesn't seem to intimidate her. She scolds one of the biggest boys as I observe. He is slumped in his chair with the expected, sullen look of a kid caught in a misdeed. She dismisses everyone for lunch, apologizing for leaving me with such a large number of needy kids who will certainly act out against me, and then . . . she is gone.

Ah jeez. When the automated call came this morning saying the job was in "third through fifth grade," I shouldn't have gambled on getting third grade. I should have known it was fifth grade, because it came in after 8:00 a.m. That means it's a job that's hard to fill. Will I never learn? Maybe it won't matter in a few weeks.

Math is bar graphs. I almost laugh out loud. *I can do bar graphs!* I think.

Thirty minutes later, I have most of the class hopelessly confused.

"Is number four 250 or 260? I don't get it!" they moan, heads in hands, their chances of getting into an Ivy League school shot to hell because a substitute teacher screwed up their math lesson one day in fifth grade. I watch the kids who never have to listen to instructions scan the worksheet, finish it, and take out books to read. They are in the minority. A scrawny boy in the front row closes his book and says, "I'll just take an F if you let me go now!" I want to tell them all to stop being weenies and ask the smart kids for help so I can hide behind the teacher's desk until math is over. But I am not a quitter, and the students' angst is getting to me. I keep trying new strategies, such as using a ruler to help clarify. They appear even more confused.

They leave the room for lunch, muttering and refusing to make eye contact with me. Not that I'm groveling and begging for forgiveness, but I wish I had done a better job of explaining.

Timing is everything when lining students up at the end of the day. If I let them get their things together and load their backpacks too early, it can get ugly. If I wait until the last two minutes before the dismissal bell rings, chaos reigns as they compete for the Most Obnoxious prize while getting ready to leave.

Today I err on the side of too early. They are in line, waiting to be released, when I see Norman, a tall, muscular boy, punch reed-thin Annamary in the stomach. She's been hanging on him, but he hits hard enough to make her fold over at the waist, wrapping her arms around herself. I can see tears forming in her eyes.

"Norman! You apologize to her immediately! That was uncalled for!" I shout, afraid that she is really hurt. The rest of the kids grow quiet, hoping to catch some of the story to reenact later.

Norman hangs his head, doing a good imitation of James Dean, the rebel. I repeat my demand.

"Whatever," he mumbles, eyes on the floor.

I realize I have to take another approach.

"Norman, I want you to understand something. You are the biggest kid in this room, and probably in the whole fifth grade. When you playfully shove someone or punch somebody, you can really hurt them. You were just goofing off, but someone else got hurt. All I'm asking is that you control your strength so you won't get in trouble, okay? Now, please apologize to Annamary."

It must have struck a chord in the kid, because he turns to Annamary, who by now has recovered and is looking adoringly at him, and says, "I'm sorry for hurting you." The dismissal bell rings, and they shoot out the door.

I'm cleaning up here and there when the teacher returns to her classroom. I tell her about math, and she laughs.

"When I subbed, math was the hardest subject to teach, because I never knew what methods the teacher was using or how to build on what the kids had already learned." Then, she adds, "Don't worry, they are fine."

"How do you manage twenty-eight kids and do them all justice?" I ask, hoping she has it all figured out.

"You don't manage," she says. "You go home every day feeling guilty, because you haven't spent enough time with each student, just those who need discipline. It's a terrible burden."

I CLOSE OUT THE MONTH of April in a first-grade classroom with all white faces. I notice it because most of my subbing experience has been in schools with many children of color. It's just odd to see how Sioux Falls looked many years ago, with a predominantly Scandinavian, Germanic, and Celtic population.

Morning Meeting in this classroom includes a supposedly short monologue by the current week's "Star Student" about something he or she finds interesting. The child can bring something from home if he or she so chooses. It's good ol' show-and-tell with a new label.

Our Star Student today is Milo. He brings a *Star Wars* book and poster, and with energy and conviction, he tells us why "Dark Vader" is his favorite character.

"Dark Vader had a laser sword, and he could fight better than anybody, but Obi-Wan wouldn't let him advance, so he got really mad. Here's when he turned into a ghost like Obi-Wan." He holds the book open to the appropriate page so everyone can see. The other children are a bit restless, since this is all very old news to them. I could nudge the boy along and wrap it up, but I have to ask some questions, because it seems as if Milo is missing the whole point of George Lucas's epic battle between good and evil.

"Milo, what do you mean 'Obi-Wan wouldn't let Darth Vader advance?'" I ask.

He repeats his mantra so quickly that I'm certain he has processed "wouldn't let him advance" as something terrible, worthy of fiery retribution.

"Milo, you know that Anakin Skywalker turned into Darth Vader because he got really mad and hurt people, right?" I ask, hoping to help him see the rest of the storyline.

"Yeah, he got mad, but it's because of Obi-Wan. Here's where Dark Vader destroyed the Republic!" he says with a smile, showing the page with the exploding planet.

I have to end his minirant and move the children on to Art, but Milo's fixation on an obviously evil villain upsets me. What is he being taught (or not taught) outside school that causes him to identify so completely with "Dark" Vader? He doesn't just want to pretend to be him so that others are scared of him; he sees the character as admirable. I wonder what George Lucas would say to Milo?

When we go outside for recess, I'm accompanied by a darling little girl who needed extra help with math and is now my best friend. Her name is Krissy, and she is well versed on the rules of the playground.

"That purple boy, he's not supposed to climb on top of the slide. And those boys can't go down the slide headfirst!" Hand-in-hand, we head to the trouble sites and remind the offenders of the rules. Krissy is so pleased with my prompt response to her instructions that she smiles wherever we go.

"Those kids can't bounce the ball against that wall, because it's too close to the windows," She proudly proclaims. "Mr. Sapp yelled at them before for doing that." We turn and walk toward the aforementioned wall, and the kids scatter. We have done our duty.

The kids come in from recess with pockets full of wood chips from the playground. I try to get them close to a wastebasket so they can get rid of the forbidden material, but it doesn't work. The floor looks like a hamster cage by the end of the day. I apologize to the custodian, who is hurrying through her chores in the room. She says it's not a problem, then launches into a diatribe about a coworker who isn't doing his share of the work. Her complaint reminds me of the corporate world, where favoritism is often the order of the day no matter how much damage it does.

I don't miss that part of working with adults. People get angry about small slights and major mistakes. It's understandable. But do they get angry enough to become . . . Dark Vader?

Chapter 19

May is a beautiful month in our part of the world. Everything is green, blossoming, and *fecund*. I heard that word in a movie, and it sounds dirty. I bet I won't find it on a vocabulary list before the school year ends.

Summer is so close that you can almost close your eyes and hear shouts from the swimming pools, smell freshly cut grass, and feel your pillow as you roll over and sleep late. As I drive to school in the morning, I repeat my May mantra: *The kids will be wild; don't expect anything else.* But I'm such a sucker for rainbows and happy endings that I don't believe it no matter how many times I say it.

I hear bits and pieces of teacher conversation as I walk down the halls in search of my assigned classroom. Some say they will tutor a few hours in the morning during the summer; others talk about trips and camping.

"We just have to get through the next couple of weeks!" I hear over and over.

The wall art and displays look ragged and ready to be tossed. No one needs to take time to fix or freshen them. The countdown has begun.

The kids in my fourth-grade classroom today are purely rotten. From the moment I announce my name, they ignore me and carry on as if they are on the playground. The teacher has left thorough notes and worksheets for the students to complete, so I shout instructions and hand out papers.

"This is so boring," mutters a skinny kid who tosses the worksheet aside and picks up a graphic magazine. His name is still taped to his desk, so I don't have to ask before I threaten him.

"Eldon, put away the magazine and get to work on the assignment, or go to the office!" I'm not afraid to get rid of the offenders early in the day.

"I was just saying what the rest of the class is thinking," he says sarcastically, slowly searching the mess around his desk for the worksheet.

The day slides downhill at a rapid rate. Two tall boys, sneering at me in practiced unison, are so belligerent that I feel a shiver of fear. I don't have time to examine the feeling, because the whole class is acting up. My back and leg pain is also getting worse, and my new pain medication isn't helping much. I'm getting discouraged.

The principal drops by during the lunch period and asks how things are going. That doesn't happen unless the class is "challenging." I tell him about Tom and Ted, the defiant boys, and he says, "Send them to me if they don't changed their behavior."

After lunch, Eldon builds a shelter for a fly that is attracted to his desk. I don't want to know what food remnants are simmering inside with his books and papers. The other kids are loudly judging him. Some are repelled by his project; others think it's cool. I figure it has his attention, so I use it as a reward. I tell him he can keep the fly house if he follows the social studies read-aloud.

Tom and Ted are laughing and tossing a ball back and forth. I send them to the principal's office, and they leave the classroom with a swagger. They don't seem too concerned about a possible punishment.

The secretary calls me a few minutes later and says, "I have two boys here who say they have no idea why they were sent to the office. Can you tell me why they are here?" The room is quiet, the first time all day. The students listen as I summarize the boys' unacceptable behavior.

The principal is in a very important meeting and cannot be disturbed. I tell the secretary that the boys cannot come back to the classroom. I must sound adamant, because she sighs and says the boys will be sent to the counselor's office. *Suppose he's busy too*, I wonder. *Do they get to hang out in the office for the afternoon, avoiding lessons? Isn't that what they wanted in the first place?*

When I hang up the phone, obviously irritated, one of the quiet boys says, "Mr. Kalberer would have sent them to the office a long time ago."

Just before dismissal, the counselor shows up with Tom

and Ted. He stands behind them as they apologize to me for their disrespectful behavior. I accept their apologies even though I would like to launch into a lecture and make them squirm a bit. But that would serve no purpose. Since it's so close to the end of the school year, there is very little work that they missed. My sending them to the office was an exercise in futility, and we all know it.

As I finish my paperwork one afternoon, I remember something I heard. I've been at a school known for its problems and challenges. Earlier, I heard the principal say to a group of teachers, "I don't believe a child comes to school wanting to fail!" He was talking about teaching children who have experienced too many failures in their lives. If we believe the child has too many obstacles in their learning process, such as parents who don't or can't help them, a deficit of food or clothing, or no permanent home, then we expect failure, and it affects how we teach.

That's true, I think. *What is the answer?*

I get second graders for my next assignment, and I am hoarse by lunchtime. During Morning Meeting, when using the prompt "What is one of your favorite toys?" Wally tells the group, "I like to play with knives and stuff." I frown and tell him that we don't talk about weapons in school. Then I point to the next child. Later in the morning, I send Wally to the office for calling another student "asshole." I'm far more surprised than the kids. The teacher next door says she heard me yelling "all morning" and urges me to "tell the truth in your notes, because the teacher really needs to know how the day went."

The afternoon science lesson is shockingly basic. I can't believe seven- and eight-year-old children have to be shown how plastic spoons float but metal spoons do not. I carry seven dishpans of water from the staff workroom and arrange the float-or-don't-float items on the table. Each child gets a chance to complete the experiment, hands-on. The water in the tubs is cloudy with dirt when we finish, and the floor is full of puddles. But the kids' hands are far cleaner than when they arrived this morning, and even the shy, immigrant children have smiled and tried to make things float. I shoo them away from the wet corner and send them on their soggy way to Music. I make another seven trips to the staff workroom to dump the water and wash the tubs, then hurry back to mop the floor.

The highlight of my day comes during reading time. An itty-bitty girl with ribbons in her hair asks if she can read to me. I eyeball the room to make sure the students are at least pretending to read. "Of course, I would love to hear you read, MaryAnne!" I answer, getting settled next to her at a corner table. With her delicate fingers tracing the words, she sings the entire *Frosty the Snowman* story to me in a voice so high that only dogs can hear the top notes. I am charmed.

KINDERGARTEN should be a safe assignment for me at this point in the school year. The snow is gone, and the teacher will have whipped the almost-first-graders into shape. They will be antsy but able to listen to me read a picture book without noisy rebellion.

Midmorning arrives, and I have yelled at the kids so much that one little boy is near tears, holding them back with a trembling lower lip. I bite my tongue and try to check my temper. I have sent the worst kid to the counselor's office, because he answered "poopy diaper" no matter what question was asked. He also smeared a wet, snot-filled tissue down the full-length mirror by the door. He may have been "experimenting with the various mediums available to him," but it was disgusting, so off he went.

The shared bins of crayons, markers, and pencils on each table contain little more than pitiful nubs, broken pieces—dried and useless things. The kids have to search for supplies at other tables. There are no more hidden stashes. Even the teacher's supply is gone. She will probably use her own money to buy baskets of extra markers and crayons in the fall, because so many families cannot afford school supplies. But everyone seems to have compassion fatigue at the end of the year.

"Wanda is being mean!" reports Betty Lou, the verbal leader of the girls. "She takes all the numbers and won't share! She had some kind of heart operation, so when she acts up, her mother lets her get away with murder!" I'm instantly sure Betty Lou is quoting her own mother. Had the woman been aware when she said it that her daughter would do a spot-on imitation in the classroom, standing with a hand on her hip and tossing her head, would she have chosen to bite her tongue? Of course Wanda hears the remark and starts to cry. All I can do is ask Betty Lou to apologize for hurting Wanda's feelings and distract them with another math exercise.

The object of the game I assign is simple: using colored cubes, the kids are supposed to give the correct answer to addition problems such as one plus two. Most of the kids are using their fingers, and none of the answers are over five. I move from group to group and observe the same counting-on-fingers process. Three plus one equals . . . ? Two plus one equals . . . ? Obviously the kids are being taught *how* to solve math problems, but what happened to *remembering* the answers so they don't have to start all over with each problem? I am not impressed with the results of what I have heard described as "the newest way to teach math." I can see that the "higher-functioning" children get the answers quickly simply because of repetition, but they are in a small minority. I have also heard concerns that testing standards have placed so great a burden on children in kindergarten and first grade that they are not able to grasp many of the concepts in the current curriculums. Is it okay for kindergartners in the last month of school to have to use their fingers to add one plus two?

Reading is next. The kids divide into five groups: Lions, Otters, Koala Bears, Monkeys, and Owls. While the kids read to themselves, I gather one little critter-group at a time around my table so they can take turns reading from an assigned book. The books are aimed at a specific level with one short sentence per page—such as "The ball is red." Most of the groups struggle with their books and try to sound out words. It's difficult for me to sit still and watch them labor over a deathly dull story that was predictable from the first page. Even the bright kids' attention wanders as a classmate's monotone voice follows the words.

Of course I want to tell all parents how to help their kids learn to read faster and love reading: *Read to them every day.* They can understand much more when listening to a story line than they can by sounding out each word. That's work. Listening to fascinating stories is not work. If you read every day, you have to find good books that interest them. You have to read in an interesting manner, not like a robot. You have to know what they enjoy, so they can eventually learn how to read for their own amusement.

In my kingdom, I will make it a law that children are read to every day. So shall it be done.

THE SCHOOL YEAR DRAGS ON. I pick up an all-day assignment to cover for a music teacher. It's one I would usually refuse, except the recording assures me that my duties will be simple: show a movie about different types of music and ask a couple of discussion questions afterward. Since each class period is forty-five minutes long and the movie will take up most of that, I will have an easy day.

The movie is somewhat interesting, and the first two classes are pretty well behaved. They whisper, but I don't swoop down on them unless they distract others. The answers they give to the suggested discussion questions are fairly thoughtful, given the time of year.

The day turns out to be a study in child development. Each age group responds with different insight. I enjoy them for the short time they are my responsibility. I'm dutifully corrected when one of the students from the gifted program tells me that the symphony I'm referring to is not Beethoven's Ninth Symphony, but rather Beethoven's Fifth. I like the fact that they're listening and engaged.

Luckily, one of the administrators informed me there is going to be a tornado drill during the afternoon, stating that the children will know what to do and where to go. When the sirens go off, we troop into the hall and are directed to crouch down by the lockers, hands over our heads, silently awaiting the "all clear." I do not crouch. I join the teachers and administrators patrolling the halls, making sure everyone is in the proper place and position. We try to quickly correct kids who are talking, but two girls from my class manage to evade the patrols. I see from a distance that they chat through the entire exercise. Like prisoners of war, they hush as soon as an adult moves near, then quickly pick up the conversation when they deem the coast clear. I'm reminded of my high school days, when it felt daring and rebellious to talk when we were told to be silent. I wonder if they can tell the difference between a sub and a real teacher by using just their peripheral vision. When I finally get a chance, I meander over to them and hold my stance. They are quiet for about five seconds before resuming their discussion. They have determined me to be nonthreatening. I have to admire that kind of vigilance, so I let them off the hook.

One of the afternoon classes reminds me that teaching is a team job, that my tendency to tough things out and suffer in silence isn't productive. They are fifth graders, and they take over the music room like a bunch of rowdy cowboys on a Saturday night. Some of the boys play with instruments that are scattered around the room, laughing and showing off. The girls hardly seem to notice. They are so deep in conversation that all they can do is toss their hair over their shoulders and find seats in corners so they can talk more. It's so Fifth-Grade-Feeling-Its-Oats that I know shouting will only provoke more acting up, so I herd them to the seating area, arms out as if I'm driving sheep to a gate.

"Come on, guys, find a place to sit," I croon, keeping my face neutral. "Come on, everyone, time to sit. Come join us, come on." I explain the movie, which of course they say they've seen, and push the play button. Most of the room settles in with minimal whispering. I correct the two worst offenders, who do not have the sense to shut up for at least ten seconds after the correction. I end up standing over them, staring at them. It is the only way to keep them quiet so that the few interested kids can hear the soundtrack.

As they line up at the end of the class period, ready to return to their room, the same two boys are talking. I tell them to be quiet, and they get snotty, repeating what I said with a smirking tone and bobbing heads. I could ignore it and dismiss them, but my exasperation level is very high.

"You two boys will remain in this room until your teacher comes to get you. At that time, you will tell her why you're still here." I dismiss the rest of the class, wondering what in the holy hell am I going to do with the two punks while we wait for the teacher. The three of us spend a very uncomfortable five minutes in the music room, avoiding eye contact.

Making a brilliant move, the teacher has called for the School Resource Officer to join us in the classroom. In full police regalia, Officer Bercier walks up to the boys and takes control by asking, "What is going on here?" I give a short description of their disrespectful behavior. When one of the boys challenges my version, I act it out. I am accurate. The boys fold. Officer Bercier doesn't use the "I am disappointed in you" speech or threaten that they'll end up in jail with someone named Gargoyle who will teach them a life of crime. Officer Bercier states facts: the boys were acting in ways that will get them in trouble; they are moving to middle school in the fall, and their behavior won't be tolerated; they know the right thing to do, and their actions have consequences. He wraps up by inviting them to the office, where they will serve detention. The teacher adds that she will have some extra work for them to complete when they have finished the sentence.

I stand silently near the teacher's desk, taking in the drama, realizing I have been afraid to reach out for help so many times during the school year, and the kids are the worse for it as much as I am.

Before the boys leave, Officer Bercier points toward me and says, "I think you have something to say to this teacher." The boys mumble apologies and leave with the officer. The teacher says, "They have been pushing the limits for a long time. I'm glad you called them on it. Thanks!" She is out the door before I can think of anything to say.

IT'S FAR TOO CLOSE to the end of the school year for some of the things I'm seeing: kids coming to school without eating breakfast; the same ones getting sick because of it and wanting to go to the office; others bringing candy for a snack. And then there are the children who wear totally inappropriate things to school, like extremely short shorts. (Kids spend much of the school day seated with crossed legs on the floor. Hello! Parents, crotch shots are not cute or adorable at any age!) Other offenders include see-through tops and torn flip-flops. Finally, what about the kids who are habitually late? Is the start of the school day sneaking up on families? Is it a surprise that a child needs to be fed before going to school?

How do countries like Japan and Germany keep students involved and interested during longer school calendars? American schools spend the first four to six weeks in the fall repeating the basic concepts taught during the preceding school year, and they allow the last two weeks of school in May to function as little more than day care with worksheets.

Today I'm in a third-grade classroom at one of Sioux Falls's largest schools. A large girl with a clipboard wanders the room until I physically block her way and ask for the clipboard so I can write a note. She seems oblivious to everything except the music she continues to hum. She isn't bothering the others, so I let her stroll.

I tell myself to relax and try to connect with the kids. When they question my directions, I show them the four pages of instructions left by their teacher, Mrs. Brindle. I read the instructions word for word in the first sentence, then substitute phrases as I go, because I'm feeling wily.

"Mrs. Brindle says, 'The students should complete the math worksheet, then gather at the north door of the gym to help wash walls. They are not allowed to eat lunch today.'"

I don't smile as I read. The kids are stunned into silence for about five seconds. As I stare at them, a few feebly protest.

"Na-ah! We always get lunch!"

"Of course you do," I say. "I just wanted to see who was listening." They erupt with relieved laughter. This technique can be used only twice per classroom, because the kids eventually become very attentive and can't be surprised.

"Mrs. Brindle wants you to complete your South Dakota alphabet book by the end of the school day tomorrow. Any student who has not finished the book will have to stay in third grade until the age of eighteen. Any questions?"

One boy says he would stay in the third grade, but when he realizes his sister would catch up with and then pass him, he changes his mind. The kids hunker down and complete the alphabet book—"A is for Aberdeen, a small city in South Dakota; B is for the Black Hills, one of South Dakota's tourist attractions. . . ." By M, the kids have lost interest, and it's obvious the parents will have to finish the work.

After recess, one of the girls tells me she is upset with a classmate.

"What happened?"

"Scott says I'm hot."

I try to keep my face neutral. "Does that make you uncomfortable?" I ask.

"Yeah, I don't like it, and I told him to stop, but he won't listen!" I want to tell her all about sexual harassment and the great strides women have made in the workplace, because the courts in our country support a person's right to work in a non-hostile environment. Instead, I tell her I'll speak to him.

"Scott, please come here." Scott is a nice enough kid, maybe a little more grown up than most of the others. "Did you tell Bernadette that she is hot?" I feel a little odd having to say the words.

"Yeah," he says, embarrassed.

"When she says she doesn't want to hear that, you have to stop, okay? Do you understand?"

"Yeah, okay," he mumbles.

I'm on my soapbox, so I have to toss in, "Stop means stop!" He wanders away, and I return to refereeing.

One of the boys causes conflict wherever he goes. Every time I look at him, I have to suppress the desire to shake my head in wonder at how difficult his life must be. His name is Rodney. His clothes are filthy, his face and hands are dirty, his hair hasn't been washed or combed in a long time, and he has a continuous flow of mucus from his nose. He cannot do the assigned work, the instructions tell me, so he is supposed to "read or draw." All day? He picks fights by kneeing the nearest boy in the crotch, then claims complete innocence.

"I didn't do nothin'!" he says when I confront him about his aggressive behavior in line. That's the only time the other kids will stand near him. It seems as if he can't control any impulses. With all the other commotion in the room, it's impossible to watch him every second.

"Mrs. M., Rodney stole my Pokémon cards from my backpack!" says one boy who swears he brought his five favorite cards for an after-school game with friends.

"I was framed!" shouts Rodney when I ask him to tell me

how someone else's cards got into his backpack. "I didn't touch his stuff! Somebody else did it!"

The other kids shun him as much as possible, and I wonder if he really was framed. There's no way for me to know, but one thing I know for certain is that this boy lives a miserable existence. As irritating as he is, my heart goes out to him. Whoever is supposed to be taking care of him is derelict in his or her duties. But am I doing my share by simply shrugging it off as someone else's responsibility?

COMBINATION CLASSROOMS are way down on my list of possible assignments after my earlier experiences (I still feel bad about the rabbit). However, the prerecorded voice on the phone this morning says it's "third through fifth grade," with nary a hint that it's a Combination Classroom.

Aww crap.

At least I will have the help of an EA who knows the kids' names and the teacher's expectations. I figure the day will be easier than last time, because the school has very few children living in poverty—but then I remember what some teachers have told me: the problems they experience with more well-off kids stem from a sense of entitlement. "The parents care and are involved, so the kids think they're pretty special," one of them remarked once.

I don't get the concept of combination classes anyway. Do you teach one lesson because the younger kids are so smart and the older kids are on the slow side? If not, how can you teach two separate lessons and still get good results? Would well-off parents rather have their kids in Combination Classrooms than transfer them to another school full of low-income families and immigrants?

So many questions, Grasshopper.

The day gets off to a rocky start. The teacher's instructions, my bible for the day, are garbled and incomplete. The EA shakes her head as we pore over the pages. "I have no idea what he means here," she says.

We check with another teacher, but she's a sub, so we just punt. One of the assignments the students have to finish is an experiment that involves designing a paper airplane that will hopefully fly farther than others. But first, we watch a video about the science of flying. I listen carefully to the narrator as he explains drag, thrust, and lift. My son was going to be a pilot. Planes had mesmerized him since he was a baby. We lived near an air force base until he was about two years old, and no matter how much of a tantrum he was ready to throw, the rumble of a fighter jet or a huge KC-135 tanker climbing into the sky would make him stop and point. His dream was to go to the Air Force Academy and fly fighter jets. I listen to the information now, because it's a connection to my son.

The kids are supposed to work in teams to make both the airplanes and posters to explain their work. Each student can design as many planes as he or she wants, but the team will vote on the three best, which will go nose-to-nose in competition with those from the other teams. A few of the teams are so dysfunctional that I have to smile. They bicker about who does what. A few kids hog all the materials while others sit silently and stare.

"I don't understand what we're supposed to do! I wasn't here yesterday, so I don't know!" is a common protest. "Just do the best you can," is all I can answer.

Some of the loudest kids are so hyper and distracting that others on their team take over and do all the work. The loudmouths complain about being excluded. It all sounds so familiar. It's a mirror of life in the corporate world.

The room comes alive with flying, flipping, diving paper airplanes. It seems to me that the kids are doing very little work.

"When you have completed your team's poster, I will take the team to the gym, and you can test the planes," I say to encourage the kids to finish. Miraculously, two teams are ready for the test flights. With all the knitted-eyebrow sternness I can muster, I tell them they must be silent in the halls and quiet in the gym, because we haven't received clearance from the office to conduct the test. "We will be quiet in the gym and leave everything as it was when we came," I say.

We creep down the stairs and slip into the gym. The late-afternoon sun is slanting through the high windows, making the light golden and surreal. I line the kids up and remind them one last time to be quiet.

One boy's airplane rips across the gym in a line drive, easily passing all others.

"Yeah, that's the winner!" he shouts so loudly that the other kids cringe, knowing he has broken the promise. I take him back to the classroom as fast as I can walk. He doesn't care—he tells everyone his plane will beat them all.

When I bring the teams back to the room, the boy who shouted in the gym cockily asks why he can't return to the gym if he promises to be quiet. I look him in the eye, and he holds my gaze.

"Really?" I ask. "You heard the rules and you made a promise to obey them. You broke the rules. The answer is no." He asks one more time before the end of the day, as though I have forgotten his earlier request. He seems genuinely shocked that his plane is out of the running. "But it's the fastest by far! It will beat everyone!"

Apparently winning is everything. It's the corporate way, after all.

Chapter 20

THE CIRCUS WAS IN TOWN RECENTLY, complete with elephant rides and roaring lions. The kids, especially the kindergartners, love to describe the guy who rode his bike up a steep ramp and did flips in the air. When they get restless and recess is still far off in the distance, I ask them to draw a circus picture and write a sentence about it. It works just about every time.

Kindergarten is such an important year. We expect so much from these students. I have to cover my mouth to hold the laughter one morning when a counselor shows up in my classroom to teach the kids about good touch and bad touch. With the little ones clustered at her feet, the counselor brings out a poster with simple drawings of a boy and a girl wearing bathing suits. She listens to several kids blurt out things like, "I have a swimming suit!" and "I'm going to take swimming lessons with my sister!" and "If you swim by yourself, you could get drowned!"

The counselor calmly draws the children's attention back to the poster.

"Boys and girls, we call the parts of the body covered by our bathing suits 'private parts.' No one can touch your private parts except you and your mommy or daddy if they're helping you in the bathtub or if you're sick. And sometimes the doctor needs to touch our private parts if we're sick."

All eyes are on the counselor except for those of Dennis, who has fallen sound asleep right under the poster.

"Boys and girls, please raise your hand and tell me what we call the parts of the body that are covered by our bathing suits?"

A couple of little boys raise their hands. The counselor smiles and calls on Roger.

"Bathing suits," he answers.

"Yes, these are bathing suits," she says, pointing to the poster. "What do we call the body parts underneath?"

Jane gives it a cautious try. "Swimming suits?"

"But what is under this boy's bathing suit?" she asks, pointing to the boy with her pen.

"Ooh, ooh, I know!" Mamie volunteers. "Boy bathing suits!"

The lesson never lands. The kids are very earnest, saying their answers slowly, drawing out "baaaathing suits," but they never quite get the "private parts" lesson. Dennis snores through it all, learning just as much as the rest of the children.

I will spend the three remaining days of the school year in one school, which is a relief. Teachers are collaborating, so my schedule is a half day in one classroom, then a half day in another after lunch. I have kindergarten the first morning. The children are more excited about a classmate's broken arm than the impending end of the school year. Little blonde Anita's arm is wrapped in a soft splint, and she tells us over and over that her daddy will be coming to get her from school so the doctor can put a "real cast" on her arm. The story of the accident holds the class's attention. They all want to touch the splint, ask if there was blood, and did she cry? It's a major distraction, and we fall behind schedule.

My announcement that we're going on a field trip to a nearby library is pretty tame stuff after Anita's dramatic story about falling down the stairs. The kids are still buzzing with memories of broken bones and bloody cuts when I notice a flagged piece of information in the teacher's notes. Apparently one of the little boys in the class has some behavioral issues and will run away if he gets upset.

A runner?! You have got to be kidding me. There are twenty-five children in this class. What do you do with the other twenty-four while you chase the runner? Am I allowed to tie the aforementioned runner to my body so he can't get away? What if he refuses to walk with me? Do I drag him? What upsets him?

I will have help, the teacher's notes tell me. Jeannie's mother will accompany the class to the library. *Well, that's better*, I grudgingly admit to myself. *I suppose we can do this.*

Jeannie's mother, Starla, arrives right on time. I read the rules for the trip with a loud voice, hoping at least a few students are listening.

"We stay together at all times. We do not cross the street

unless the teacher says we can. We do not yell. We raise our hands and wait to be called on before we speak."

As I line up the children, counting heads and trying to keep a file of their little faces saved in my brain, the principal comes to tell me there will be a fire drill this morning and to make sure we are back from the library in time to participate.

What are these people smoking? A sub in a large kindergarten classroom, a field trip, *and* a fire drill during the last week of school?

She must mistake my gaping mouth and bugged-out eyes for an expression of acknowledgment—that I can take twenty-five kindergartners to the library (which is two blocks away), keep them in a group for forty-five minutes, and get them back to their classroom in time to march with the rest of the schoolchildren to some unknown, specific area of the schoolyard while the fire alarm is going off. She nods and hurries off.

Starla, my sole source of support and comfort, is deep in a smiling conversation with her daughter while the class bubbles around her. I have a sinking feeling that she will be of little help, and even worse, I will have to be cordial to her and refrain from snarling when I call for help. I won't be able to say, "What the hell are you doing? Do you know you're supposed to help with *all* the children, not just your child? Get those kids out of the trees, and haul their little hinders to the sidewalk!" Nope. I will have to smile and use my best kindergarten-teacher voice to say, "Starla, you're doing a great job following the class! Would you like a sticker? Now, could you please round up the children who are playing in the mud puddles? Thank you so much!"

The walk to the library takes longer than expected, because

it rained last night, and earthworms are all over the sidewalks. Some kids are fascinated, some are scared, and a few just follow in a daze. I try to take the potential runaway child's hand, but he pulls away and wraps his arms around himself.

"Don't try to touch him, 'cause he won't like it, and then he might run away," reports Mary Margaret, a darling redhead with glasses who is obviously a class spokesperson. "And he gets nervous if you yell at him."

"What other things make him nervous?" I ask. Why not get the whole list?

"Just if he has to eat things he doesn't like," Mary Margaret says in a grown-up tone. This is old news, and her attention shifts to a classmate. Score one for me, though; he won't have to touch food on my shift.

When we arrive at the library, a librarian greets us and says she has a "special story to read to us, and with a special helper—a puppet!" That news item is good for about thirty seconds of the kids' attention.

The library is small, so the children can't wander off without adult intervention. However, they *can* tap on the self-checkout computer, hang on the desks and chairs, and wrestle with each other as the librarian, in a sickly sweet singsong voice, tells the five-year-olds about the nonfiction area of the library, describes in detail how their mommies and daddies can put books on hold, and explains how to check out music from the CD library.

Starla, my helper, continues to gaze with rapt wonderment at her daughter, unaware of the chain of boys hopping like frogs around her. One little girl persists in telling me she has to go to the bathroom, so I send Starla as the escort. Starla encourages her child to go along "just in case."

God, please grant me patience.

I debate whether to whisper a reminder of our time line to the librarian when she finally says, "Boys and girls, are you ready for the story?" I join in the very loud, "Yeah!" We follow her into a small room, and the kids settle on the floor. The story she has chosen isn't even a new book, so half the kids shout that they've heard it. One little boy crawls to me, tugs on my arm, and says, "I want to go home now." Yes, darling, we all do. I ask if he's sick. He tells me he is tired, so I let him lie on the carpet in the corner. Mistake. They all end up wanting to lie down, and there isn't enough room. The librarian stops reading for a moment, because there is so much commotion. Then, her story drags on.

The puppet she promised us is a stuffed-animal character from the story that sits in her lap as she reads. The kids all want to hold it, but she is firm. The thing stays with her. It is so lame that I refuse to back her up. Talk about false advertising!

Midstory, Anita's father arrives to pick her up for her doctor's appointment. He isn't happy, because he drove to the school, expecting to find his child there. He, like all working parents, has allotted just enough time to pick up Anita and get to the clinic. He has lost valuable time, he tells me, driving to the library. Anita says good-bye to her little sympathizers as he whisks her out the door. We now have lost more time.

Finally, finally, the librarian releases us. We are behind schedule, so I try to hurry the kids down the sidewalk. The fire alarm goes off when we are across the street from the school, not inside the classroom as instructed. Crap. I still don't know which area of the schoolyard this class is supposed to go to for the final count. Kids are pouring out of all doors.

"I have a stomachache!" wails a little girl.

"You can go to the office when this is all done, okay?" I answer, scanning the wave of children for an adult who can help us.

"This way!" shouts a woman who is leading small children. "Follow us!"

By the time we gather on the grass, another girl has a headache.

"Suck it up!" says the teacher. Then, she leans in toward me. "She always has a headache."

The administrator is not happy with my tardiness. She reminds me that I was supposed to get the children back to school before the alarm rang. I want to ask her what brilliant minds decided a substitute teacher would be a good fit for this morning's schedule?

With my teacher's notes in hand, we follow the hundreds of children back into the school. According to the notes, we are supposed to go straight to the art room. We do. The art teacher looks incredulously at me, saying, "You're not supposed to be here! I have another class coming! Let me see those notes!" as if I cannot read. When she decides the notes are wrong, she steps into the hall and bellows at the music teacher, asking if K04 is supposed to be in her room.

"Yeah, they are. Why are they with you?" the music teacher asks, again, with a tone intended to make someone feel stupid. That person is me.

With the kids safely in the hands of a teacher who knows the rules, I go back to the classroom, gather my purse and lunchbox, and find a quiet corner to eat and read.

The kids will be wild. Don't expect anything else.

The afternoon finds me in a third-grade classroom with thirty, that's *three-zero*, children. A couple of them are my height, five foot four. Holy crap! But the teacher is a bright spot on the substitute horizon. She tells me that she subbed for seven years before she got a full-time teaching position. Seven years. I would stick pencils in my eyes if I had to sub for seven years!

She has lined up the afternoon with projects that must be finished by the end of the day. "The students know exactly what they can and cannot do," she explains as the kids listen silently. Then, she turns to them. "If Mrs. M. gives me anything other than a perfect report on your behavior, you will suffer the consequences we discussed earlier." She says it with conviction. The kids keep their eyes on her as she scans their faces, leaving a final nonverbal message. When she leaves the room, I sense no change in the energy levels, no insubordination brewing. They continue with their assignments. I would have traded a kidney last fall to land in a situation like this. I am almost afraid to sit in the teacher's chair and . . . what? I'm not going to read my book in front of the students. I sit down, feeling sort of silly and superfluous.

I read the teacher's notes. I see that two boys cannot use the bathroom if anyone else is in there; they must go alone. What did they do to earn that restriction? And then I see news that makes my day: the students have a one-hour art period this afternoon! I will savor the gift of having one whole hour without the usual responsibility.

The rest of the afternoon passes without a single incident. I thank the teacher profusely. She seems like such a normal, decent, dedicated person. But seven years of subbing . . . maybe she has had her memory wiped. Maybe she escaped from Area 51 and is hiding here in Sioux Falls from the Feds.

One day down, two to go.

THE KIDS WILL BE WILD. DON'T EXPECT ANYTHING ELSE.

Second graders are my charges for the next morning, and I am pleasantly surprised by their behavior with me and with each other. They are polite and inclusive of everyone. No one comes crying about being left out of games at recess. They choose partners quickly for Math, leaving no child standing in a corner with a hurt look or slumped shoulders, something I often see.

This is an illusion, I tell myself. Why, at the end of the school year, am I placed in two classrooms in two days that do not require me to raise my voice or get in the face of a kid who is out of control?

As further proof that I am in the Land of Make-Believe, the second graders tell me that their teacher makes them use soap and scrub their hands before they go to lunch. I want to do handstands and cartwheels! I have argued with children all year as they insisted that using a squirt of antibacterial gel is just as good as proper hand-washing. Some teachers had given up the fight; they just sent the kids off to eat with filthy hands.

These second graders not only wash their hands, but they police the bathrooms and pick up paper towels that have been tossed on the floor. I smile as I lead them to the lunchroom. Life is good.

I eat my lunch in a staff workroom for the third time this year. The place is full of subs, so I don't feel like an outcast. Almost all of the women are retired teachers. Some seem relaxed and happy to be back in "their" school; others chat about previous assignments. I get a clear message that many of these teachers haven't subbed in the tough schools in Sioux Falls. I don't want to sound as if I survived the Hunger Games, so I ask them first where they have worked. Yup. None of them know what it's like to work with a room full of needy kids who demand so much more of them than they could ever possibly provide.

I shift my questioning and ask the woman seated next to me if she has ever worked in a Cluster Classroom.

"Yes, but only as an EA," she replies. "And none of the children were in wheelchairs. I didn't think I was qualified to do anything else."

Ah-hah. No one told me I had to be qualified.

I spend half the day in a classroom with the EA who stepped in and calmed the kicking boy who trapped me in a corner last fall. Her name is Dawn, and today she is helping a boy in a wheelchair. As I start a movie for the kids (it's the last week of school, so we're all coasting), Dawn carefully positions the boy so he can see the movie as well as the rest of the children. It's a time-consuming job, because the boy's head is twisted at an angle.

During a break, I remind her of how effective she was when she helped me in a difficult situation and how inspired I was by her calm, focused approach. She shrugs it off, repeating that it's hard to know what to do when you don't work with the child every day.

Today, I welcome recess duty. The weather is warm but breezy, a nice change from the hot classrooms. I'm reminded of my son again as I watch F-16 fighter jets crisscross the sky, leaving white trails. Then, I see a tall, lanky boy lope easily across the playground with a stride that looks just like Ian's did. It's a good thing I'm wearing sunglasses, so I can hide the tears.

The closer we get to the last day of school, the more hyped the kids get. Without the pressure of lesson plans, I have to become resourceful when their energy levels hit the ceiling. I call for jumping jacks, running in place, and sit-ups—then push-ups for the hardy few who haven't staggered back to their desks, breathing heavily. We take more drink-and-bathroom breaks. I read chapter books to them as often as I can get away with it. I'm taking it easy.

AND SUDDENLY IT'S THE LAST DAY of the school year for me. Tomorrow is Field Day for all the children; then there is a half day of getting report cards and saying good-bye. The plan for today is movies and games. Some future OCD sufferers want to clean out their desks, and I encourage it. With paper towels and soapy water, they burn up time and proudly show the results of their work.

I spend the last stuffy afternoon sorting books after the

children leave. The teacher assures me that I don't have to stay, but I'm so programmed to tidy up the classroom and write notes before I leave at 3:30 that I tell her I'm happy to finish the job. We chat as I work in my corner, and she files and writes at her desk. It's such an anticlimactic end to a life-changing experience.

If someone had asked me at the beginning of the year whether I was going to sub for the entire nine months, I would have snorted "No way!" I was certain that "something else" would turn up. Now, I can hardly believe that I lived through it all.

I limp down the long hall for the last time, wondering if I've done permanent damage to my degenerating spinal disks. My tote bag of supplies—pencils (I will never get over the indignation I felt when I couldn't find pencils for all the kids!), Band-Aids, wipes for the kids' smudged and smeared eyeglasses, erasers because there were never enough, and a chocolate bar that I'd forgotten—drags on the floor. The importance of this last trip to the office to get my paperwork isn't lost on me, but the heat in the hall makes me count steps like Gunga Din in the desert.

The secretaries are cheerful as always, maybe even more so, because another school year is coming to a close. They ask if they will see me next year, and I try to be kind, even diplomatic. I smother the "Hell no!" in the back of my throat and tiredly smile.

"I have no plans at this time, I guess," I answer. "I'll see how I feel after I rest up." That seems ambiguous enough, so we exchange pleasant wishes for a good summer. I totter off to my car. As I wait for the air-conditioning to kick in, the enormous weight of all the stories immobilizes me. I feel as though I'm supposed to do something with all the experiences: the words, the faces, the details that add color and laughter, the smells and sounds that conjure up a school year on the front lines. I came to this job pretty broken, still bleeding fresh grief from my son's death. I think he is giving me permission to be a mother to these stories, to make sure they "grow up and contribute to society."

Of course I think the stories are priceless, but they aren't worth anything unless they are shared. Now, the stories belong to you as well.

Acknowledgments

I WANT TO THANK THE TEACHERS in the Sioux Falls school district who reached out to help me while I was subbing, as well as Rhonda Iddings, the SEMS (Substitute Employee Management System) coordinator who never lost patience with my ineptitude. My teachers in elementary and high school who encouraged me to write deserve my unwavering thanks. My family and friends have earned my heartfelt appreciation, because they believed in me when I didn't. The greatest thanks go to my highly professional, detail-oriented, creative, all-around-good-guy editor Matthew J. Beier of Epicality Books, LLC, who shepherded me through the independent publishing process without ever letting me hear him scream or cry because I knew so little. Finally, thank you to my amazing proofreader, Christine Zuchora-Walske!

And to all the children who shared a classroom with me: Thank you, you little turkeys!

PEGGY MASTEL

About the Author

Recess Is My Best Subject is Peggy Mastel's first book. Born and raised in a small town in North Dakota, Peggy developed her storytelling skills early on in life to guarantee that she would be noticed by her large family. After holding jobs in sales, marketing, broadcast reporting, and employee training, she became self-employed. She lives with her husband and three dogs in Sioux Falls, South Dakota, and is currently working on her second book, a novel.